CW00607269

Politics of South Asia

Series Editors
Sumit Ganguly, Department of Political Science, Indiana University
Bloomington, Bloomington, IN, USA
Ronojoy Sen, Institute of South Asian Studies, National University of
Singapore, Singapore, Singapore
Neil DeVotta, Department Politics and International Affairs, Wake
Forest University, Winston-Salem, NC, USA
Katharine Adeney, School of Politics & International Relations,
University of Nottingham, Nottingham, UK

This book series focuses on the contemporary politics of South Asia. To that end it covers a range of subjects including but not limited to electoral politics, party systems, political economy, social movements, ethnic and religious conflicts, foreign policy, inter-state dynamics and migration. Publications in the series are theoretically grounded with intellectual rigor, combining propositions from the fields of political science and international relations, with sound regional and area knowledge.

The series publishes full-length monographs, edited volumes, as well as shorter Palgrave Pivots, that are cutting edge, as well as accessible.

More information about this series at
https://link.springer.com/bookseries/15911

Pradeep Peiris

Catch-All Parties and Party-Voter Nexus in Sri Lanka

palgrave
macmillan

Pradeep Peiris
Department of Political Science &
Public Policy
University of Colombo
Colombo, Sri Lanka

ISSN 2523-8345   ISSN 2523-8353 (electronic)
Politics of South Asia
ISBN 978-981-16-4152-7   ISBN 978-981-16-4153-4 (eBook)
https://doi.org/10.1007/978-981-16-4153-4

This Palgrave Macmillan imprint is published by the registered company Springer Nature
Singapore Pte Ltd.
The registered company address is: 152 Beach Road, #21-01/04 Gateway East, Singapore
189721, Singapore

PREFACE

Before my rebirth as a political scientist, I was a survey researcher assisting many local and foreign civil society organizations to research on various social and political injustices. Once I was approached to design and carry out a knowledge, attitude and practices survey (also known as KAPS survey) on Sri Lankan political parties. Following many research instruments modelled on Western scholarship, I designed a survey and carried it out by employing state-of-the-art survey techniques. The findings not only made almost no sense, even a novice like myself could recognize that there is something wrong in the behaviouralist and institutionalist approaches in understanding the way political parties function in non-Western societies.

This rather uncomfortably memorable blunder prompted me, when invited to pursue a doctoral research, to embark on studying the party-voter nexus in Sri Lanka. Having transited to the Social Sciences from the domain of the Natural Sciences, it took almost six years for me to complete my doctoral research. However, since defending my doctoral thesis, I found myself happily distracted by various other preoccupations despite my supervisor, Prof. Jayadeva Uyangoda's polite but persistent nudges to update and publish my work. After a lapse of almost six years, I woke up from my long slumber to realize that the oligopolistic dominance of the UNP and SLFP is under serious threat for the first time in the history of independent Sri Lanka. I was admittedly more worried about how this new development affects the findings of my doctoral study than its ramifications on the country's democracy! Therefore, I quickly resumed my filed research in the period from April 2019 to September 2020 in the original field locations to capture the dynamics surrounding the SLPP and SJB's emergence. The result was that the study came to reflect not only the electoral heydays of the UNP and SLFP, but also the arrival of new 'coalition centres', which in turn lent itself to an analysis of the formation, sustenance and disappearance of the party-voter nexus in Sri Lanka's catch-all parties.

It would be unforgivable if I do not say a few words about the scholars who have studied Sri Lankan political parties before me. My respect for them as well as my admiration for their nuanced analysis grew exponentially as I was reaching the end of my research. Most of these observations are valid to a great extent even to date, clearly demonstrating that the political system has not undergone a significant transformation despite parties and the electoral system having experienced numerous changes. At the end of my study, therefore, I have had to concede that I am more sceptical than ever before about the capacity of the Sri Lankan political parties to bring about just, fair and egalitarian social change.

Colombo, Sri Lanka   Pradeep Peiris

ACKNOWLEDGEMENTS

This is my first book as well as the publication of my doctoral research study. Obviously, therefore, I have a long list of people to thank not only for their help to conduct the research and write this book, but also for the numerous sorts of assistance that have made it possible for me to pursue an academic project of this nature. I am humbly thankful to all who motivated, guided and advised me throughout the entire process of producing this book. Some have paved the way for this doctoral research, many helped me to successfully complete it, and then a few volunteered to provide the critical assistance needed to produce this book.

First and foremost, my deepest sense of gratitude and appreciation goes to Prof. Jayadeva Uyangoda not only for been an excellent doctoral supervisor but also for been the role model for my academic pursuit. I would also like to remember Dr. Paikiasothy Saravanamuttu who introduced me to the academic path by hiring me to the Centre for Policy Alternatives to form and oversee its opinion polling division, Social Indicator, and providing me with the opportunity to obtain training at a number of foreign research institutes.

I am also especially indebted to Professor Kristian Stokke for his guidance and for his generous friendship that has enriched my academic career. In addition, my sincere appreciation goes to Professor Olle Tornquist and the University of Oslo, for their generous fellowship that enabled me to focus on my studies fulltime. I would also like to thank Prof. William Mishler, through whom I got introduced to behavioural political science, for introducing me to the cleavage-based party literature during the early stages of my doctoral studies. Prof. Mick Moore, thank you for introducing me to party literature that is based on rational choice theory. I also fondly remember my PhD buddies, Dr. Minna Thaheer and Dr. Keerthi Ariyadasa, with whom I shared the humour, excitements and frustrations through the challenging period of our doctoral studies.

I remember with a great deal of gratitude the assistance I received from Kithsiri Wickramasinghe, Bandula Threemavithana and D.P. Werawatta in conducting my field research in the Dedigama, Weligama and Kelaniya electorates. This study would not have been possible without their assistance and the generosity as well as the hospitality of their families and friends during the course of my fieldwork. I also take this opportunity to thank my colleagues Hasika Jayawardena, Shamindrini Sivananthan, Anupama Ranawana, Marimuttu Krishnamoorthy, Kumudu Priyankara and Shashik Dhanushka Silva for the support extended to me during the doctoral research this book is based on. All the assistance extended and facilities provided by Dr. Kumari Jayawardena and her staff at the Social Scientists' Association are also remembered with utmost gratitude. I am hugely grateful to Andi Schubert and Dr. Minna Thaheer for the invaluable assistance extended throughout the writing stage of my doctoral thesis.

This book would not have been possible without the critical intervention of two individuals. It was Neil DeVotta who suggested that this research is worth publishing with an international publisher and that I should approach Palgrave Macmillan to that end. Thank you, Neil, not only for encouraging me to work on this book, but also for your meticulous guidance throughout the publication process. Hasini Lecamwasm is the other person without whose help, encouragement and sometimes polite threats this book would not have been realized. Her exceptional skills in editing and generosity with her time enabled me to convert my thesis into book format.

I would also like to thank the reviewers of my manuscript for providing invaluable comments that have truly helped improve the clarity and strength of the argument that I make in this book. This section would not be complete if I fail to thank Vishal Daryanomel and Aishwarya Balachandar of Palgrave Macmillan for their assistance throughout the publishing process.

Last but not least, I thank my wife, son and daughter for all the support they extended to me during the difficult time of this research and more importantly for their enduring patience with me in spite of my continued absence and distance over the years of writing this book.

CONTENTS

LIST OF FIGURES

LIST OF TABLES

CHAPTER 1

Introduction

This book explores the party-voter relationship of two political parties in Sri Lanka, the United National Party (UNP) and the Sri Lanka Freedom Party (SLFP), from the perspectives of both these parties and their voters. Thereby, it attempts to examine how the party-voter nexus between these two parties—the UNP and SLFP—and voters has formed, sustained and eventually ceased as well.

Although Sri Lanka has one of the longest and most active party systems in South Asia, scholarly and systematic understanding of how they function, organize and mobilize, as well as how people choose their party and candidates, remains considerably low (Shastri and Uyangoda 2018). This study, by examining the party-voter nexus of catch-all parties, can be seen as an attempt to make a small but important contribution to the scholarship on political parties in Sri Lanka. To this end, I focused on the following puzzle as my point of departure.

THE PROBLEM

The 1956 victory of the Sinhala nationalist SLFP effectively ended the decades-long electoral domination of the UNP that espoused a conservative liberal ideology and sought to protect the interests of the propertied classes. During the early years of two-party electoral competition, these two parties clearly advocated starkly distinct policies for the country's economy and national question: The UNP stood for a liberal market economic policy and, broadly speaking, an ethnically plural society (Wilson 1975; Kearney 1973; Jupp 1978; Shastri 2018). Westernized urban elites and the intermediate classes—financial, business and trading classes along with civil servants—formed the UNP's main support bases (Shastri 2018). On the contrary, the SLFP clearly represented the interests of Sinhala nationalist forces, accordingly advocating a nationalist-socialist economic policy (Jupp 1978). The SLFP successfully brought "together wider congeries of social strata in the Sinhalese society, who were culturally indigenous, middle class, lower middle class, or poor in social terms and who had remained excluded from political power under colonial rule as well as post-independence UNP administration" (Uyangoda and Ariyadasa 2018: 136). However, since the 1990s, the SLFP too has embraced the liberal market economy that the UNP has been advocating since long before. Therefore, despite election-time rhetoric, it is apparent that the distinction maintained by these two parties along the axis of economic policy no longer exists. The clear difference in ideological and policy terms that they exhibited in relation to the ethnic conflict during the 1950s and 1960s also faded away after the 1980s. In this connection, both parties appear to have failed to maintain a consistent policy, swinging between liberal pluralism (for instance, during the regime of President Kumaratunga and Prime Minister Wickramasinghe) and majoritarian Sinhala nationalism (for instance, during the time of Presidents Jayewardene and Rajapaksa). What is fascinating is that despite not maintaining distinct ideological and policy positions, these parties have not only presented themselves as the main opposition to the other, but also managed to polarize the Sinhalese electorates accordingly and capture an overwhelming majority of the votes therein.

In order to address this important puzzle in the Sri Lankan political party system, this book attempts to examine the party-voter nexus from the point of the party as well as voter. This study not only investigates the rationale behind parties and voters forming and maintaining such relationship, but also the rationale behind ending it. To understand this relationship from the point of political parties, this study seeks answers to two questions: (i) How do the UNP and SLFP organize their party organizations and organizational networks at the electorate level, and how have they changed over time? and (ii) How do the UNP and SLFP activate their party organization to mobilize the electorate for electoral support, and how have they changed in response to changes in the electoral system? In addition, to understand the relationship from the point of the voter, the study poses another two questions: (i) How do voters for the UNP and SLFP make their electoral decisions and choices, and what causes them to change such decisions and choices? (ii) How is party allegiance to the UNP and SLFP formed and sustained over time in Sinhalese constituencies? These questions investigate how the party-voter nexus of the UNP and SLFP has been formed and maintained for seven decades. The emergence of two new parties, the SLPP and SJB, to replace the old ruling parties has opened up opportunity to investigate the role and rationale of the party and the voter in ending the party-voter nexus as well. It has particularly been useful in examining as to why the supporters of the SLFP and UNP decided to desert their party and join a new party instead of other existing parties, and the extent to which the organizing strategies and ideological positions of these new parties differ from the ones they stemmed from.

Essentially, then, this book is an attempt to glean how Sri Lanka's two main parties (which have now reincarnated as two new parties) have managed to command the loyalty of the majority of Sinhalese voters despite being catch-all parties for more than seven decades. In addition, this study on the party-voter nexus provides valuable insights into how political parties mediate at the local level in shaping the state-society relationship in Sri Lanka. As an extension to this problem, this study also treats the question of new parties emerging out of these existing ones, without really altering the nature of the party system, which may be identified as a 'bipolarized multiparty system'.

POLITICAL PARTIES, CITIZENS AND DEMOCRACY

The genesis of the Sri Lankan political party system is directly linked to the introduction of universal franchise in 1931 by the colonial government in anticipation of transition of power to locals (Wriggins 1960; Woodward 1969; Kearney 1973). As E. E. Schattschneider (1942: 1) in his seminal work *Party Government* argues, democracy is "unthinkable" without parties. However, political parties can also be observed as an inevitable by-product of democracy. Commenting on the function of political parties in Sri Lanka, Uyangoda states that "Sri Lanka's political parties have been products of two of the enduring legacies of modernity – democracy and ethnicity" (2012b: 1). However, despite the consensus amongst scholars on the intertwined, mutually enriching and enduring relationship between democracy and political parties, radical democrats such as M. N. Roy (2006) argue for politics without parties. Roy states that since the whole purpose of the party system is to capture power either through constitutional means or though armed insurrection, parties have debased democracy to demagogy (Roy 2006: 51).

At first glance, it may seem easy to define what a 'political party' is. In reality, however, this is quite complex as it is hardly an objective task (White 2006). According to Downs, "a political party is a team of men seeking to control the governing apparatus by gaining office in a duly constituted election" (Downs 1957: 25). Nevertheless, White reminds us that there are many legitimate political parties that exist for reasons that have little to do with winning elections (White 2006). As Edmund Burke, political theorist and member of the British Whig Party conceptualized it, "[A] party is a body of men united, for promoting by their joint endeavours the national interest, upon some particular principle in which they are all agreed" (cited in White 2006).[1] Even though Burke's classical conceptualization offers a more comprehensive definition than the positivist and utilitarian approach of Downs (1957), it still does not provide a clear answer to the question of *what parties ought to be doing*.

According to Weber, 'power' is the chance for a man or a group of men to realize their own will in a communal action even against the resistance of others who are participating in the action (Weber 1958: 180). In this light, four types of political power can be identified, namely political coercion, political authority, political influence and political manipulation (Birch 1993: 139). Weber asserts that classes, social groups and parties are phenomena that are part of the distribution of power within a community (Weber 1958: 181). Like the "genuine place of *classes* is within the economic order and the place of *status groups* is within the social order", Weber argues, "*parties* live in the house of power" (Weber 1958: 194).

Since the late 1920s, elites and interest groups have been forming political parties in Sri Lanka with the primary aim of winning elections to capture power or consolidate their existing power. Calvin Woodward (1969), a pioneering scholar of Sri Lankan political party scholarship, describes this phenomenon as shifting the "politics of notable to parties of notables". It was in this backdrop that the UNP that was formed in 1946 dominated politics until the emergence of the SLFP in 1951. Like Rajini

Kothari's (1964) concept of the "congress system", the UNP functioned as the dominant party for a good decade at the national-level electoral legislative politics. However, the 1956 victory of the SLFP-led coalition not only marked the end of years of UNP dominance, but also laid the foundation for a two-party system in Sri Lanka that was to last for many decades (Shastri and Uyangoda 2018). As Uyangoda (2012b) observes, governments of post-independence Sri Lanka have largely been formed by coalitions, and the UNP and the SLFP, under the two-party system, have been the 'coalition centres' until the 2020 election victory of the SLPP. In order to understand in part the larger question of how these parties managed to retain their support bases over so many decades despite being catch-all parties, I next pay attention to the emergence and organizational strategies of the UNP and SLFP.

Party Organization

James Jupp's book, *Sri Lanka: Third World Democracy* (1978), now a classic, provides a detailed account of party organization in Sri Lanka. In addition, scholars such as Kearney (1973), Wilson (1975), Hettige (1984), Moore (1985) and Gunasekara (1994) also have contributed to the scholarship on the dynamics of party organization of the UNP and SLFP. Observing the party system in the 1970s, Jupp claims that both parties changed from the classic "parties of notables" to something much closer to the British pattern of a disciplined national structure based on enrolled mass membership (Jupp 1978: 89). He further states that "by 1970 the textbook proposition that the British type of electoral and parliamentary system that forces a two-party confrontation was largely true outside of Tamil areas" (90).

Jupp also emphasizes the highly centralized nature of political parties, while admitting the powerful role played by local notables. He says that central committees have increasingly intervened in local selection and disputes, limiting but by no means eliminating the power of local notables (90). The major parties, despite differences in terminology and ideological tradition, have built up pyramidal structures in which their most powerful inner bodies are dominated by Members of Parliament (99). This group is either called the politburo or the working committee, and they are drawn from a larger national executive committee. The members of the executive committee are elected from an annual convention that is composed of delegates from local branches (99). According to

Jupp's analysis of party structures, he appears to suggest that all the main parties organize themselves along the lines of what Duverger character-izes as 'direct' parties. He elaborates on the various ancillary organizations attached to the main parties and their roles in the decision-making process of the party. Jupp also says that trade union ancillaries play a small part in party affairs, and those who had control of the policies and organization of the two major parties were inevitably politicians (109).

Robert Kearney's (1973) analysis of party organization structures of the UNP and SLFP is somewhat different to Jupp's. He claims that party organization in Ceylon in the 1960s tended to be loose and informal. Unlike Jupp, Kearney does not seem to believe in the existence of strong institutional structures. He notes that "M.P.'s predominate amongst the party officers and appear to control extra-parliamentary organization" (125). Describing the functioning of political parties in reality, Kearney says:

> Periodic party conferences serve as instruments for generating enthusiasm among the party's activists and local stalwarts and provide the leadership with a platform from which to enunciate party policy. Conferences seem intended to present an appearance of party unity and enthusiasm, and seldom seriously ponder alternatives of policy, leadership or strategy (125).

This analysis is confirmed by the observations of other scholars who have studied village politics in Sri Lanka such as Hettige (1984), Spencer (1990) and Gunasekara (1994).

Many scholars (Jupp 1978; Wriggins 1960; Kearney 1973; Wilson 1975; Jiggins 1979; Gunasekara 1994; Jayanntha 1992) have also high-lighted the influential role played by Buddhist monks in Sinhalese political parties. Their role has been pivotal in sustaining traces of the feudal system in all Sinhalese parties including the Communist LSSP (Jupp 1978: 93). Making an interesting observation, Jupp argues that Sri Lankan party organization structures contribute to the reproduction of old Kandyan feudal obligations within the modern Parliamentary mass-party system (93). The role of temples and Buddhist monks in the political party organization is succinctly elaborated on by Tamara Gunasekara in her ethnographic work in Ranagala (Gunasekara 1992). Furthermore, Uyan-goda (2010a) points out that Buddhism is the most politicized religion in Sri Lanka. Associations of Buddhist monks have also formed powerful ancillary organizations for the main political parties (Jupp 1978).

The Party-Voter Nexus

Scholars of party politics from the structural-functionalist school describe parties as manifestations of the social cleavages that exists in any given society. As Lipset and Rokkan (1967) have argued in their pioneering scholarly work on voter allegiance, voters rally around political parties that they feel represent the social cleavages they belong to. Therefore, parties consciously construct their identity and take policy positions to place themselves in this multi-dimensional map of social cleavages made up of divisions running along lines of class, caste, ethnicity, religion, region and ideology (Lipset and Rokkan 1967). However, voters accord varying priority to these cleavages and the level of importance for each cleavage can change across time and space (6). Nevertheless, in this background, it is important for political parties to maintain clear differences in order to amass votes on the basis of social cleavages.

Take the centre-periphery cleavage in Sri Lanka for instance. In the early stage of the nation-building process, centre-periphery cleavages pitted the national culture against ethnic, linguistic or religious minorities in the provinces and the peripheral sectors of society (Lipset and Rokkan 1967; Dalton 1996). In the Sri Lankan context, conflict on the basis of ethnicity, language and regionalism initially reflected the centre-periphery cleavages that sprouted as consequences of the nation-state building process stemming from and following 400 years of colonial rule. The conflict that emerged between the English-educated, Western intelligentsia and local vernacular village elites around the time of the transition from colonial to self-rule has features similar to the 'centre-periphery' kind of social cleavage (Wriggins 1960; Woodward 1969; Wilson 1974, 1975; Kearney 1973; Jupp 1978). The 'Sinhala only' policy of S.W.R.D. Bandaranaike and the acquisition of Christian schools under Mrs. Bandaranaike could be considered as some of the policies that resulted from this conflict.

Caste is another example. In a country like Sri Lanka in which society had been organized under feudalist structures for centuries, caste plays a crucial role in day-to-day social relations, and in electoral politics in particular (Wilson 1975; Jupp 1978; Jiggins 1979; Hettige 1984; Gunasinghe 1990; Jayanntha 1992; Gunasekara 1994; Uyangoda 2010a; De Zoysa 2013). As Tamara Gunasekara states, "class segregation is less obvious and, to some, less discomforting than caste discrimination, but is nevertheless evidence that inequalities of birth status remain today, as they were at the turn of the century, a significant basis for structuring behaviour in rural society" (Gunasekara 1994: 114). However, caste is not only a matter of status, but also, to an extent, a determinant of the villager's economic class as well. Newton Gunasinghe illustrates the dialectical relationship between caste and class in Kandyan village society (Gunasinghe 1990). Therefore, in an agrarian democracy like Sri Lanka, caste is a powerful social cleavage, and Jiggins (1979) commented about its potential for party mobilization in the countryside. Studying the role of caste in Sri Lanka's early elections, Jiggins (1979) says that the largest caste in terms of numbers has generally been able to return a representative from its fold to Parliament (Jiggins 1979). Reiterating Jiggins' point, Gunasinghe states that "no major political party dares to put forward a candidate who is not a member of the numerically dominant caste in the area" (Gunasinghe 1990: 144).

Social cleavage theorists believe that once a voter forms party loyalty and interest groups establish party ties, the potential for dramatic partisan change lessens and the parties become self-perpetuating institutions (Dalton 1996). This model of the party-voter relationship had a significant influence on electoral research, as scholars found that social cleavages are powerful determinants of voting behaviour. There is a significant body of literature that examines the role of social cleavages in respective societies in engendering party support. Torcol and Mainwaring argue that although cleavages have a social component, they are politically constructed, and therefore, it is the political factors that shape party systems and social and political conflict (Torcal and Mainwaring 2000).

However, parties are no longer the same institution that they once were (Schmitter 2000; Randall 2006). Dahl is sceptical of a simple application of the cleavage model, as the strength of the cleavage also determines the type of party system that ultimately emerges as cleavages become politicized (1966: 378). The partisan stability that the social cleavage model assumes became conventional wisdom as the very same party system began to undergo dramatic changes (Dalton 1996). Dalton further states that the ability to predict voting choices through traditional social cleavages is waning, and hence, a higher level of unpredictability of voting is expected. In addition, increasing social differences or conflict can be observed within political parties instead of amongst parties. On the one hand, this has triggered the formation of new political parties by dissident factions of old parties. For example, in Sri Lanka, the Jathika Hela Urumaya (JHU), a Sinhalese-Buddhist nationalist political party, sprang out of the old capitalist UNP at a time when the UNP was distancing itself from Sinhalese-Buddhist nationalist politics (Uyangoda 2010a).

Given the emergence of these new dynamics, a new lens through which to view parties is needed. Interestingly, and as briefly introduced above, the UNP and SLFP in Sri Lanka have seen increasing convergence of their policy and ideological positions, irrespective of which they also managed to maintain their respective voter bases until very recently. This was made possible by the catch-all strategies pursued by both parties, resulting in them paying increasingly less attention to targeting specific cleavage groups as they did during the first few decades of two-party electoral competing. 'Catch-all' is a concept that Otto Kirchheimer (1966) coined to describe the loss of clearly distinguishable class and ideological identities of European political parties.

Anthony Downs (1957), a pioneering Rational Choice Theorist, claims that political parties in a democracy formulate policies strictly as a means of gaining votes rather than to serve any particular interest group. Therefore, politicians' social functions are accomplished as a by-product of their private motives—to attain income, power and enjoy the prestige of being in office. In this model, all actors—the party, the politician and the voter—play an active role in the party-voter nexus for the purpose of maximizing the utility for self. Even though Downs does not present parties as having any interest in creating a particular type of society, he does not deny the existence of ideology in democratic politics. However, according to him, "many of the particular characteristics of those ideologies may be deduced from the premise that parties seek office solely for income, power and prestige that accompanies it" (Downs 1957: 141).

Kitschelt and Wilkinson (1997) view the phenomenon from another angle, arguing that "in many political systems, citizen-politician linkages are based on direct material inducements, targeted at individuals and small groups of citizens whom politicians know to be highly responsive to such side-payments and willing to surrender their vote for the right price" (Kitschelt and Wilkinson 1997: 2). According to Kitschelt and Wilkinson (1997), in affluent democracies, parties often tend to operate through programmatic accountability, while parties in poorer democracies often tend to practice clientelism. Furthermore, according to them, parties make more of an effort to build principal-agent linkages of accountability whenever 'competitiveness' is intense. The extent to which this competitiveness translates into more programmatic or clientelistic responsiveness is contingent upon the level of development in society. Democratic institutions and particularly electoral systems also matter in the linkage between principal and agent. However, Kitschiest and Wilkinson argue that as long as socio-economic, competitive and political-economic configurations are conducive for clientelism, politicians may come up with tactics to implement such linkages under all sorts of formal institutional arrangements. In relation to Sri Lanka, Dilesh Jayanntha (1992) makes a similar point in his PhD work on *Electoral Allegiance in Sri Lanka*, where he observes that "elections were fought not on the grounds of party ideology but, instead, they entailed rival patrons mobilising their different local networks" (5).

Almost all the scholars who have worked on Sri Lankan political parties have identified the powerful role that patron-client relationships play in forming and maintaining the party-voter nexus (Wriggins 1960; Woodward 1969; Kearney 1973; Wilson 1975; Jupp 1978; Jiggins 1979; Jayanntha 1992; Uyangoda 2010a). James Scott (1972), a distinguished scholar who has studied patron-client networks in South and Southeast Asia in great depth, states that "if we are to grasp why political parties seem more like ad-hoc assemblages of notables together with their entourages than arenas in which established interests are aggregated, we must rely heavily on patron-client analysis" (92). Scott defines the patron-client relationship as:

> An exchange relationship between roles – may be defined as a special case of dyadic (two-person) ties involving a largely instrumental friendship in which an individual of higher socio-economic status (patron) uses his own influence and resources to provide protection or benefits, or both, for a person of lower status (client) who, for his part, reciprocates by offering general support and assistance, including personal services, to the patron (Scott 1972: 92).

Having defined the patron-client relationship, Scott observes that "the dynamics of personal alliance networks are as crucial in the day-to-day realities of national institutions as in local politics" (92). According to Jupp (1978), who analysed Sri Lanka's political party system prior to the introduction of the PR system, "the major parties are bound together by patronage, symbolism, group loyalty and the exigencies of the single member electorate" (96).

Siri Hettige (1984), based on his ethnographic research conducted in Nilthanna, says that the traditional patronage networks involved in landlord-tenant relationships are not relevant or important any longer. Instead, what is important is "the networks of political patronage that link the villager with higher authorities who control the scarce resources to which the villagers have no direct access" (158). In this context, patronage networks are useful for the mobilization of votes for political parties as well as their candidates. Often, as far as patron-client, network-based party mobilization is concerned, the party in the government enjoys significant advantages over opposition parties as they have a monopoly over state resources (Jayasuriya 2000). Therefore, by early 1980s, both the UNP and the SLFP seemed to have assumed the character of catch-all parties in order to become efficient election-engineering machines.

Despite the lack of a widely agreed definition for catch-all parties, they are ideologically centrist, dispersed and flexible over time (Mainwaring and McGraw 2018). Reflecting on catch-all parties, Wolinetz (2002) argues that "those parties which were once accustomed to the regular support of electorates of *belonging*, find that both the relative size and loyalty of these electorates have shrunk, and electronic media deny parties control over the political agenda" (159). Catch-all parties have become vulnerable to the vagaries of the electorates who have detached themselves from previous strong bases by adopting a strategy to compete for votes on the basis of their leaders and the effectiveness of their policies (148). Analysing the contemporary political developments in the Europe, Katz and Mair (2009) argue that political conditions encouraged parties to foster depoliticization and hence also—most crucially for the cartel argument—made it that much easier for the parties to cooperate and collude. Katz and Mair (2009) succinctly summarize the concept of cartel party:

> the concept of the "cartel party" was first proposed as a means of drawing attention to patterns of inter party collusion or cooperation as well as competition, and as a way of emphasizing the influence of the state on party development. The cartel party is a type that is postulated to emerge in democratic polities that are characterized by the interpenetration of party and state and by a tendency towards inter-party collusion. With the development of the cartel party, the goals of politics become self-referential, professional, and technocratic, and what substantive inter party competition remains becomes focused on the efficient and effective management of the polity. Competition between cartel parties focuses less on differences in policy and more on the provision of spectacle, image, and theatre. (755)

Although general political commentaries on the functioning of Sri Lankan political parties confirms the existence of characteristics similar to cartel parties, contemporary party literature lacks systematic inquiry into the party-voter nexus that involves reflecting on current realities. In addition, while both the cleavage theory and the rational choice model are very useful in understanding the changing dynamics of party-voter relations, treating the relationship as either purely the result of rational calculations, or simply a product of social cleavages ensnares the analysis on one side of the objective-subjective, structure-agency and micro–macro dualities. Therefore, in order to capture the nuanced yet complex reality of the party-voter nexus, this book employs the following theoretical framework that transcends such dichotomies while embracing their analytical value.

THEORETICAL APPROACH

The theoretical framework utilized in this study draws inspiration from both the Social Cleavage Theory and Rational Choice Theory, particularly since they have found resonance with scholars who have studied voter behaviour in various democracies across the world. While the social cleavage theory emphasizes the importance of social structures in determining the voting decision, the rational choice theory gives greater prominence to the agency of the political party, politician and voter in determining electoral choice. Although the structuring effect of social divisions on political identities and interests is undeniable, the agency exercised by political actors also plays a key role in the construction and mobilization of the collective (Stokke and Peiris 2010). Therefore, it is clear that any attempt to understand the party-voter relationship must transcend the structure/agency dualism and be built on a theoretical framework that accommodates both structure and agency into its analytical categories. Therefore, I draw extensively on Bourdieu's seminal work on the 'theory of practice' and its main concepts in order to conceptualize a theoretical framework to understand and analyse the practice of party politics in local settings.

Pierre Bourdieu and the Theory of Practice

Bourdieu's approach to understanding the structure/agency debate is very similar to Giddens in many ways.[2] Unlike structuralists and agency-oriented theorists who focus mainly on either society/structure or individual/agent, in his structuration theory Giddens pays primary attention to "recurrent social practices" (Ritzer 1996: 528). Bourdieu also rejects the structure/agency opposition and states that "the most steadfast intention guiding my work has been to overcome the opposition between objectivism and subjectivism" (Bourdieu 1989: 15). However, Bourdieu makes an important move away from Giddens' theory of structuration in terms of the way he conceives the structure. Bourdieu makes a three-fold conceptual substitution to Giddens' work: from 'rule' to 'strategy' (governed by habitus); from 'resources' to 'forms of capital'; and from 'institutions' to 'fields' (Stokke 2002: 5). According to Bourdieu, what people do—their social practice—is constituted by and constitutes their dispositions (habitus), the capital they possess and the field within which they operate (Maton 2008: 51). Using an equation as a heuristic device, Bourdieu presents his conceptualization of social practice as: (Habitus * Capital) + Field = Practice (Bourdieu 1984: 101) (Fig. 1.1).

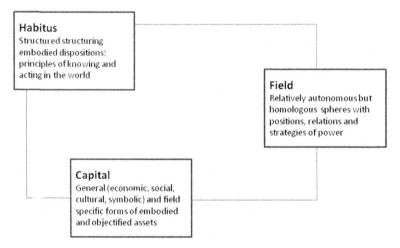

Fig. 1.1 Key concepts in Bourdieu's theory of practice[3]

Habitus
Habitus is the mental or cognitive structures though which people deal with the social world. People are endowed with a series of internalized schemes though which they perceive, understand, appreciate and evaluate the social world (Ritzer 1996: 540). People use these schemes to produce social practices and to perceive and evaluate them. Hence, habitus is, dialectically, a "product of the internalisation of the structures" of the social world (Bourdieu 1989: 18). Habitus is acquired as a result of long-term occupation of a position within the social world, and thus, habitus varies depending on the nature of one's position in the social world. As Ritzer states:

> The habitus allows people to make sense out of the social world, but the existence of multitude of habitus means that the social world and its structures do not impose themselves uniformly on all actors. (Ritzer 1996: 540)

The habitus is acquired, particularly through childhood socialization, and constituted through the unreflexive and mundane processes of habit formation. These dispositions of habitus are acquired, structured, durable and transposable. As in the case of Giddens' structuration theory, Bourdieu also mainly focuses on the *social practice* that mediates between habitus and the social world. It is the practice that creates the habitus as well as the social world. As Ritzer states, "practice tends to shape habitus, habitus, in return, serves to both unify and generate practice" (Ritzer 1996: 541).

Making a departure from the work of mainstream structuralist thinkers, Bourdieu jettisons determinism in his formulation of this theory. The habitus merely suggests what people should think and what they should do instead of determining their action. The principles on which people make their choices and choose the strategies that they employ in the social world are provided by the habitus. According to Bourdieu, "people are not fools; however, they are not fully rational either; they act in a reasonable manner as they have practical sense" (Ritzer 1996: 541).

Fields
The *field* is a network of relations amongst the objective positions within it (Bourdieu and Wacquant 1992: 97). The relations exist apart from individual consciousness and will, and they are not interactions and

intersubjective ties amongst individuals (Ritzer 1996: 542). Bourdieu conceives of the social world as comprised of multiple fields with varying degrees of autonomy in regard to each other (Stokke 2002: 7). As Stokke further states:

> Fields should not be understood as bounded domain but rather as a relational space of positions (occupied by actors) and relations of power (forces) between these positions. Positions grant access to different general forms of capital (economic, social, cultural or symbolic) as well as field specific forms of capital (e.g. political capital) which define relations of domination, subordination or equality between the positions. (Stokke 2002: 7)

Bourdieu sees the field, by definition, as an arena of battle and he says that "the field is also a field of struggle" (Bourdieu and Wacquant 1992: 101). The occupants of these fields, individuals and institutions, are engaged in continuous struggle to either safeguard or improve their positions. They may also engage in preserving or transforming the configuration of positions and the forces within the field (Stokke 2002: 7). These positions and power relations, in a particular field, are defined by the forms of capital that are allocated to those who are occupying those positions.

Bourdieu's main focus is on the relationship between the habitus and fields. He sees the relationship as twofold: on the one hand, field conditions the habitus, and on the other hand, the habitus constitutes the field as something that is meaningful, has sense and value, and is worth the investment of energy (Ritzer 1996: 543).

Forms of Capital
Capital also plays a key role in Bourdieu's conceptualization of social practice. The key aspects of the fields—positions and forces—are defined by the various forms of capital the occupant—individual or institution—possesses (Fig. 1.2). According to Bourdieu, capital presents itself in three fundamental forms: (i) economic capital, (ii) social capital and (iii) cultural capital (Bourdieu 1984). Economic capital is constituted by material wealth in the form property or money, shares, etc. Social capital refers to social resources in the form of networks and contacts that are based on mutual recognition. Cultural capital refers to the information assets in the form of knowledge and skills acquired through socialization and education. As Bourdieu argues, "these fundamental forms of capitals are

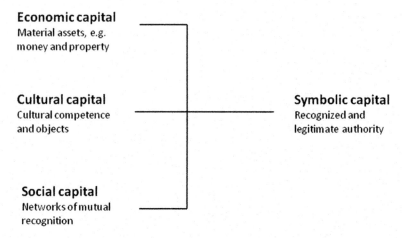

Economic capital
Material assets, e.g.
money and property

Cultural capital
Cultural competence
and objects

Symbolic capital
Recognized and
legitimate authority

Social capital
Networks of mutual
recognition

Fig. 1.2   General forms of capital with possible conversions[4]

different forms of power, but the relative importance of the different form will vary according to the field" (Bourdieu 1984). These forms of capital can convert to other forms, i.e. converting economic capital to social capital or cultural capital or vice versa. However, there is a rate of exchange for this conversion that varies from one field to another. Bourdieu considers a fourth capital, symbolic capital, which is a product of all three of the above forms of capital (Bourdieu 1984). Symbolic capital refers to legitimate authority in the forms of prestige, honour, reputation and fame. Interestingly, these forms of capital also constitute and are constituted by the disposition in the habitus (Stokke 2002: 8). Hence, capital is dialectically related to the constitution and operation of both the field and the habitus.

Doxa
Another important concept in Bourdieu's theory of practice is that of doxa, which is the combination of both orthodox and heterodox norms and beliefs—the unstated, taken-for-granted assumptions or 'common sense' behind the distinctions we make (Deer 2008a). Doxa happens when we "forget the limits" that have given rise to unequal divisions in society: it is "an adherence to relations of order which, because they structure inseparably both the real world and the thought world, are accepted as self-evident" (Bourdieu 1984: 471). As Deer states, "*doxa*

is more specifically used to account for action and practice in traditional social organizations where the near perfect correspondence between the social structures and mental structures, between the objective order and the subjective organizing principles, make the natural and social world unquestionable" (Deer 2008a: 121).

As Deer describes, in a field the doxa takes the form of an unrecognized unconditional allegiance to the 'rules of the game' on the part of social agents with similar habitus (Deer 2008a: 122). He further states that "*doxa* creates, in contrast to the notion of rules accepted by a majority, which posit the emergence of a field of opinion where different legitimate answers can be given to explicit questions about the establish order" (Deer 2008a: 122).

Any attempt to summarize Bourdieu's theory of practice in a way that can be applied across academic disciplines is undoubtedly a futile attempt. Therefore, what I have discussed so far should be considered as some key concepts that are useful to analyse the party-voter relationship beyond the structure-agency dichotomy. Bourdieu's key concepts—habitus, field, capital and doxa—provide a conceptual framework to comprehend how parties, politicians and voters play the 'game of party politics' in Sri Lanka.

Social Capital and Network Politics

In order to better comprehend the local political practice in my field locations, I would also like to introduce the concept of 'network politics' into this theoretical framework. The role of patronage networks in Sri Lankan villages, and local and national politics has often been commented on by scholars (Woodward 1969; Jupp 1978; Jiggins 1979; Hettige 1984; Jayanntha 1992). As Scott suggests, it is important to inquire into the nature of network politics in order to understand how bureaucracy or political parties function in post-colonial, agrarian and developing societies[5] (Scott 1972: 92). Therefore, in the following paragraphs, I will attempt to conceptualize network politics, by using Bourdieu's concepts of social capital and field, to strengthen the theoretical framework of this study.

Bourdieu's concepts of habitus, field and capital can be used to conceptualize the practices of actors and the power relations between them. These concepts also help to explore the logic of different and overlapping social fields that constitute the arenas of everyday politics and the multiplicity of practices, institutions, discourses and networks that make up the local political space (Selboe 2008: 60). Social capital is "the aggregate of the actual or potential resources which are linked to the possession of a durable network of more or less institutionalised relationships of mutual acquaintance and recognition" (Bourdieu 1986: 248). According to Bourdieu, these relationships may exist only in the practical state, in material and/or symbolic exchanges which help to maintain them. He further states that "they may also be socially instituted and guaranteed by the application of a common name (the name of a family, a class, or a tribe or of a school, a party, etc.) and by a whole set of instituting acts designed simultaneously to form and inform those who undergo them; in this case, they are more or less really enacted and so maintained and reinforced, in exchanges" (Bourdieu 1986: 249).

A network of connections is neither inherited nor constructed. Instead, personal relations and social networks are mainly the products of the unconscious strategies of individuals to create or maintain social relationships that may be beneficial in the short or long term. As Bourdieu states:

> the network of relationships is the product of investment strategies, individual or collective, consciously or unconsciously aimed at establishing or reproducing social relationships that are directly usable in the short or long term, i.e., at transforming contingent relations, such as those of neighborhood, the workplace, or even kinship, into relationships that are at once necessary and elective, implying durable obligations subjectively felt (feelings of gratitude, respect, friendship, etc.) or institutionally guaranteed (rights). This is done through the alchemy of consecration, the symbolic constitution produced by social institution (institution as a relative – brother, sister, cousin, etc. – or as a knight, an heir, an elder, etc.) and endlessly reproduced in and through the exchange (of gifts, words, women, etc.) which it encourages and which presupposes and produces mutual knowledge and recognition. (Bourdieu 1986: 250)

A person may "strengthen his or her position, power and possibilities through nurturing social relationships or being member of a group" (Selboe 2008). However, through continuous engagement in socializing, social actors have to work hard to achieve the mutual recognition and solidarity that they hope to enjoy as part of the social network. Therefore, it requires the time and energy of social actors to accumulate and reproduce social capital, and to access the potential and associated material or symbolic profits (Selboe 2008).

As discussed thus far in this section, my theoretical framework of the study has attempted to move beyond the positivism/post-positivism duality. This framework has allowed me to maintain a vantage point that synthesizes macro- and micro-views as well as structure-oriented and agency-oriented understanding throughout the research.

THE STUDY METHODOLOGY AND METHODS

This study integrates both qualitative and quantitative methods in order to transcend the 'objective-subjective' dichotomy that has dominated social inquiry. Bourdieu's theory provided me with a very important point of entry to the research, as his work is animated by the desire to overcome the 'false' opposition between 'objectivism' and 'subjectivism' (Ritzer 1996). In order to overcome the objectivist-subjectivist dilemma, Bourdieu draws our attention to *practice*, which he sees as an outcome of the dialectical relationship between structure and agency (Ritzer 1996: 537).

Furthermore, with his idea of reflexivity, he espoused the need for objectifying the subject as well as the object (Deer 2008b). Here, he points out that the researcher must deploy the same "epistemological thinking tools" to his/her own position and processes as those deployed in order to produce knowledge on the object of research (Grenfell 2008: 226). For Bourdieu, this also means that the researcher's 'thinking tools' must be influenced not only by theory but also by his/her practice in the field. According to him:

> We must try, in every case, to mobilize all the techniques that are relevant and practically usable, given the definition of the object and the practical condition of data collection ... The long and the short of it is, social research is something much too serious and too difficult for us to allow ourselves to mistake scientific *rigidity*, which is the nemesis of intelligence and invention, for scientific *rigor* and thus to deprive ourselves of this or that resource available in the full panoply of intellectual tradition of our discipline and of the sister disciplines of anthropology, economics, history, etc. ... Needless to say, the extreme liberty that I advocate here ... has its counterpart in the extreme vigilance that we must apply to the conditions of use of analytical techniques and to ensuring that they fit the question at hand. (Bourdieu and Wacquant 1992: 227)

Since this research was influenced by "the definition of the object as well as the practical condition of data collection", Bourdieu's epistemological stance introduced above proved to be a significant influence on the research methods I employed to inquire into the agency of voters, politicians, political actors and political parties as well as the structural conditions within which they exercise their agency. As such, this study has employed a pluralist research methodology, utilizing both qualitative and quantitative methods in data collection and analysis including in-depth interviews, FGDs, observations, consulting secondary sources, as well as a survey research component using survey data collected by the Social Scientists' Association (SSA) in Sri Lanka and the Centre for the Study of Developing Societies (CSDS) in New Delhi, India. The initial round of the field research was carried out from 2010 to 2014 as part of my doctoral research. In order to capture the latest electoral dynamics, another round of field research was conducted during 2020 in the same filed locations.

The study paid special attention to the ethical aspects of research since party-voter relationship is a very sensitive subject, especially in a patronage democracy like Sri Lanka. Therefore, all the respondents interviewed were referred to by pseudonyms. In addition, political actors at each selected ward were carefully selected with the help of three informants of the three field locations. In order to learn about the life histories of these villages, I spent more than two years visiting the three field locations and befriending villages of all walks of life. Due to the caste and class dynamics in Sinhalese villages, I approached my respondents through the existing networks and thereby made them feel comfortable about sharing their stories. To ensure accuracy and address possible bias, the information gathered during interviews were triangulated through various other sources.

Selecting Field Locations

The field work for this study was conducted in three electorates—Dedigama, Weligama and Kelaniya. The decision to conducting my fieldwork in these three electorates enabled comparisons not only across 'space' but also, to a certain extent, across 'time'. In this study, I have attempted to compare the party-voter relationship under the PR and FPTP electoral systems. However, in order to carry out this comparison effectively, it was important to conduct this research in electorates where prior knowledge on party-voter relations is available. Therefore, the Dedigama, Weligama and Kelaniya electorates emerged as ideal field sites since both Janice Jiggins (1994, 1979) and Dilesh Jayanntha (1992) have studied party politics in these electorates. Jiggins' work examines the function and dynamics of party politics in Dedigama (1974, 1979), while the Weligama and Kelaniya electorates were extensively studied by Jayanntha (1992) and broadly by Jiggins (1979) as well.[6]

All three electorates are located in the country's wet zone. Dedigama is home to a largely agrarian, Kandyan Sinhalese population, whereas the majority of the population in the coastal electorate Weligama is agrarian, low-country Sinhalese. Kelaniya, in contrast, is mainly an urban, low-country Sinhalese constituency. The choice of these electorates is informed by a desire to capture the diverse and complex dynamics at work amongst Sinhalese constituencies, such as their regional ties (Kandyan and low-country), locality (urban and rural) and economic activity (agriculture, fisheries and industry) (Fig. 1.3).

STRUCTURE OF THE BOOK

This book examines the dynamics of the party-voter nexus in relation to the UNP and SLFP, the two main parties that have been ruling Sri Lanka, alone or as main coalition partners, for over seven decades after independence. The findings and analysis of the study are organized under five themes that are presented under five distinct but interconnected chapters. The first two chapters focus on how the UNP and the SLFP have organized the party and mobilize votes at the electorate level. The next two chapters discuss how voters make their choice in terms of voting and party allegiance, while the final chapter examines the context and the process through which supporters of the UNP and SLFP have deserted their parties. Therefore, these five chapters together describe how the party-voter nexus of these two parties with their supporters was formed, sustained over time and lost as well.

Chapter 2 examines the party organizational structures and strategies of the UNP and SLFP at the level of the electorate, focusing on their transformation over the past few decades. Contrary to the prevalent understanding of party organization, it argues that the organizational strategies of parties are often determined more by political conditions than structural conditions, which may largely be attributed to the agency

Fig. 1.3 Field
locations of the study

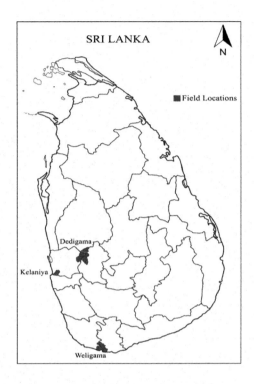

of party leaders. This chapter argues that the party structure at the electorate level is extremely feeble and, at best, loosely organized. Electoral organizers rely heavily on local political actors who are economically and/or culturally notable figures at the local level. Additionally, the focus of the two main parties has shifted from building a strong membership base to attracting votes for the next election. This leads to the reproduction of the feeble nature of the party organization at the local level, which in turn has diverted attention from the establishment of a strong party organizational structure to an emphasis on mere party mobilization.

Chapter 3 examines how the party organizational structures of the UNP and SLFP are deployed in order to mobilize electoral support, and how these party mobilization strategies have been devised in response to changes in the electoral system. The chapter closely analyses the party organizer's role in facilitating access to state patronage for certain social groups, which earns them symbolic capital as leverage for social/ political returns. As such, their focus is typically on local political actors—or 'nodal points'—rather than voters themselves. Through patronage, brokerage and particularization, these actors have emerged as important figures in the everyday life and political decisions of the local community. These mobilization strategies have been supplemented by the PR system which has intensified intraparty competition more than interparty competition, inevitably opening up more opportunities—and given more incentives— for the two dominant parties to mobilize numerically small social groups within the district.

Chapter 4 looks at the practice and logic of voting from the point of view of the voter, during and after an election, as an individual and member of the community. It posits that voters have two types of interests—identity and material—and which of the two gets prioritized largely depends on their level of dependency. Voters with higher levels of dependency are more likely to rely on material interests, while those with lower levels of dependency rely more on their identity interests when making electoral choices. The level of dependency in turn is not only determined by the life history or personal choice of the individual voter, but can also be shaped, to a certain extent at least, by state policies and through the choices of political actors. Within this framework, the ultimate electoral choice is dictated by the function of cultural structures, economic networks, family status and the status of the neighbourhood amongst other things. As such, rational public cynicism about politicians and political parties is forced into irrationality within certain logics and practices of voting.

Chapter 5 examines how party allegiance towards the UNP and SLFP is formed and sustained over time in Sinhalese constituencies, particularly given their being classified as 'catch-all' parties. It differentiates between voting behaviour and party allegiance, whereby party allegiance is not understood as an intended result of the electoral mobilization strategies of the two dominant parties, but rather as an inevitable offshoot of the process that leaves a more enduring emotional imprint on the voter. The sustenance of party allegiance, however, takes place as a result of two processes. On the one hand, the function of the organizational strategy of the party embeds these loyalists into the party's political actor network. On the other hand, party allegiance is also sustained through the handing down of party identification from one generation to the next. These processes are interconnected and interdependent social practices that are ritualized within Sri Lankan society. This differentiation between voter and party allegiance is crucial in order to understand the continued ability of both the SLFP and UNP to maintain their support bases irrespective of whether they are in power.

Chapter 6 discusses the emergence of the SLPP at the 2018 Local Government election as an offshoot of the SLFP and the SJB at the 2020 Parliamentary election as an offshoot of the UNP. It examines how and why supporters of the UNP and SLFP deserted their parties to join two new political fronts that emerged as the new 'coalition centres'. The weakening of the party institution and party discipline as a result of relying heavily on patronage-based politics while distancing from programmatic politics made both parties vulnerable to the politics of new entrants. Especially in the absence of a large electorate that is emotionally attached (like the kind afforded by the FPTP system), catch-all parties find it difficult to retain the interest/ loyalty of their local-level support bases. These new parties cannot be seen as parties that emerged to represent a socio-political class or socio-cultural group that has not been represented in the Sri Lankan party system so far. They are both clearly founded upon the bases of their old parties. The only distinction is that with the emergence of these new parties, the leadership of the country's rule has shifted to a new brand of politicians who are not connected to any of the Colombo-based, Westernized old political dynasties. Therefore, in terms of the party-voter nexus, it can be said that by deserting the UNP and the SLFP and joining not their rival groups but rather their own respective 'reincarnations', their supporters did not so much breach the nexus as renew it.

In sum, this book will deepen our understanding of the nuanced and complex subject of party-voter relations, with a focus on Sri Lanka. Scholars of Sri Lankan political party studies have thus far provided valuable accounts of the factors that matter when forming and maintaining the party-voter nexus. This study complements these analyses by explaining why and how such factors matter in forming, maintaining and ending the party-voter nexus. The electoral success behind the main parties has been their ability to address the material and identity interests of voters optimally. Their capacity to form a government automatically qualifies them to deliver the material interest of the voter, as state resources are the main source of patronage. Maintaining ideological plurality by forming wider coalitions with identity-based parties, these main parties invite voters from a wider spectrum of identities—be they caste, ethnicity, religion or class. For this, they have to deliberately maintain a feeble institutional structure that is disperse and flexible over time and ideological position, and a party organization strategy which relies largely on political actors. Although assuming such a character has enabled them to be powerful vote generating machines, its cost has been that these catch-all parties have become vulnerable to desertion of their support bases. However, the study demonstrates that even though voters are willing to desert their party, they are not quite ready to take a risk to desert the system within which the party-voter nexus is formed and maintained. In this context, though they have the capacity to amass votes, parties like the UNP and SLFP—and now the SLPP and SJB—cannot venture into programmatic initiatives unpopular amongst majority voters. As much as main parties mastermind the electoral engineering process, then, they are also very much at its mercy.

Notes

1. "Thoughts on the Cause of the Present Discontents" (1770), in Paul Langford, ed., *The Writings and Speeches of Edmund Burke*, Oxford: Clarendon Press, 1981, 317.
2. In his structuration theory, Anthony Giddens (1984) made an articulated effort to integrate structure and agency. In his famous book, *The Constitution of Society*, he states that "every research investigation in the social sciences or history is involved in relating action [or agency] to structure … there is no sense in which structure 'determines' action or vice versa" (1984: 219).

   Unlike structuralists and agency-oriented theorists who focus mainly on either society/structure or individual/agent, in his structuration theory Giddens pays main attention to "recurrent social practices" (Ritzer 1996: 528). The core of the structuration theory, with its focus on social practices, is the theory of relationship between agency and structure (Ritzer 1996: 529). According to Giddens, agency and structure cannot be conceived as apart from one another; they are two sides of the same coin. All social actions involve structure, and all structures involve social action. As Ritzer puts it, "agency and structure are inextricably interwoven in ongoing human activity or practice" (Ritzer 1996).

   According to Giddens' structuration theory, social practices are recursive and they are "not brought to being by social actors, but are continually recreated by them via the very means whereby they

express themselves as actors. In and through their activities agents produce the conditions that make these activities possible" (Giddens 1984: 2). Further, Giddens states that human agents are reflexive. That is to say that the human actor, being reflexive, "is not merely self-conscious but is also engaged in the monitoring of the ongoing flow of activities and social conditions" (Ritzer 1996: 528).
 3. Stokke (2002: 9).
 4. Stokke (2002: 10).
 5. In this case, he refers to 'patron-client' networks in Southeast Asia, Latin America, Africa and poorer parts of Europe.
 6. Jayanntha used pseudonyms to refer to the electorates where his fieldwork was conducted. He discussed electoral allegiance in Weligama under the pseudonym Bluville, and Kelaniya was discussed using the pseudonym Red Town (1992).

REFERENCES

Adrian, Wolfgang, 1987, "Some Reflections on the Role of Political Parties in a Democracy," in *Political Party System of Sri Lanka*, Colombo: Sri Lanka Foundation Institute.
Birch, Anthony. 1993. *The Concepts and Theories of Modern Democracy*. London: Routledge.
Bourdieu, Pierre. 1984. *Distinction: A Social Critique of the Judgment of Taste*. Cambridge, MA: Harvard University Press.
———. 1986. The Forms of Capital. In *Handbook of Theory and Research for the Sociology of Education*, ed. J.G. Richardson. New York: Greenwood Press.
———. 1989. Social Space and Symbolic Power. *Sociological Theory* 7: 14–25.
Bourdieu, Pierre, and L.J.D. Wacquant. 1992. The Purpose of Reflexive Sociology (The Chicago Workshop). In *An Invitation to Reflexive Sociology*, ed. P. Bourdieu and L.D.J. Wacquant, 61–225. Chicago: University of Chicago Press.
Dahl, R.A. 1966. *Political Oppositions in Western Democracies*. New Haven: Yale University Press.
Dalton, R.J. 1996. The History of Party Systems. In *Citizen Politics: Public Opinion and Political Parties in Advanced Western Democracies*, ed. R.J. Dalton, 2nd ed., 149–164. Chatham, NJ: Chatham House.
Deer, Cecile. 2008a. Doxa. In *Pierre Bourdieu: Key Concepts*, ed. Michael Grenfell. Durham: Acumen.

———. 2008b. Reflexivity. In *Pierre Bourdieu: Key Concepts*, ed. Michael Grenfell. Durham: Acumen.

de Zoysa, K.P. 2013. *Caste Matters: Democracy, Caste and Politics in Sri Lanka After the Promulgation of the 1978 Constitution: A Case Study of Sinhala Society*. Unpublished MA thesis, University of Colombo.

Downs, Anthony. 1957. An Economic Theory of Political Action in a Democracy. *The Journal of Political Economy* 65 (2) (April): 135–150.

Giddens, Anthony. 1984. *The Constitution of Society: Outline of the Theory of Structuration*. Oxford: Polity Press.

Grenfell, Michael, ed. 2008. *Pierre Bourdieu: Key Concepts*. Durham: Acumen.

Gunasekara, T. 1992. Democracy, Party Competition and Leadership: The Changing Power Structure in a Sinhalese Community. In *Agrarian Change in Sri Lanka*, ed. James Brow and Joe Weeramunda, 229–260. New Delhi and Newbury Park/London: Sage.

———. 1994. *Hierarchy and Egalitarianism: Caste, Class and Power in Sinhalese Pleasant Society*. London: The Athlone Press.

Gunasinghe, N. 1990. *Changing Socio-Economic Relations in the Kandyan Countryside*. Colombo: Social Scientists' Association.

Hettige, S. 1984. *Wealth, Power and Prestige: Emerging Patterns of Social Inequality in a Peasant Context*. Colombo: Ministry of Higher Education.

Jayanntha, D. 1992. *Electoral Allegiance in Sri Lanka*. Cambridge: Cambridge University Press.

Jayasuriya, L. 2000. *Welfarism and Politics in Sri Lanka*. Perth: School of Social Work and Social Policy, University of Western Australia.

Jiggins, J. 1979. *Caste and the Family in the Politics of the Sinhalese 1947 to 1976*. London: Cambridge University Press.

Jiggins, J. 1994. Dedigama 1973: A Profile of a By-Election in Sri Lanka. *Asian Survey* 14 (11) (November): 1000–1013.

Jupp, J. 1978. *Sri Lanka: Third World Democracy*. London: Cass.

Katz, R., and P. Mair. 2009. "The Cartel Party Thesis: A Restatement", of "Perspectives on Politics." *American Political Science Association* 7 (4): 753–766.

Kearney, R.N. 1973. *The Politics of Ceylon (Sri Lanka)*. Ithaca and London: Cornell University Press.

Kirchheimer, O. 1966. The Transformation of Western European Party Systems. In *Political Parties and Political Development*, ed. J. La Palombara and M. Weiner, 177–199. Princeton, NJ: Princeton University Press.

Kitschelt, Herbert, and I. Steven Wilkinson, eds. 1997. *Patrons Clients and Policies, Patterns of Democratic Accountability and Political Competition*. Cambridge: Cambridge University Press.

Kothari, Rajini. 1964. The Congress System in India. *Asian Survey* 4 (12) (December): 1161–1173.

Lipset, S.M., and S. Rokkan. 1967. *Party Systems and Voter Alignments: A Cross-National Perspective*. New York: The Free Press.

Mainwaring, B., and S. McGraw. 2018. How Catchall Parties Compete Ideologically: Beyond Party Typologies. *European Journal of Political Research*. https://doi.org/10.1111/1475-6765.12307.

Maton, Karl. 2008. Habitus. In *Pierre Bourdieu: Key Concepts*, ed. Michael Grenfell. Durham: Acumen.

Moore, M. 1985. *The State and Peasant Politics in Sri Lanka*. Cambridge: Cambridge University Press.

Randall, Vicky. 2006. Political Parties and Social Structure in the Developing World. *Handbook of Party Politics*. Sage. http://www.sage-ereference.com/hdbk_partypol/Article_n33.html. Accessed 6 April 2010.

Ritzer, George. 1996. *Sociological Theory*. New York: McGraw-Hill.

Roy, M. N. 2006. Politics without Party. In *India's Political Parties*, ed. Peter DeSouza and E., Sridaran, 51–57. New Delhi: Sage Publications India Pvt. Ltd.

Schattschneider, E. 1942. *Party Government*. New York: Farrar & Rinehart.

Schmitter, P.C. 2000. Parties Are Not What They Once Were. In *Political Parties and Democracy*, ed. Larry Diamond and Richard Gunther, 67–89. Baltimore and London: The Johns Hopkins University Press.

Scott, C. James. 1972. Patron-Client Politics and Political Change in Southeast Asia. *The American Political Science Review* 66 (1) (March): 91–113.

Selboe, Elin. 2008. Changing Continuities: Multi-Activity in the Network Politics of Colobane, Dakar. Unpublished PhD thesis, University of Oslo.

Shastri, A. 2018. United National Party: From Dominance to Opposition and Back. In *Political Parties in Sri Lanka: Change and Continuity*, ed. A. Shastri and J. Uyangoda, 100–133. New Delhi: Oxford University Press.

Shastri, A., and J. Uyangoda, eds. 2018. *Political Parties in Sri Lanka: Change and Continuity*. Oxford: Oxford University Press.

Spencer, Jonathan. 1990. *A Sinhala Village in a Time of Trouble, Politics and Change in Rural Sri Lanka*. Delhi: Oxford University Press.

Stokke, Kristian. 2002. *Habitus, Capital and Fields: Conceptualizing the Capacity of Actors in Local Politics*. Oslo: University of Oslo, Department of Sociology and Human Geography.

Stokke, Kristian, and Pradeep Peiris. 2010. Public Opinion on Peace as a Reflection of Social Differentiation of Identity in Sri Lanka. In *Democracy in Practice: Representation and Grassroots Politics*, *CPD Journal*, vol. II, no. 10, 37–68. Yogjakarta: University of Gadjah Madha.

Torcal, M., and Scott Mainwaring. 2000. The Political Recrafting of the Social Bases of Party Competition: Chile in the 1990s. Working Paper 278, September.

Uyangoda, Jayadeva. 2010a. Politics of Political Reform—A Key Theme in the Contemporary Conflict. In *Power and Politics: In the Shadow of Sri Lanka's Armed Conflict*, ed. Camilla Orjuela, 29–78. Sida Studies No. 25. Sida.

———. 2010b. *Samaajeeya Manawa Vidya Paryeshana: Dārshanika saha Kramavedi Handinveemak*. Colombo: Social Scientists' Association.

———. 2010c. It Was Election Time. *Polity* 5 (3 & 4): 3–9.

———. 2012a. The State in Post-Colonial Sri Lanka: Trajectories of Change. In *The Political Economy of Environment and Development in a Globalized World: Exploring Frontiers*, ed. D.J. Kjosavik and Paul Vedeld, 345–373. Colombo: Social Scientists' Association.

———. 2012b. The Dynamics of Coalition Politics and Democracy in Sri Lanka. In *Coalition Politics and Democratic Consolidation in Asia*, ed. E. Sridharan, 161–240. New Delhi. Oxford University Press.

Uyangoda, J., and K. Ariyadasa, 2018. Sri Lanka Freedom Party: Continuity Through Ideological and Policy Shifts. In *Political Parties in Sri Lanka: Change and Continuity*, ed. A. Shastri and J. Uyangoda, 134–158. New Delhi: Oxford University Press.

Weber, Max. 1958. Class, Status and Party. In *From Max Weber: Essays in Sociology*, ed. H.H. Gerth and C.W. Mills. New York: Oxford University Press.

White, J.K. 2006. What Is a Political Party? In *Handbook of Party Politics*. Sage. http://www.sageereference.com/hdbk_partypol/Article_n33.html. Accessed 6 April 2010.

Wilson, A.J. 1974. *Politics in Sri Lanka, 1947–1973*. London: MacMillan.

———. 1975. *Electoral Politics in an Emergent State: The Ceylon General Election of May 1970*. London: Cambridge University Press.

Wolinetz, Steven. 2002. Beyond the Catch-All Party: Approaches to the Study of Parties and Party Organizations in Contemporary Democracies. In *Political Parties: Old Concepts and New Challenges*, ed. Richard Günther, José Ramón Montero, and Juan Linz, 136–165. Oxford: Oxford University Press.

Woodward, Calvin A. 1969. *The Growth of a Political System in Ceylon*. Cambridge: Cambridge University Press.

Wriggins, W.H. 1960. *Ceylon: Dilemmas of a New Nation*. Princeton, NJ: Princeton University Press.

CHAPTER 2

Dynamics of Party Organization at the Level of the Electorate

An examination of party organizational structures and strategies of the UNP and SLFP at the level of the electorate will enable an in-depth understanding of the role, function and formation of party organization. Therefore, I focus on the transformation of party organization strategies of the two political parties during the past decades. Contrary to the prevalent understanding of party organization, I argue that there are multiple organizational strategies within a party that are often determined more by political conditions than structural conditions. In a shift from the traditional approaches of scholarly inquiry into party organization, I place emphasis on understanding the agency of party leaders. I hold these leaders responsible for designing and implementing the organizational strategies at multiple levels of the party hierarchy, instead of attributing this to a rigid hierarchical structure that each party may claim to possess at its headquarters.

To this end, I have drawn from the function of parties in the electorates of Dedigama, Weligama and Kelaniya, probing into the organizational structure and strategies adopted by the UNP and SLFP at the electorate level. Interviews with a cross section of voters have been relied upon to explain how the two parties are organized within each electorate. This information was gathered from three successive generations and spans several decades from the 1960s and 1980s to contemporary times.

© The Author(s), under exclusive license to Springer Nature   31
Singapore Pte Ltd. 2022
P. Peiris, *Catch-All Parties and Party-Voter Nexus in Sri Lanka*,
Politics of South Asia,
https://doi.org/10.1007/978-981-16-4153-4_2

The study of the organizational dynamics of the two parties reveals the process of transformation of their organizational strategies and structures in the past four decades, necessitated by changes in the electoral system and structures of governance. It provides greater understanding of the internal dynamics of organizational structures and strategies of the two main political parties in Sri Lanka. To probe into these issues, I examine the basic components of party organization under the following themes: (i) electorate organizer, (ii) inner circle and (iii) grassroots party leadership, branches, membership and ancillary organizations.

Party Organization in Electorates

The role of party organization at either the constituency or electorate level is not limited to merely managing its leaders and the membership. In political parties such as the UNP and SLFP, the party hierarchy regards the recruitment and managing of local leaders (village political leaders or community leaders) as more important than managing the general membership of the party. Traditionally, party membership is also accorded equal importance with leadership in the organizational literature of the party. However, in mass parties such as the UNP and SLFP where clientelist politics is practised, the party organization and membership do not receive the same attention as found in the literature on Western political parties. This aspect requires detailed discussion, and this will be developed later in the chapter.

In both parties, the party organization within the respective electorates functions more as a vote-garnering mechanism than as an institution designed to manage members. The organizational strategy of the party at the electorate level is invariably dependent on the discretion of the organizer of the electorate. Hence, the nuts and bolts of party organization at the electorate level differ from one electorate to another, although there is general uniformity in the national organizational structure. The party organization at the local level in the case of the UNP and SLFP is invariably context specific and is often flexible. At times, they exist as parallel networks. Yet, active politicians of the two parties present their respective organizational structures as well-structured and hierarchical,[1] largely thanks to having the local politician at its apex (it helps supporters define the 'line of command' within the electorate). However, closer scrutiny of the organizational dynamics within an electorate confirms that party organization within the electorate is not static, but rather context specific and less hierarchical. It is useful to understand the conventional conceptualization of the party organization structure as a point of departure in the inquiry of the actual party organization in the electorate.

Figure 2.1 depicts the conventional understanding of the party organizational structure. As shown, both the UNP and SLFP maintain a hierarchical structure of positions, and various formalities such as working committee meetings and development management committee meetings as functions of the party organization in the electorate. The electorate organizer is supposed to function with his inner circle that comprises various advisors and assistants. Directly under the organizer, there is a group of local council members (and sometimes potential local council candidates) who are responsible for one or more wards in the electorate. Under each local council member (or second-level leader), party branches are formed and each branch has its office bearers, such as chairman, vice chairman, treasurer, secretary and council members, in addition to officials of the ancillaries such as youth committees and women's committees (Fig. 2.1).

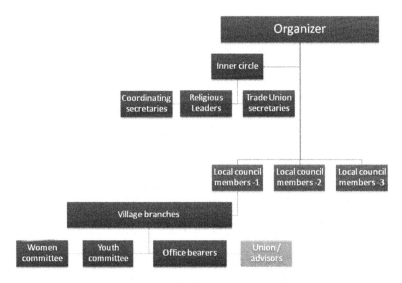

Local level formal party organization structure under the FPTP before 1978

Fig. 2.1 Party organization structure in the electorate—the traditional model

This formalization of the party organization began only after the mid-1970s. As many scholars have observed, the emergence of political party organization in any society goes through a common trajectory from "personal followings of the aristocracy", to "parties of notables", to "parties of plebiscitarian democracy" (Weber 1958; Duverger 1954). Woodward observes a similar trajectory in the Ceylonese party system and states that by the late 1950s parties had moved from notable dependency to parties based on mass voters (Woodward 1969: 275). However, the influence of the notables did not disappear. By the 1970s, recognizing change in the socio-political context, both parties felt the need for their party organization structures to reach the masses instead of depending only on followers of the notables. Traditional leaders, who built up their political capital largely on their economic capital (wealth) of the feudal past, lost their positions when the economy at the village and national levels transitioned into a market economy.[2] Access to public office and capital in the form of state resources replaced the personal wealth of politicians—an ingredient essential for patron-client relations in politics. Hence, by the 1970s, what mattered most was the scope and extent of personal or state capital that the politician could access. It was under the leadership of J.R. Jayewardene that the UNP began to set up village-level branch offices in order to strengthen its bases against the ruling coalition led by the SLFP. The SLFP also began its formal party organization at the village level, at least in the electorates I did my field work in, following the Sinhalese youth uprising of 1971 led by the JVP. However, these village-level formal party organizational positions as well as activities, such as setting up branches and appointing branch officials, usually remain dormant, only coming to life with elections. Usually, they tend to temporarily disappear soon after an election.

Electorate Organizer

Electorate organizers have attracted, more than anyone else, the attention of scholars who ventured into analysis of Sri Lankan political parties (Woodward 1969; Wilson 1975; Jupp 1978; Jiggins 1979; Jayanntha 1992; Coomaraswamy 1988). In most of these studies, members of Parliament and electorate organizers have been taken as the basic unit to examine the dynamics of politics in respective electorates. The analysis of electorate organizers undoubtedly provides valuable insights into the politics of electorates. However, in order to obtain a deeper understanding of the politics of an electorate, the analysis should be extended beyond the structural inquiry to examine organizer agency in the electorate.

Establishment of Electoral Leadership

As the field study suggests, the assumption that electoral organizers emerge from their electorates to assume political leadership is not entirely correct. As mentioned above, Woodward speaks of how the absorption of political notables to the ranks of parties transformed the "politics of notables" to "parties of notables" (Woodward 1969). However, when the two-party system was entrenched after the formation of the SLFP, local party leadership expanded to include non-traditional elites. With the expansion of electoral representation, parties also continued to recruit their local-level leadership from within and beyond their traditional bases. Often, the selection of electorate organizers rests on the discretion of party leadership at the centre rather than the will of the party organization at the electorate level. In such instances, it does not matter whether the person selected is from the electorate or from outside. Of course, individuals such as Panini Illangakoon and Montague Jayewickrema of Weligama, R.S. Perera and U.S. Perera of Kelaniya, and M.P. Herath of Dedigama were appointed as electorate organizers in electorates where they were natives.

However, all other organizers appointed as electorate organizers in these three electorates were not originally from them. Therefore, as far as the UNP and SLFP are concerned, electorate organizers were not always a product of the electorate and were often 'parachuted' in from outside to lead the party, to suit the interests of the national party leadership. Therefore, the organizer's loyalty to the incumbent leadership is far more important than his/her relation to the electorate. Similarly, there is no tradition of electing organizers by the party membership either. Instead, electorate organizers are selected by the party leadership based on their own criteria from amongst those who have shown electorally valid credentials and strong allegiance to the party leader.

Electorate Leadership—Dedigama

Dedigama was known as the stronghold of the Senanayakes. Family connections between the Senanayakes and Wijewardenes helped Dudley Senanayake, son of the country's first Prime Minister D.S. Senanayake, to inherit the Dedigama seat from Sir Francis Molamure[3] (Jiggins 1979: 72). Until Dudley Senanayake's death in 1973, he managed to win the Dedigama seat in all the elections he contested despite the considerable opposition he had to face. Dudley Senanayake banked on the feudal networks in the electorate although he himself was not from a traditional feudal family.[4] He belonged to a family of landed elite of the *goigama* caste that had accumulated wealth under colonial capitalism after the mid-nineteenth century. His father's family home was the famous *Bothale Walawwa* in Meerigama, which is adjacent to his Dedigama electorate. Family contacts and the name of his father were of great assistance to the young Dudley Senanayake. British educated, Dudely Senanayake grew up in Colombo as an urban professional. Later, he purchased the Narangoda estate, the largest rubber estate in Dedigama, and gradually established his base in the electorate.[5] He received substantial support because of the fame of his father and his cousin, Sir John Kotelawela, who was a wealthy graphite-mine owner as well as a prominent national politician at the time. According to Senanayake's surviving loyalists in Dedigama, he did not have a support base in Dedigama until he was appointed as the electorate organizer.[6] Therefore, it can be said that Dudley Senanayake, the very first electorate organizer of Dedigama, was an outsider 'parachuted' into the electorate. His father's close association with important Buddhist temples in the electorate enabled him to earn a great deal of cultural capital as well. For example, D.S. Senanayake called on the chief priest of the Dedigama Viharaya accompanied by Senanayake, Jr. He told the chief monk that from then onwards, his son was in the safe hands of the priest, and that he expected the monk's support for his son's electoral success.[7] Even to date, many temples remember Dudley Senanayake's good work and services to them.[8] No doubt the political capital of Dudley Senanayake was a direct outcome of the social and economic capital that he inherited (Table 2.1).

Except at the 1956 election, the SLFP failed to win the Dedigama electorate until 1994. For the 1956 election, S.W.R.D. Bandaranaike approached M.P. Herath to contest the Dedigama seat. M.P. Herath was an ordinary *goigama* government official whose only political credential was the office he held as chairman of the Warakapola village council. M.P. Herath was a strong UNP member until Dudley's temporary retirement from politics in 1953 (Jiggins 1974: 1004). As confirmed by several old SLFP members, it was his own brother who threw rotten eggs at S.W.R.D. Bandaranaike and led a mob to disrupt the campaign when Bandaranaike went to Dedigama to campaign during the 1952 election.[9] His brother was, at that time, the superintendent of the Narangoda estate, which belonged to Dudley Senanayake.[10] According to Siriwardane, who was a young Bandaranaike enthusiast at that time, he witnessed M.P. Herath being given Rs. 60,000 by S.W.R.D. Bandaranaike to campaign

Table 2.1 Dedigama party organizers

UNP			SLFP		
Name	Period	Caste	Name	Period	Caste
Dudley Senanayake	1947–1973	goigama	M.P. Herath	1953–1960	goigama
Rukman Senanayake	1973–1975	goigama	Deshapriya Senanayake	1960–1965	goigama
Nissanka Wijeratne	1975–1989	goigama	Dharmasiri Senanayake	1965–2000	goigama
Manoda Wijeratne	1989–2006	goigama	Athauda Seneviratne	*	goigama
Champika Premadasa	2006–2010	wahumpura	Manoda Wijeratne	*	goigama

*The period is not clear

for the 1956 election. However, M.P. Herath's victory could be attributed more to the nationwide swing in favour of the SLFP than to his personal appeal.

Due to bitter internal party conflict over the issue of succession after his father's sudden death in 1952, a heartbroken Dudley Senanayake left the country leaving his cousin, Sir John Kotelawela, to lead the 1956 general election (Jupp 1978: 59). Later, it was Wimala Kannangara from Kegalle who unsuccessfully contested from Dedigama for the UNP at the 1956 election. However, later M.P. Herath defected to the MEP with Philip Gunawardena and contested and lost the 1960 election under the MEP. Under the leadership of Mrs. Bandaranaike, Deshapriya Senanayake was appointed as the SLFP organizer of Dedigama. Deshapriya Senanayake was a lawyer from the Rambukkana electorate. Although his caste claim was contested by many UNPers, SLFPers believed that he belonged to the *goigama* caste. As in the case of M.P. Herath, Deshapriya Senanayake was also appointed by the national party leadership instead of emerging from the electorate, and both of them represented the intermediate classes that entered the political sphere following the 1956 election victory of the SLFP. However, unlike M.P. Herath, Deshapriya Senanayake never won the Dedigama seat despite working with SLFP party supporters to strengthen the party in the electorate. After losing the 1965 election, Deshapriya Senanayake left for China, passing the responsibilities of party organization on to his brother, Dharmasiri Senanayake, who was not a stranger to the electorate, having been his brother's secretary for years.

Dharmasiri Senanayake received the fullest support from party leadership as he had been close to Mrs. Bandaranaike for a long time. In fact, young Dharmasiri Senanayake was more popular than his brother due to his charming personality and hard work. For the first time, SLFP supporters in Dedigama felt that they had found a stable party organizer best suited to challenge Dudley Senanayake.[11] Siriwardane, an ardent loyalist of Dharmasiri Senanayake, recalled how the latter refused to accept the offer of Mrs. Bandaranaike to contest the Minuwangoda electorate, which he could have won comfortably at the 1970 election.[12] Therefore, even though Dharmasiri Senanayake was also from another electorate, his long years of presence and hard work allowed him to earn the loyalty of those who had supported S.W.R.D. Bandaranaike since 1956.[13] Despite his hard work and popularity amongst SLFP supporters, he could not win the Dedigama seat until 1994.

According to the chief priest of the Dedigama temple, although Dudley Senanayake commanded the support of most of the prominent temples in the electorate, Dharmasiri Senanayake did not hesitate to visit those temples.[14] He maintained a healthy relationship with temples in the electorate. Therefore, after the death of Dudley Senanayake, most Buddhist temples that supported Dudley Senanayake shifted their loyalty to Dharmasiri Senanayake. Unlike Dudley Senanayake, Dharmasiri Senanayake did not possess as much economic capital and primarily depended on the social capital he had acquired by cultivating personal social contacts. He also used state resources and his political contacts to provide patronage goods, such as jobs, land, promotions and easy access to the bureaucracy.[15] A good example is his appointment as chairman of a leading state corporation after his defeat in the electorate, even though his party, the SLFP, formed the government. He capitalized on these political appointments to maintain a steady flow of incentives that kept his patron-client relations with party loyalists in Dedigama.

Following the death of Dudley Senanayake, there was popular consensus amongst UNP supporters that someone from the Senanayake family should be offered the position of party organizer. Against this background, the then leader of the UNP, J.R. Jayewardene, appointed young Rukman Senanayake, a nephew of Dudley, to contest the 1973 election. This election turned out to be a violent by-election where the coalition government used all its powers to deny the Dedigama seat to the UNP

(Jiggins 1974). Despite the strength and resources deployed by the coalition government, Rukman Senanayake managed to secure a victory. He was supported by grieving Dudley loyalists who voted for him despite the widespread threats and intimidation by a desperate SLFP leadership.[16]

Despite Rukman Senanayake's victory at the Dedigama by-election and the popular support of the constituency, J.R. Jayewardene decided to offer the electorate to Nissanka Wijeratne, one of his personal loyalists. Wijeratne was a senior civil servant and a former *diyawadena nilame* (lay incumbent) of the Temple of the Tooth, which is the most prestigious religious-civilian post in the country. It is believed that Rukman was sidelined due to the political rivalry between the Jayewardene and Senanayake families.[17] It is said that Rukman was seen as a potential threat to J.R. Jayewardene's leadership. Nissanka Wijeratne did not have any family connection to Dedigama. However, he was regarded as an educated civil servant with a *goigama* feudal background (his wife belonged to a feudal family of the *Dunuvila Walawwa*).

At the beginning, Nissanka Wijeratne had to face stiff resistance from the old UNP loyalists. However, he was clever enough to win the support of the UNP rank and file and to appropriate the political network that Dudley Senanayake had developed over decades in the electorate. His association with the Dalada Maligawa as the *diyawadana nilame* gave him an advantage in winning the support of the UNP organizational network connected to the temples in the electorate. In fact, some of those temples were administered under the Dalada Maligawa, and the incumbents of those Buddhist temples took part in the selection of the *diyawadane nilame*. Against this backdrop, compared with his rivals, Nissanka Wijeratne had stronger ties with the Buddhist temples in the electorate. His impressive educational background and reputation as a senior civil servant helped his cause. Thus, it was his cultural (education) and social (contacts with the bureaucracy and Buddhists) capital which Wijeratne later successfully converted to political capital.

His son, Manoda Wijeratne inherited the post of electorate organizer following Nissanka's retirement from active politics in the late 1980s. Manoda Wijeratne had earlier worked as his father's coordinating secretary for many years. He continued with the networks that his father had developed to advance his political career. However, as years passed, most of the old personalities in this network retired from active politics, leaving those positions to be filled by young members either from the same families or from the same communities. In 2006, Manoda Wijeratne crossed over to the SLFP and contested the 2010 Parliamentary election from that party, but lost. The vacancy created by Manoda's defection was filled by Champika Premadasa, a businessman from the *wahumpura* caste. Compared with all those who had held the UNP organizer position in the past, Champika Premadasa's profile is radically different. He had a long political history with the SLFP before joining the UNP. Unlike his predecessors, he is not from an affluent family or a higher class background. However, in common with all the others, Champika Premadasa is also not from the Dedigama electorate. Before he assumed the position of electorate organizer in Dedigama, he represented the adjoining Rambukkana electorate in the provincial council. Although he entered politics as a rich businessman, he had amassed his wealth while emerging from very humble beginnings. He had started his life as an ordinary *beedi mudalali* (person who sells beedi, a cheap variety of cigarette made out of beedi leaves). It was the new UNP leader Ranil Wickremasinghe who appointed Premadasa to the post of Dedigama electorate organizer. He was uniquely fortunate to inherit almost the entire UNP organizational structure in Dedigama. In addition, his much publicized differences with the chief minister of the Sabaragamuwa Provincial Council (both were strong SLFP supporters in the past) and his new social standing as a rich businessman gave him publicity, which he capitalized for electoral advantage. Interestingly, while the UNP lost the Dedigama electorate in the 2010 Parliamentary election, Champika Premadasa managed to get elected to Parliament, while Manoda Wijeratne who had much stronger and longer ties with the Dedigama electorate was badly defeated. This will be discussed later in detail.

If we turn once again to the SLFP leadership in the electorate, Dharmasiri Senanayake led the SLFP in Dedigama until his death in 2001. Athauda Seneviratne, who was a long-time member of the Lanka Sama Samaja Party (LSSP), later joined the SLFP and was appointed as the SLFP organizer, replacing Senanayake. He was a school teacher from the *goigama* caste before entering full-time politics. Even though he was not a veteran SLFPer, he was not a total stranger to the SLFP as his party, the LSSP, had been a traditional electoral ally of the SLFP. Prior to his appointment as the Dedigama organizer, he had represented the Ruwanwella electorate in Parliament since 1970. Interestingly, except for M.P. Herath, none of the electorate organizers of Dedigama from both the UNP and SLFP had emerged from the Dedigama electorate. All were

Table 2.2   Weligama party organizers

UNP			SLFP		
Name		Caste	Name		Caste
Montague Jayewickrema	1947–1970	karawa	Panini Illangakoon	1952–1977	goigama
Chandra Premaratne	1970–1977	goigama	Chulapadmendra Dahanayaka	1977–1982	goigama
Montague Jayewickrema	1977–1988	karawa	Jayantha Wikramasuriya	1982–1990	karawa
Madurapala Ediriweera	*	karawa	C.A. Jagath		goigama
Ronnie De Mel	*	karawa	Sujith Jayewickrema	1990–1993	karawa
Mahinda Wijesekara	*	karawa	Saman Weeraman	*	goigama
			Mahinda Yapa Abeywardana	*	goigama

*The period is not clear

introduced to the electorate from outside, appointed by their respective party leaderships at the centre (Table 2.2).

Electorate Leadership—Weligama
Montague Jayewickrema is undoubtedly the most popular political leader in the history of Weligama. He inherited the popularity and wealth of his maternal grandfather, *Mudaliyar* Samaraweera, who was a very rich landlord and well-regarded philanthropist. The Jayewickrema and Samaraweera families enjoyed a prestigious position in Weligama and the surrounding area due to their wealth, social service and the honorary position that *Mudaliyar* Samaraweera received from the colonial government. Hence, getting into politics for Montague Jayewickrema just meant a continuation of the status of the family that they had enjoyed for many years amongst different communities in Weligama. Even though Jayewickrema belonged to the *karawa* caste, which constituted less than 15%[18] of the Weligama electorate, he commanded a great deal of support from the *goigama* majority throughout his political career in Weligama. He entered politics by becoming the Chairman of the Weligama Urban Council in 1936. Except for the 1970 election, he was the UNP organizer for Weligama until the late 1980s. He was first elected to Parliament in

1947 and then held various senior cabinet portfolios until 1989 when he was appointed as the Governor of the North Western Provincial Council by then President Ranasinghe Premadasa. At the 1970 election, Jayewickrema decided to contest from the Haputale electorate due to his growing unpopularity in Weligama.[19]

The vacant electoral organizer post was given to Chandra Premaratne who hailed from a non-Weligama, non-*karawa* (*goigama*) and less popular elite background. However, Chandra Premaratne lost the Weligama seat at the 1970 election, as the UNP too was defeated badly nationally and reduced to just 17 seats in Parliament. However, Jayewickrema's decision to contest from Haputale did not help him to return to Parliament. Later Jayewickrema returned to Weligama and reorganized his home electorate quite successfully by attracting young village youth and community leaders to his organizing network. By that time, especially the youth, but all communities in general, were utterly frustrated with the economic embargos and political victimization at the hands of SLFPers who virtually controlled the distribution of subsidies through *samupakara* (cooperative) shops. Therefore, reorganizing the electorate was not that difficult a task for Montague Jayewickrema. In 1977, he was again elected to Parliament and given a senior ministerial portfolio under President J.R. Jayewardene.

However, when President Premadasa assumed leadership of the UNP in 1988, he wanted to give more space to his own loyalists within the party by sidelining politicians such as Montague Jayewickrema, the loyalist of his predecessor. When Jayewickrema took up appointment as Governor of the North Western Province, Premadasa appointed Madurapala Ediriweera, who was one of Montague's close supporters, as the UNP organizer in Weligama. Even though Ediriweera had been one of Montague's trusted foot soldiers, he was a miniscule political actor, compared with the wealth and social standing of his political patron. Madurapala Ediriweera was also a member of the *karawa* caste and represented the coastal belt of Weligama. President Premadasa approached him as he was the only available alternative to replace Jayewickrema. At the height of the second uprising of the JVP during 1987–1989, many seniors left politics due to the violence. In the midst of it, Madurapala Ediriweera succeeded in getting elected to Parliament in 1989 with just 8,562 votes out of the 451,926 registered voters in Matara District.[20] Although Ediriweera commanded neither the economic capital nor the network of the landed gentry and family network of Jayewickrema, he was popular in the electorate. This was because he was in the inner circle of the powerful politician Jayewickrema and also was Mayor of the Weligama Urban Council. He was directly involved in the distribution of clientelistic goods that Jayewickrema had generously distributed amongst his supporters, allegedly (mis)using his ministerial positions for decades.

However, Ediriweera could not consolidate his status as the electorate organizer in Weligama for long. After defecting to the UNP in 2001, Mahinda Wijesekara was appointed as the organizer for Weligama by the party leadership. He was widely considered as the leader of the *karawa* caste by that community in Weligama.[21] Prior to his defection to the UNP, he was the SLFP organizer of the Devundara electorate. Mahinda Wijesekara certainly was more popular than Madurapala Ediriweera. Amongst the coastal communities, he was popular as a fearless leader and someone from their community. He capitalized this popularity for his electoral organizing in the district. However, unlike Jayewickrema and Ediriweera, Mahinda Wijesekara did not have family roots in the electorate other than his strong caste connections which he capitalized to a great extent. After he returned to the SLFP in 2006, the UNP was without a strong electorate organizer there. The discussion so far indicates that the UNP leadership in Weligama has always been from the *karawa* caste. Interestingly, although the UNP leadership in the electorate did not slip out of the *karawa* caste, the social status and wealth of the leadership changed over the decades, from rich landlord families to middle-class professionals. As Tara Coomaraswamy (1988) has observed, landed political elites were replaced by new elites who accumulated their wealth after joining the profession of politics.

Unlike the UNP, the party leadership of the SLFP in the Weligama electorate shifted to many hands of both the *goigama* and *karawa* communities. S.W.R.D. Bandaranaike approached his cousin Panini Illangakoon, when he formed the SLFP, to organize the Weligama electorate and contest Montague Jayewickrema. Panini Illangakoon was the only son of Mudaliyar Illangakoon who was the chief *mudaliyar* (*Maha Mudali*) for the Southern Province under the British colonial government. Therefore, Illangakoon inherited the wealth of his father, which spread across the entire Province. Until he was approached by the SLFP leadership to contest the 1952 election for the Weligama electorate, he was very much a Communist Party (CP) loyalist. However, he accepted the invitation of his cousin and took the responsibility to lead the SLFP in Weligama. Unlike Jayewickrema, Illangakoon did not have an extended family network across the electorate. Despite possessing substantial economic capital and representing the caste of the majority of Weligama voters, Illangakoon managed to win only two elections. It should be noted that even the 1956 and 1970 election victories cannot be considered as his personal electoral wins, because during these elections there was a groundswell of support for the SLFP at the national level. Complications and controversies regarding Illangakoon's personal life affected his political career, and as a result people including SLFP loyalists began to distance themselves from him.

Later the leader of the SLFP, Sirimavo Bandaranaike, appointed Chulapadmendra Dahanayake as the Weligama SLFP organizer, as Panini was no longer favoured by the party's national leadership. By then, Panini Illangakoon had lost the wealth and popularity he had enjoyed for decades in Weligama. Dahanayake was a lawyer from the *goigama* community. However, he was neither from the landowning class nor from the Weligama electorate. Soon after the 1977 defeat, Dahanayake made strenuous efforts to reorganize the SLFP party organizational network. This was partially to counter the post-election violence unleashed by UNP supporters. However, later he changed his allegiance to the UNP during the 1982 presidential election. For the first time in Weligama, the SLFP appointed two electorate organizers to replace Dahanayake. Mr. C.A. Jagathchandra from the *goigama* caste was appointed to Weligama East, and Jayantha Wickramasuriya from the *karawa* caste was appointed to Weligama West. Neither of them hailed from rich landed or feudal families like Illangakoon. However, C.A. Jagathchandra was a well-known personality due to his family background and family connections to the famous Anagarika Dharmapala, who led the Sinhala Buddhist revival movement in the early years of the twentieth century. Jayantha Wickramasuriya was a businessman involved in the citronella industry and married to a wealthy business family that owned a bus company.

However, within a few years, the SLFP leadership appointed Sujith Jayewickrema, a nephew of Montague Jayewickrema, as the Weligama SLFP organizer. Sujith Jayewickrema inherited some degree of symbolic capital from his family legacy in Weligama and especially from his uncle Montague, but he did not possess the same wealth and landlord network that his uncle enjoyed. Despite his family background and wealth, Sujith Jayewickrema could not win the 1989 election that was marred by extreme violence. As Sujith Jayewickrema quit politics, Saman Weeraman was appointed as the Weligama organizer in 1993. Saman Weeraman was a lawyer practising at the Matara court. He hailed from the *goigama* caste. Mahinda Yapa, the Chief Minister of the Southern Provincial Council and ex-UNP strongman who defected to the Prajatantravadi Eksath Jathika Paksaya (breakaway faction from the UNP led by Lalith Athulathmudali and Gamini Dissanayake during the time of President Premadasa), joined the SLFP and took over the organizing work of the Weligama electorate to contest the 1994 election. Mahinda Yapa is originally from the Hakmana seat in Matara District and did not have many family connections in the Weligama electorate. Thanks to the PR system, he continued to be elected to Parliament by amassing votes from other electorates despite his weak popularity in Weligama.

Electorate Leadership—Kelaniya
In many respects, the Kelaniya electorate stands in contrast to both Dedigama and Weligama. Its close proximity to Colombo, the capital city; its diverse socio-economic composition and a rapidly expanding migrant population; its drastically changing geographical map over the past five decades; and the completely non-agrarian economic base of the electorate that rests on industrial and service sectors.

The highly respected statesman Sir D.B. Jayatilaka represented Kelaniya in the State Council from 1931 to 1943. Upon his resignation to accept the post of Sri Lankan High Commissioner to India in 1943, J.R. Jayewardene became the representative in the State Council for Kelaniya. At the interim election held on 18 April 1943, J.R. Jayewardene contested E.W. Perera, a nationally reputed Catholic leader, and managed to win the election with the help of Buddhist temples in the electorate. Neither J.R. Jayewardene nor E.W. Perera was originally from the Kelaniya electorate. However, J.R. Jayewardene's mother and grandmother were linked to the powerful Kelaniya temple. Elina Rupasinghe, J.R. Jayewardene's wife, was from the Kelaniya electorate, and he used his wife's coconut estate, Manelwatta, for his political activities (de Silva and Wiggins 1988: 140). At the 1952 election, the newly formed SLFP put forward Wimala Wijewardene to contest J.R. Jayewardene. In that election, Jayewardene had a comfortable victory despite Wimala Wijewardene being supported by the Kelaniya temple. Wimala Wijewardene's husband was a relative of J.R. Jayewardene, and he was from the family of the chief patrons of the Kelaniya temple. In addition, her close association with the chief incumbent of the temple, Buddharakkitha, was known to many in the electorate. Therefore, Wimala Wijewardene, despite being a Catholic, received strong support from the network connected with the Kelaniya temple. After the 1952 defeat, Wimala Wijewardene moved from Kelaniya to start organizing the Meerigama electorate. The victory of R.G. Senanayake at the 1956 election ended J.R. Jayewardene's 13-year representation of Kelaniya in the legislature. In this election, R.G. Senanayake contested for both the Kelaniya and Dambadeniya electorates. R.G. Senanayake had no connection with the Kelaniya electorate. He was the son of a national hero, F.R. Senanayake. It is believed that R.G. Senanayake contested in Kelaniya due to personal animosity between him and J.R. Jayewardene. However, J.R. Jayawardene continued to be the electoral organizer for Kelaniya until the March 1960 election (Table 2.3).

At the March 1960 election, he won a slim victory against the young and less experienced R.S. Perera. Like all previous party organizers (from the SLFP and UNP) in Kelaniya, R.S. Perera was also a Sinhalese from the *goigama* caste. Unlike previous SLFP party organizers, he was the first organizer who was originally from the Kelaniya electorate. Even though J.R. Jayewardene managed to win that election, the slim margin he gained against novice politician R.S. Perera signalled his declining popularity in the electorate. According to Jayanntha, J.R. Jayewardene and his advisors recognized this election result as an "illusionary victory" (Jayanntha 1992: 167). Therefore, at the July 1960 election, three months after his victory in Kelaniya, he decided to move to Colombo South. A.W.A. Abeyagoonasekera was appointed to Kelaniya as the new UNP electorate organizer. Compared to the stature of J.R. Jayewardene, Abeyagoonasekera was a nonentity. Nevertheless, he enjoyed considerable popularity amongst the party rank and file since he managed to defeat Pieter Keuneman, the prominent leftist, at the Colombo Municipal Council election in 1959.[22] Like J.R. Jayewardene, Abeyagoonasekera was originally not from Kelaniya electorate. However, later, he purchased land and went to live in Kelaniya. R.S. Perera continued to win the Kelaniya electorate until 1977, despite being a Catholic in a Buddhist-majority electorate and also without support from the Catholic Church. Following the sudden demise of Abeyagoonasekera in a plane crash, party loyalists in Kelaniya proposed K.S.N. Perera, a Sinhala Buddhist lawyer of the *hunu* caste for the post.

The new UNP leader, J.R. Jayewardene, decided on his nephew Ranil Wickremasinghe, who is a Sinhala Buddhist and of the *goigama* caste. However, Ranil Wickremasinghe did not serve long in Kelaniya. He took

Table 2.3 Kelaniya party organizers

UNP			SLFP		
Name	*Time Period**	*Religion/Caste*	*Name*	*Time Period**	*Religion/Caste*
J.R. Jayewardene	1947–March 1960	Buddhist/*goigama*	Wimala Wijewardene[1]	1952	Buddhist/*goigama*
A.W.A. Abeygunasekara	July 1960–1977	Buddhist/*goigama*	R.G. Senanayake[2]	1956	Buddhist/*goigama*
K. D. Cyril Mathew	1977–1984	Buddhist/*wahumpura*	R.S. Perera	1960–1970	Catholic/*goigama*
U.S. Perera	1989–1994	Catholic/*goigama*	Erin Senanayake	1977	Buddhist/*goigama*
Pradeep Hapangama	1994–2001	Buddhist/*goigama*	M.K.J. Nandasena	1989–2001	Buddhist/*goigama*
Athula Nimalasiri Jayasinghe	2004	Buddhist/*wahumpura*	Sripathi Sooriarchchi[3]	2004	Buddhist/*goigama*
Suranimala Rajapakse	2010	Buddhist/*goigama*	Mervyn Silva	2007–2010	Buddhist/*salagama*

*Time period range covers parliamentary elections, rather than exact years of appointment
1 Wimala Wijewardena was a Catholic, although she was later married to a Buddhist, and organized her electoral work with the help of the chief incumbent of the Kelaniya temple
2 Even though R.G. Senanayake contested as an independent candidate for Kelaniya in the 1956 election, the SLFP supported him as its candidate
3 His wife is a Catholic, and it is believed that his father is Tamil

up the post of electorate organizer of the newly created Biyagama electorate (carved out of a large part of the Kelaniya electorate) where the
majority belonged to the *goigama* caste. The post of Kelaniya electorate
organizer of the UNP was filled by a strong J.R. Jayewardene loyalist
and *wahumpura* caste Buddhist, Cyril Mathew. This was the first non-
goigama appointment either the UNP or SLFP had made as electoral
organizer in Kelaniya. With his wife being from Kelaniya, Cyril Mathew
had a large network of relations and community in Kelaniya. It was
believed that he would attract the support of *wahumpura* voters who
constituted a substantial proportion of the Kelaniya electorate. Since R.S.
Perera declined to contest the 1977 election, the SLFP nominated Erin
Senanayake, widow of R.G. Senanayake, a few months before the election.
Therefore, Erin Senanayake did not function as the electorate organizer of
the SLFP in Kelaniya but was 'parachuted' in only for the election. Cyril
Mathew scored an easy victory at this election against Erin Senanayake.
However, given the landslide swing towards the UNP in 1977, the victory
of Mathew is not considered as a personal achievement (Jayanntha 1992:
177). After the defeat at the 1977 elections, internecine turf wars amongst
the national leadership of the SLFP weakened its electoral organizing
activities in Kelaniya. Despite his popularity in the electorate, by late
1984 J.R. Jayewardene removed Cyril Mathew from his post. The position was then given to young Nimal Samarasinghe, who was a Sinhalese
Catholic and native Kelaniya resident from the *goigama* caste. However,
due to the violence-marred politics in the background of the second
JVP uprising during 1987–1989, he left party politics. The leader of the
UNP, Ranasinghe Premadasa, appointed U.S. Perera as the UNP electorate organizer in Kelaniya. He is also a Sinhalese Catholic from the
Kelaniya electorate and belongs to the *goigama* caste. U.S. Perera made
his entry into politics through leftist politics. He was popular as the chal-
lenger to the much-experienced national politician J.R. Jayewardene in
the 1960s.

Later, he joined the UNP and under Cyril Mathew held various political posts. The SLFP appointed H.K.J. Nandasena, a *goigama* Sinhala
Buddhist who was originally from Deniyaya in Matara District. Although
he was from outside the Kelaniya electorate, he married into a family in
Kiribathgoda, in the electorate. Although the UNP won the Kelaniya electorate at the 1989 Parliamentary election, U.S. Perera was not elected to
Parliament, mainly because he could not obtain enough preferential votes

under the proportional representation system. This was the first election held under the PR system.

For the 1994 election, the UNP appointed Anura Pradeep Hapangama as its electorate organizer. He was a resident of the Kelaniya electorate and belonged to the *goigama* caste and a Sinhala Buddhist family. He was earlier the SLFP electorate organizer of the adjoining Mahara electorate and had been a Member of Parliament since the 1989 election. Pradeep Hapangama was a popular politician during this time in the Kelaniya electorate and was also the *Basnayake Nilame* of the Vibhishana Devalaya of the Kelaniya temple. The SLFP won the Kelaniya seat at the 1994 election. Thanks to the PR system, both K.H.J. Nandasena and Pradeep Hapangama were elected to Parliament. Both led their parties at the 2000 and 2001 elections, and both failed to be elected to Parliament due to their diminishing popularity amongst their respective party supporters. For the 2004 election, the SLFP appointed Sripathi Sooriarchchi, a former Navy officer who was an outsider to Kelaniya, as the electorate organizer. He presented himself as a Sinhala Buddhist from the *goigama* caste. Nevertheless, his wife is a Sinhalese Catholic while his father was allegedly Tamil. The UNP appointed Athula Nimalasiri Jayasinghe (*Loku Athula*), a former deputy minister of the rival SLFPer, as the Kelaniya electorate organizer. He was a *wahumpura* caste resident of the adjoining Mahara electorate and one of the high-ranking leaders of the JVP during the 1971 insurgency. At this 2004 election, the SLFP-led UPFA coalition won the Kelaniya seat and Sripathi Sooriarchchi was elected to Parliament. However, after he fell out with President Rajapaksa, Sripathi Sooriarchchi was replaced by Mervyn Silva as the SLFP's Kelaniya electorate organizer and remains its organizer to date. Mervyn Silva is the first non-*goigama* SLFP electorate organizer in Kelaniya. He is a Sinhala Buddhist from Hambantota District and belongs to the *durawa* caste. He is yet another electorate organizer who is completely new to the electorate. However, at the 2010 election, he was reelected to Parliament with a massive preferential vote. The UNP appointed Suranimala Rajapakse, a former UNP minister and the former Biyagama UNP electorate organizer of the Kelaniya electorate, to contest Kelaniya at the 2010 election.

The above survey of electorate organizers reveals some important aspects of the post of electorate organizer of both the UNP and SLFP. The organizer is the most important link in the chain of the party organization at the level of the electorate. Electorate organizers do not necessarily belong to the community in the electorate; nor do they rise from the rank and file of the party organization in a particular electorate. It is the national leadership of the party that selects and appoints the electorate organizer. Therefore, loyalty to the party leadership is the most important qualification to be a party organizer. Although other skills and capabilities are important, they are of secondary importance when measured against allegiance to the central leadership of the party. Most importantly, the caste and the religion of the party organizer do not always need to have a direct correlation with the caste and religion of the majority in the electorate. Hence, it is not the social structural profile, but how the electorate organizer manipulates and addresses the social structural conditions of the electorate that determines the success as an organizer. This will be discussed later in detail.

THE BASIC COMPONENTS OF PARTY ORGANIZATION IN ELECTORATES

As the field study in the electorates of Dedigama, Kelaniya and Weligama indicates, the basic components of the formal party organizational structure at the electorate level comprise: (i) the electorate organizer, (ii) inner circle of the organizer, (iii) grassroots leadership, (iv) members and (v) ancillary organizations. In the party organization of the electorate, the organizer is the pivotal element and the driving force. This is to say that the electorate organizer formulates and executes strategies based on personal experience in politics and how he/she understands the political history of the electorate. However, these organizing strategies are executed while conforming to the broad structure at the centre. Electorate organizers always have a group of confidants who form an inner circle. The inner circle often comprises professionals rather than local politicians. These are persons with the capacity to either raise funds or provide funds themselves, who have some professional expertise to function as secretaries, and who are equipped to offer advice to the organizer or to enhance the symbolic capital of the organizer. However, these individuals are not always engaged in local-level party politics.

The field study also shows that local or provincial council members or candidates are the most important segment of the party cadre that leaders employ to manage party organization across the electorate. These local council members represent geographically smaller units or wards within the electorate. Usually, local council members who manage to be elected to a Municipality, Urban Council or *Pradeshiya Sabha* are appointed to oversee ward-level party activities. Often, one local council member may have to oversee several wards. Party branches at the ward level usually comprise a chairperson, secretary, treasurer and three committees to include elders, women and youth. In addition, some have trade union representation, often enabling school teachers to play an important role as advisors at this lowest level of the party organization structure. Office bearers of these branches and their ancillary units are supposed to be elected democratically, even though this is hardly the practice. All the individuals who play various roles in the party structure can be referred to as office bearers of the parties. Therefore, it is very common to consider the people who associate and participate in this party organization as being members of the party.

However, the concept of party membership with regard to these two parties is misleading on many grounds. While this aspect will be dealt with later, it should be noted that the electorate-level organizations of the UNP as well as the SLFP do not intend to recruit and maintain a membership base. The voters too do not want to commit themselves to being card-holding members of either of the two parties that depend on a mass base instead of active party cadre. Unlike at the centre, the role of ancillary organizations at the electorate level is somewhat ambiguous. Temple committees, funeral societies, farmers and fishermen's societies and labour unions within the electorate are typically the organizations that serve as ancillary organizations of the parties at the electorate level. Most of these elements of the party organization become activated only during an election campaign, especially during national elections. In between elections, the functions of various party organizations and organs are confined to a small group of people who hold positions in the party structure. This limited presence of the party organization structure becomes even less prominent and terribly unattractive when the party is in the opposition. However, as long as the party is in power and active in government, the party organization in that electorate is likely to remain active and functional (regardless of winning or losing).

Inner Circle

Regardless of whether they are leaders at national, regional or local levels, all leaders maintain their own inner circles or coteries. Hence, it is not surprising to observe that politicians even at the electoral level tend to maintain their own inner circle quite independent of the party structure.

It is common for family members, relatives and long-time associates to comprise the inner circle of a politician. They are not necessarily representatives of a particular constituency, although some do represent certain community groups in the electorate. What qualifies these individuals to be in the inner circle is not their political strength in the electorate, but their loyalty to the politician and their expertise in election engineering. Their role is largely to administer the electoral enterprise of the leader by managing the networks of local elites and community leaders. These individuals play a crucial role in implementing the strategies of the electorate organizer while insulating the organizer from any pressures that arise from grassroots leadership and party supporters. Loyalty is the topmost qualification of these individuals. Hence, often the inner circle is constituted of family members and relatives. In general, electorate organizers are engaged in a constant struggle to improve their standing while holding on to their current position. In this context, they not only challenge politicians in the upper echelons of political power but are also challenged by their subordinates within or outside the party. In this volatile competition for power, those in the inner circle not only assist the electorate organizer in challenging seniors in the hierarchy, but they also shield him/her from any potential challenge from those aspirants for power from the junior political leadership in the electorate. During election campaigns, members of the inner circle negotiate with grassroots leaders to garner the votes of communities the latter represent. This is achieved by offering material as well as non-material benefits.

Those in the inner circle also negotiate with businessmen and other wealth producers to raise funds for an election campaign under the guidance of their leader. In return, they promise various clientelist goods once (re)elected. During elections, they play a vital role in activating an electoral web that collects funds from those who have wealth but not votes, and garnering votes using clientelistic strategies from those who possess no wealth but their votes. They are usually professional electoral engineers who the electorate organizer depends on. At the same time, they are the first to benefit from political patronage in the event of their party forming the government or entering into a coalition that forms the ruling alliance. The benefits and perks to members of the inner circle depend on the portfolio that their organizer receives from the party leadership. If their electorate organizer is appointed as a senior minister, usually individuals in the inner circle fill most of the top posts of the departments and institutes that come under that particular ministry. Hence, these individuals receive a great deal of access to state resources that they can use to distribute clientelist goods amongst their supporters and those who funded their electoral campaign. The point that needs to be highlighted here is that they are not only important to electorate organizers, but are also essential contacts for grassroots organizers and voters who expect patronage of the party and of the politicians.

Robert Senanayake (brother of Dudley Senanayake), Dharmasiri Senanayake (brother of Deshapriya Senanayake) and Erel Jayewickrema (brother of Montague Jayewickrema) are examples of families serving in the inner circle of politicians. Of course, if one looks at today's politics, countless such examples can be seen. Some keep their spouse or children in the inner circle as secretaries or in other powerful positions. An example from my field work is Nissanka Wijeratne, who used his two sons, first Anurudda and then Manoda, as his secretaries. Manoda Wijeratne and Mahinda Wijesekara are examples of electorate organizers who appointed their spouses to the inner circle.[23] In addition, most of them used family members and loyal experts in their party in the inner circle. Those who occupy the inner circle hold significant authority in matters of electorate organizing and often act as the link between the party organizer and others. The authority that members of the inner circle exercise also depends on the personality of their organizer. For example, the authority of the inner circle is relatively higher in the case of a weak electorate organizer than of a stronger one. Those who occupied the inner circle of Panini Illangakoon exercised a great deal of authority and sometimes they even slipped out of his control.[24] Illangakoon was generally a weak electorate organizer due to various scandals and contrivances. On the contrary, Mahinda Wijesekara was relatively a strong personality and not only the inner circle, but the entire Weligama electorate organization, was kept under his strict supervision. It was widely believed that those who served in Illangakoon's inner circle engaged in various activities abusing Illangakoon's powers that eventually made their leader very unpopular in the electorate. Even though Mahinda Wijesekara did not have many relatives in his inner circle, except his wife, his strong management style always kept the inner circle under tight control.

The social composition—ethnicity, caste and class—of the inner circle of the electorate organizer often contributes to his/her image. It also provides a strong indication about the electorate organizer's sense of representation. For example, by nurturing *wahumpura* caste people in his inner circle, Kelaniya UNP organizer Cyril Mathew let his caste loyalty be known to the electorate and hurt the sentiments of *goigama* caste, grassroots leaders of the UNP in the electorate.[25] Similarly, during early electorate organizing, Dudley Senanayake kept individuals from the *goigama* and *radala* background in his inner circle. Hence, this contributed to the common perception that the UNP and Dudley had special loyalty to people from the *goigama* and *radala* caste families. Later, perhaps after realizing its negative effect on the election campaign, Dudley Senanayake began to approach local leaders who represented communities of other marginalized caste groups.[26] The presence of Errol Jayewickrema, who was married to an Kandyan *goigama* woman, in the inner circle of Montague Jayewickrema, helped him to reach out to the *goigama* majority in the electorate despite his *karawa* caste identity. It is said that Montague often identified himself as '*api govi-karawe*' (We are *goigama-karawa* people). This was to highlight his links to the *goigama* Kandyan community through his brother's family. Interestingly, inner circles of Jayewickrema and Illangakoon, who represented two rival parties and two different caste groups, were dominated by individuals of the *karawa* community. This angered the *goigama* and *durawa* communities in the Weligama electorate, as they felt that *karawa* people 'called the shots' despite their population strength being far below that of the *goigama* and *durawa* caste communities.[27]

Therefore, it is common for politicians to appoint family members, relatives and long-time associates to the inner circle who will play key roles in assisting the politician in organizing the electorate. These individuals extend maximum loyalty, while some of them could even provide technical advice on election engineering. Ironically, party loyalty is not an essential factor for these individuals despite their key role in the party organizational structure in the electorate.

Capacity to Unleash and Counter Violence

No political party in Sri Lanka today maintains a party militia as part of the party organization. Studying political parties in Europe in the 1960s, Duverger (1954), however, included the party militia as part of the party organization.[28] In the past, some Marxist parties paraded in uniforms, carrying flags on May Day. Even those colourful and pseudo-revolutionary parades of Marxist parties have waned by now. Other than those symbolic parades, no political party publicly acknowledges any association with or maintaining a militia as Duverger describes. However, while not matching Duverger's definition of militias, politicians of the UNP and SLFP are known to have the capacity to unleash or counter violence. It is quite common to use weapons in these encounters. In this context, despite the absolute silence of or denial by political parties, it is important to note the capacity of political parties and electoral organizers to maintain such facilities of coercive persuasion as part of their electoral competition strategy.

Despite impressive records of voter turnout, violence has become integral to the process of elections. No election in contemporary times has been devoid of violence. Paikiasothy Saravanamuttu, the convener of the Centre for Monitoring Election Violence (CMEV), succinctly illustrates the dilemmatic cohabitation of democracy and violence in Sri Lanka as follows:

> It must also be emphasized that whilst electoral violence and malpractices has been a growing problem over the last four decades, the Sri Lankan electorate has maintained a deep and abiding faith in the electoral process as turnout figures consistently in the range of 55-86% confirm. (Saravanamuttu 2008: 53)

Therefore, the dilemma in Sri Lankan democracy is that in spite of election violence and malpractice, voters show a great deal of interest in participating in elections.

It is important to acknowledge the nexus between electoral competition and violence in order to have a pragmatic understanding of political parties such as the UNP and SLFP and their electoral strategies. It is not difficult to observe that parties and politicians maintain contacts with thugs/gangs as an integral part of their party organizations.

Before the 1970s, both parties relied on the allegiance of village *chandiyas* (thugs) who often operated in isolation and had minimal access to firearms. But today, those village *chandiyas* have been replaced by organized gangs/thugs wielding sophisticated weapons. These thugs/gangs usually do not represent a political party nor subscribe to the goals of a political party. Instead, they maintain links with individual politicians on the basis of private relationships. Politicians use them in the course of electoral competition in the electorate and sometimes beyond the electorate to symbolize the coercive power they have at their command. This has become a part of Sri Lankan electoral campaigns. In return, these gangs and thugs enjoy various benefits such as money, patronage goods (liquor licences, land) and immunity from police action whenever required. The intensified interparty and intraparty competition that has been triggered by the introduction of the PR system has made access to the capacity for violence an important element in electoral politics. Often politicians use thugs not only to counter violence from opponents but also to initiate violence for electoral benefit. By unleashing violence at polling booths that are regarded as unfavourable to a particular politician, on election day or the day before, the politician can change the overall electoral result in that particular electorate. Often voters refrain from going to the polling booth if they anticipate violence. In such situations, the opposition politician should have the capacity to counter the violence or unleash more violence to send a strong message to supporters and potential voters that he/she can assure their security. Even though it is popularly believed that electoral violence began to intensify from 1978 (Saravanamuttu 2008), it is wrong to conclude that violence is only a recent phenomenon in Sri Lankan electoral politics.

Jiggins (1979: 72) quotes the then Minister of Home Affairs Felix Dias Bandaranaike who described the disgraceful act of Kotelawala/Senanayake who emptied a latrine bucket into N.H. Keerthirathne's house while preventing people of lower-caste groups from reaching the polling booths. This incident is claimed to have taken place in the second election that was held in 1936, where Keerthirathne from the *bathgama* caste contested Dudley Senanayake for the Dedigama electorate.

The history of competitive party politics in Sri Lanka is full of such acts of coercion and violence, and these examples highlight only the most harmless forms of violence. The point I highlight here is that often political parties and politicians maintain their own bands of thugs to exercise coercive power in the highly charged competitive electoral environment. For example, under the leadership of Montague Jayewickrema, Bandara, a close loyalist of Jayewickrema, was often accused of violence committed against members of the opposition.[29] While most politicians maintained their capacity to unleash or counter violence, the methods they employed and the degree of what they achieved varied from one politician to another. For example, some politicians accommodated such individuals in their inner circle. Others maintained surreptitious links while keeping them well outside the organizational network.

Those who did not have access to thugs in the electorate obtained them from outside in order to counter the violence of their opponents.

During the 2004 Parliamentary election, a candidate from Kegalle District hired two gunmen from Colombo to counter campaign violence by the rival candidate.[30] This helped boost his popularity amongst party loyalists and independent voters because he was seen as a leader capable of protecting his supporters and loyalists on his home turf. According to a coordinating secretary to a minister, his minister used gangs from Colombo to contain a protest campaign staged by unemployed graduates at an exhibition he organized in his district.[31] This particular minister is well known in the district for his capacity to unleash violence against his political opponents. However, in this instance, he brought in gangs from Colombo in order to shroud his involvement in the attack.

Therefore, although there are no formal militia-like groups maintained by most politicians of the UNP and SLFP, they sustain their capacity at least to counter the violence of their opponents. Strategies of maintaining these capacities vary from one politician to another. Some politicians openly associate with thugs and gangs and sometimes offer various positions to them in the party or its ancillaries. Others maintain their links very low key. If the party is in government, often the links between the politicians and thugs/gangs are visible. Thugs and gangs are often quite open about their associations with the government politician as that provides them extra clout, power, resources and, more importantly, the necessary immunity to exercise violence. Thugs and gangs find it difficult to survive by only depending on politicians of the opposition. Those groups who have links only with opposition politicians, for obvious reasons, operate very low key. Therefore, often popular thugs and gangs in the electorate or districts invariably remain the servants of politicians of the ruling party. This element of party organization at the electoral level is not common amongst parties other than the UNP and SLFP.

GRASSROOTS POLITICAL LEADERSHIP: FROM VILLAGE ELITES TO BROKERS

In the colonial societies of South Asia and elsewhere, colonial rulers imposed a system of administration that facilitated what was often called the "indirect rule" of an alien power (Robinson 1975: 2). As Hettige describes in relation to Sri Lanka, traditional administrative officials, operating at various levels, who linked subjects with the government in the process of administration (Hettige 1984: 129), collected revenue, maintained law and order, constructed essential infrastructure and also imposed rules, regulations and taxes on the local communities on behalf of their higher authorities (Ibid.). This created an enormous gap between the villagers and administration. This did not change much after the withdrawal of those alien rulers (Wriggins 1960; Hettige 1984).

While this chasm remained largely constant, Hettige says that new political institutions, such as political parties, universal franchise, local government and other local bodies, facilitated the emergence of new links between local communities and higher authorities (Hettige 1984: 129–30). However, he contends that despite the new links, the gap between communities and the higher authority remained intact because the channels of communication were dominated by local-level mediators (Hettige 1984: 129–30). These local-level actors played the role of representing the community as well as being the conduit of higher authorities. Hettige's conclusion that the role of these actors (mediators, village elites and influentials) was largely as brokers of higher authorities, rather than as genuine representatives of the local people, has much merit (Hettige 1984: 129–30). It is through these actors that political parties, especially the UNP and SLFP, penetrated the villages in expanding their support base (Hettige 1984; Gunasekara 1992; Moore 1985; Silva 1992). My field work suggests that competitive politics in Sri Lanka compelled the electorate organizers of the two main parties to depend on these actors to build their party structures in the villages.

The term 'grassroots political actors' used in this analysis refers to individuals who derive their political power by representing both politicians and the community. Public perception of the personality of these grassroots political actors varies from one social setting to another. Over time, the modalities that formed and shaped the grassroots political leadership have also changed. Roberts (1997: 194) argues that wealth and access to political power were key to the formation of national elites. However, Bourdieu provides a much broader scheme with the concept of symbolic capital to understand elite formation at the grassroots level. According to Bourdieu, 'symbolic capital' is a product of economic, cultural and social capitals. He argues that a person can acquire one form of capital using another form of capital (Bourdieu 1984: 47). For example, the economic capital of an individual could help him/her build more contacts with important people and then acquire a good deal of social capital. However, there is an exchange rate in the exchange of capitals. Further, the contribution of these capitals to symbolic capital differs from one field to another. For example, in a rural setting, perhaps, cultural capital might have a slight edge over economic capital, and this could differ from urban settings where economic capital might be more important than cultural capital. Even within the same field, the contribution of these capitals in forming symbolic capital varies over time. This scheme of capitals that Bourdieu conceptualizes is very helpful in understanding the formation of grassroots leadership and their political life.

Competition amongst grassroots political actors in villages gradually increased after the expansion of the franchise to all communities in the 1930s. Since party competition came into full force, especially after the emergence of the SLFP, competition amongst grassroots political actors became more aggressive. In the early stages of electoral competition, politics was largely centred on the individuals who exercised 'indirect rule' in villages under colonial rule. During that time, at the village level, politics rested on local notables such as the *mudaliyars, korales, vel vidanes* and rich landlords, who enjoyed authority over villagers due to the state recognition/positions they received from colonial rulers (Jupp 1978; Hettige 1984; Gunasekara 1992). This eminence was also established over the wealth that they had accumulated from the colonial economy. As a majority of the villagers worked for these individuals in their cash crop estates or paddy lands, the former continued to seek the patronage of these landed families. In addition, villagers were subject to the authority of colonial-feudal officials such as *mudaliyars, korales* and *vel vidanes* (Jupp 1978). In this backdrop, these local village notables enjoyed a great deal of influence over the communities of their respective villages. In the case of coastal towns, wealthy business families—of the fishing industry or other ones—played the same superior role that landlords in agrarian villages played. These grassroots political actors represented the villages and linked them with the politicians who contested elections for the State Council. The network of these grassroots political actors also depended on the political power that national political elites held in order to receive various forms of patronage to maintain their wealth and status in their villages (Jayanntha 1992). The domination of old village political actors was challenged as a consequence of the intensified competition amongst national elites for state power. Hence, political competition at the local level extended to a new segment of village influentials, such as caste leaders, monks and indigenous doctors, and government servants such as teachers and postmasters. In contrast to the old elite, this new type of political operatives did not possess economic capital and access to political authority. They represented the intermediate classes in the rural economy.

Their authority and influence were based mainly on cultural capital—their social status as respected individuals in the village, such as the Ayurvedic physician, senior government servant, school master or the village temple monk. S.W.R.D. Bandaranaike found this class rivalry between the old feudal and capitalist village elites and the community leaders of the rural intermediate classes (Jupp 1978) to be a great opportunity to exploit for his own leadership ambitions. The SLFP mobilized these village actors against the UNP's old band of village elites to win a landslide victory in 1956. By no means does this mean that all village political actors who supported the SLFP in 1956 were from intermediate classes, nor does it mean that they did not have access to wealth and political power. For example, M.P. Herath, ex-chairman of the Warakapola cooperative shop, managed to mobilize support not only from the intermediate classes[32] thatthe SLFP popularly mobilized, but from families of the old rich as well (Jiggins 1974). It is also important to note that all those newly mobilized village political actors did not represent a totally new social group; instead, they stood as an alternative leadership to the same social groups who were earlier represented only by the wealthy classes in the villages.

However, this apparent difference of the grassroots leadership of the UNP and SLFP soon began to fade as both parties began to expand their village leadership bases by approaching individuals from the intermediate classes. On the one hand, the change in the rural economy and policy reforms introduced by successive governments also made the traditional elite hierarchy increasingly redundant, while allowing a new band of village political actors to emerge. At one level, the old feudalist and capitalist classes lost their wealth and access to political power that they had enjoyed in the past, and hence did not appeal to the villagers as they earlier had. People found themselves becoming less dependent on the old village leadership in their day-to-day social lives due to the availability of new economic opportunities and avenues to access political authority. In this context, a new breed of village political leadership who became politically active from 1956 continued to grow and serve in both the UNP and SLFP village political actor networks. Usually, national politicians distributed clientelistic goods to their voters through the village political leadership while entertaining those political actors with even more exciting clientelistic goods. This is not to say that politicians did not practice clientelistic politics with their old traditional elites. As Jayanntha (1992) argues, clientelistic politics was practised even before this new segment of villagers came into being. However, often the distribution of clientelistic goods such as political appointments to government departments, job opportunities, promotions, government land or impunity for illegal activities did not trickle down beyond those elites. This new segment of village political actors not only expanded access of the village community to the political authority in the electorate and thereby increased access to resources of the state, but they also gave an opportunity for national politicians to represent different social cleavages such as caste, ethnicity, religion and class in their patron-client network. The following photograph of the Mirissa village council taken in 1967 shows how various socio-cultural groups such as different caste groups, economic strata and geographic diversity were represented in a village council (Fig. 2.2).

The formation of new village political actors should be understood as a result of two mutually independent parallel efforts of local community leaders and national politicians. Local community leaders wanted to play a larger political role in the electorate by asserting more authority, replacing old feudalist-capitalist village political actors. At the same time, due to growing electoral competition, national politicians also aspired to expand their representation in the electorate. Party organizers in each electorate played a very sophisticated role in identifying and nurturing grassroots elites. It was a prerequisite for individuals who rose to be the new segment of elites to possess the right volume of some form of capital (or a combination of economic, cultural and social capital) in addition to their interest to hold a leadership role in the village.

However, they are baptized as political actors only when they are recognized and successfully connected to the political authority in the electorate. Once they have been baptized as village political actors, they enter the elite struggle in the field of politics in that electorate. In the elite struggle, as Bourdieu argued, in order to advance their position in the field of politics or to retain their current position, they have to struggle by acquiring more political capital (Jenkins 2002). For this, village political actors have to struggle to acquire more symbolic capital, largely using their private economic capital or by forging access to state capital. Those who have close access to the political authority, even if they do not possess other forms of capital, usually enjoy the status of a 'village influential' amidst poor villagers, as they secure and retain some form of access to state resources. For example, Montague's driver Kulathunga in Weligama and Nissanka's driver Nimal from Algama in Dedigama command respect in their respective villages as able political actors. In fact, Kulathunga was

Names (left to right)	Caste and Family
1. M.M. Garwin	A *goigama* member, son of rich landlord Arthur Weerakoon, who provided a livelihood to most of the villagers from and around Kotuwila
2. M.P. Somapala	A *goigama* member
3. Henapala Wijesuriya	A *karawa* member
4. Francis Weerasuriya	A *karawa* member
5. M. Arnis (chairman)	A *durawa* member
6. K.G. Jinadasa	A *durawa* member
7. D.K. Amarapala	A *durawa* member and the driver of Montague Jayewickrema
8. A. Hewavitharana	A *goigama* member
9. K. John Silva	A *karawa* member

Fig. 2.2   Members of the Mirissa Village Council in 1967

elected to the Mirissa *Gam Sabha* (see above picture) in 1965 with other rich political actors in the village who possessed considerable wealth or some form of cultural capital.

LIFE STORIES OF GRASSROOTS POLITICAL LEADERS

The following two stories collected during the field research provide an insight into how grassroots leadership has emerged and the role of the village political actor network on which the party organization in an electorate is founded.[33]

Story of Siriwardena from Ragalakanda[34]

Siriwardane is a *goigama* caste village political actor from Ragalakanda village in Dedigama. His father was the *vel vidane* of Ragalakanda village, and being a notable family in the village, they were quite understandably supporters of the UNP before 1956. The young Siriwardane and a few of his classmates had gone to see an election campaign event of S.W.R.D. Bandaranaike under the influence of a radical school teacher. According to Siriwardane, at that time, although he had not even reached voting age, he was determined to support Bandaranaike, especially after they got a chance to talk to him personally. Despite the objections of his family, he supported M.P. Herath, the SLFP candidate for Dedigama in the 1956 election. During this time, the UNP campaign was organized by a notable of the village called Mohotti Nilame who represented the only *walawwa* in the village. Mohotti Nilame was a rich descendent of an aristocratic family and commanded a great deal of respect amongst villagers due to his economic and social capital which he inherited by being a member of the village headman's family. He was also a member of the *Gam Sabha* at that time. Siriwardane admitted that he found it difficult to convince people of his village—who were from the same caste—as they were strong UNPers at the time. However, eventually he managed to convince some people from nearby lower-caste villages—*bathgama* and *kumbal*—by promising to provide a road, several public wells and a temple (as these low-caste communities were not welcome in the *goigama* temple). He says that after M.P. Herath won the election, he managed to get the political leadership of the electorate to provide what he had promised to those people. He recalled how he contested for the *Gam Sabha* election in 1965. According to him, the main competition in the village was between the two *goigama* caste notables of the village—Mohotti Nilame and Siriwardane. Apparently, Mohotti Nilame got another person to contest Siriwardane, as it was too embarrassing for him to contest with someone who was new to village politics and who commanded less status—as Siriwardane was merely the son of a *vel vidane*, who was lesser in social standing. However, according to Siriwardane, Mohotti Nilame spent lavishly on the election campaign of Siriwardane's contender and, in fact, even senior figures such as Robert Senanayake—the brother of Dudley Senanayake—visited the village in support of the UNP candidate. The UNP spent a lot of money on the election campaign and even entertained the villagers with meals, liquor and cigarettes, while Siriwardane continued his strategy of canvassing personally at houses, especially of low-caste communities. According to him, some of his UNP relatives had told him straightforwardly that they were not going to vote for him, so he paid more attention to the poor, underdeveloped, lower-caste villages in the area. According to Siriwardane, the poor villagers respected him because of his father, who was the old *vel vidane* of the village and had helped them in the past. As the *vel vidane*, Siriwardane's father was entitled to receive a share from every farmer—called *huandirum*—which, according to Siriwardane, had been distributed by his father to poor villagers who were merely labourers without paddy land. Despite himself hailing from the *goigama* caste, his candidacy failed to receive the *goigama* votes that were loyal to the UNP, while on the other hand he succeeded in receiving the support of lower-caste groups on the basis of the patronage which his father had extended using his official status.

Siriwardane became the SLFP party organizer of Kahabiliyawa in 1968. He claims to have enlisted the youth of his area in support of the SLFP's electorate organizer, Deshapriya Senanayake. He had to contend with the electoral violence of the UNP in his village. When Philip Gunawardena withdrew from the coalition government of the MEP in 1959, M.P. Herath, the then member for Dedigama, too crossed over to the Mahajana Eksath Peramuna. Siriwardane and others who remained loyal to party leader Bandaranaike began to support Deshapriya Senanayake, who was entrusted by the party to organize the SLFP base in Dedigama. However, Siriwardane says that they were closer to Deshapriya's brother Dharmasiri Senanayake, as he was involved in party organization work in Dedigama. While describing his political history, he expressed a great deal of respect for and loyalty to Dharmasiri Senanayake. Even though Dharmasiri Senanayake lost the election in 1970 when the SLFP obtained a significant victory across the country, the SLFPers in the electorate did not feel that they had lost, as their party was in the government. Due to his close relationship with Sirima Bandaranaike, Dharmasiri was appointed as Chairman of the Tourist Board where he provided over 2,000 jobs to SLFP supporters in the electorate. Even though the SLFP lost the seat, since it was their party that was in the government, Dharmasiri and his organizers managed to provide various clientelist goods to their supporters. During the 1970 SLFP regime, lands were distributed amongst their supporters in the areas of Mangedara and Alauwatta. Siriwardane claims that those lands were distributed amongst SLFP supporters as well as UNPers who were in the opposition. During this time, a teaching job was given to his nephew whose family was made of UNPers in the village. Despite 16 petitions by SLFP supporters, Dharmasiri Senanayake decided to give the job to Siriwardane's nephew. Later, the family switched loyalty to the SLFP and supported Dharmasiri Senanayake. Siriwardane says many villagers came to receive benefits but not all switched to the SLFP. In addition, Dharmasiri Senanayake managed to get the necessary funds from the SLFP and its ministers for *Gam Sabha* members to conduct their projects, as well as for those members to meet the demands of their constituencies despite failing to win the electorate. Siriwardane claimed that after the death of Dharmasiri Senanayake, they (perhaps referring to the individuals who held positions in the Dedigama SLFP organizing elite network) were sidelined from active SLFP activities. He is not pleased with the current leadership of the SLFP—he claimed he is a member of Bandaranaike's SLFP—and is not actively supporting the electorate organization. He continued to vote for the SLFP and assisted various party MPs in his personal capacity. He claimed that he did not accumulate wealth by dabbling in politics, but he managed to educate his children and got them government jobs with the help of various SLFP ministers. Four years ago, his youngest daughter was given a government job by minister and SLFP organizer of Dedigama, Athauda Seneviratne, even before she received her degree certificate. Siriwardane claims that he helped Athauda Seneviratne's election campaign on several occasions despite him not being connected to the electorate's party organization structure.

The story of Siriwardane illustrates how the SLFP penetrated the support base of the UNP in its early years through new grassroots leadership and consolidated itself as a national political party. The narrative of his political career confirms the observations of scholars of Sri Lankan politics (Wilson 1975; Jupp 1978) who maintain that the SLFP, despite its rhetoric, is not a political party that is exclusively of the poor and the oppressed. Even in its early formative years, the SLFP approached affluent and wealthy families to offer leadership in their villages to build its party organization. This narrative is used later to demonstrate the dynamics of grassroots political leaders of the SLFP.

Story of Berty Gunapala from Waddeniya[35]

Berty Gunapala is a village political actor from the *wahumpura* caste who represented the political actor network of the UNP over a long period in Waddeniya village, Dedigama. It should be noted that an over-whelming majority of the Waddeniya village belongs to the *wahumpura* caste community, and this village is surrounded by villages dominated by *goigama* and *bathgama* caste groups in addition to *wahumpura*. Berty's family members had been popular anti-UNPers who rebelled against the caste suppression that prevailed at that time. Since most of the higher-caste village notables were UNP supporters, Berty's father openly worked against the UNP. Due to this, most of the *wahumpura* caste villagers rallied around his father, granting him considerable symbolic power—largely based on social capital. Berty fell out with his father on his marriage and left the family and the village. Later, he returned to the village and became a popular social worker with the help of some of his relatives and several *goigama* families in the village. He became the *Gramodaya Mandalaya* (village welfare board) Chairman with the support of the chief monk of the temple and with the assistance of notable *goigama* families in the village. As the chairman, he had the opportunity to interact with various government officers, and amongst them, the District Revenue Officer (DRO) of the Kegalle Government Agent's office was especially helpful to him. This DRO helped Berty, using his public office, to successfully carry out social service programmes in the Waddeniya village. Berty recalled how that DRO later approached him seeking his assistance for Dudley Senanayake's electoral campaign. According to Berty Gunapala, he had felt obliged to agree to this request as he had received so much support from him in the past. On the other hand, he says that he had felt this would be a good opportunity to serve the people that he represented even better, with the assistance of a national leader like Dudley Senanayake.

On the eve of the election, Berty and other village political actors went to the *Bothale Walawwa* (in Meerigama, Gampaha District), the house of the Senanayakes, to attend the election organizing meeting. Berty's representation was mainly of the *wahumpura* caste in the area, although he played an active leadership role only in the village. Since then, Berty became the main contact person of the UNP in the area and particularly for the *wahumpura* community that was spread out in that part of the electorate. During the tenure of Dudley Senanayake, Berty managed to bring in a considerable volume of clientelistic goods such as jobs, land and government welfare benefits to the village, and particularly the community he represented. During this time, he served as a member of the village *Gam Sabha*. After Dudley's death, Nissanka Wijeratne also approached him, and despite his initial opposition to the appointment of Nissanka, he played an active role until Nissanka retired from politics. When Manoda Wijeratne, son of Nissanka, took over the leadership of the electorate, Berty stepped down, leaving his son and some of his young assistants to assume their role in Waddeniya village.

The story of Berty Gunapala highlights how the UNP, which was widely described as the party of the feudal class and landowners during early elections, expanded its support base to include subordinate caste groups in the face of the challenge presented by the SLFP. This story helps to reiterate the common strategy adopted by both parties to influence various groups by enlisting village-level leadership to leverage the social dynamics within the village. Berty Gunapala and Siriwardane represent the grassroots political leadership during the time when the UNP and SLFP were consolidating their respective popular bases in the two-party system of electoral competition. After 1970, these social dynamics became more complex and elaborate as a result of the socio-economic changes that Sri Lanka experienced.

PARTY BRANCHES

Until the early 1970s, neither the UNP nor SLFP maintained systematic party branches beyond electorate organizers' offices in electorates. This was the network that the party organizer maintained across the electorate on the basis of family ties, friendship and their clients. Patron-client relationships provided the main basis for party organization in electorates. Even though I used the word 'party organization', this was very much an 'electoral organization'—a mechanism to collect votes at the election. The policies of the party were almost never discussed as an item on the agenda at those meetings, nor were they given any importance. Instead, voters and their political actors in the village discussed what they needed from the party and the politician—individual needs or collective needs. They would also discuss how to mobilize the election campaign and ensure the victory of the party in order to secure patronage for individuals and the community.

As electoral competition increased, parties, especially the UNP and SLFP, began to employ more sophisticated methods in their electoral organization. In the wake of the JVP rebellion in 1971, the SLFP began to set up youth committees at the electorate level that were directly linked to the party's youth wing at the head office. Under the leadership of

J.R. Jayewardene, by 1974 the UNP also began to organize the party at the polling-booth level as part of its party reorganizing drive. Electoral organizers were advised to set up party branches in each electorate and elect office bearers for positions such as secretary, treasurer and leaders of the youth and women's wings. However, despite the new terminology, these branches were also very much based on the old village political elites that the electorate organizer used to work with. Interestingly, these branches become active usually after an election is announced. When parties are preparing for an election, especially a Parliamentary or Presidential election, electorate organizers activate their village-level branches, elect office bearers and organize pocket meetings to mobilize supporters. These branches are almost nonexistent at other times, leaving party organizing activities to the grassroots elites and a few individuals who are part of the electorate organizer's elite network.

Since the 1970s, ruling parties began to strengthen their party representatives at the village level by entrusting various state powers to them. The SLFP government brought the state bureaucracy under the direct control of the ministers with the abolition of the Public Service Commission under the First Republican Constitution, which made the bureaucracy subservient to the authority of politicians. After a landslide victory, J.R. Jayewardene also continued this practice and in fact further strengthened the powers of local politicians and party organizers. He wanted his village-level party officers to play a key role in their respective villages. As a result of J.R. Jayewardene's vision, villages were once again brought under the direct control of the political authority. The only difference was that they were not the old feudalist-capitalist elites, but the new village political leadership who rose from the intermediate classes by replacing the old landlords and feudal officials. Village political actors who represent the ruling party elite network in the electorate had a great say in the lives of the villagers, especially the ones from economically poor and backward groups. Connections to such actors became vital for villagers to acquire basic needs such as a job or promotion, school admission, and in some areas to enable peaceful living conditions without any harassment.

In this context, pressure mounted on those village political leaders who continued to search for new avenues to have access to state power and state capital to meet those demands. The old segment of village elites who had in the past risen to the elite status in the village due to their cultural capital and personal wealth was no longer relevant in this context of a highly demanding environment. This opened up more space for a new segment of village political actors to emerge. Many continued to come forward to compete for the new village elite positions by acquiring access to state capital through various means. In order to survive, these village political actors were compelled to provide comparatively higher benefits to their respective communities than their competitors. Hence, one's own economic capital and capacity to have access to state capital became more important than ever before. Particularly, since the introduction of the 'open economy', the needs of the electorate intensified and became more complex. It was observable how the ruling parties made people dependent on the grassroots political elites, while the needs of the villagers also increased exponentially under the open economy. Under this new condition, grassroots elites of the ruling party enjoyed many advantages, while remaining as 'village influentials' became extremely difficult and challenging for those in opposition parties.

MEMBERSHIP

Any discussion on party organization invariably assumes the existence of party membership, as this is considered an essential and basic element of a political party. However, in reality, party membership of the UNP and SLFP is often very different from the understanding of the classical political party by scholars such as Maurice Duverger (1954). Particularly, in parties such as the UNP and SLFP, despite their pronouncement of the existence of party membership in their party constitutions, there is hardly any serious effort to maintain party membership systematically. On the other hand, those who claim to be members of these parties hardly play the role that traditional party members are supposed to perform. Of course, the role of a party member is hard to define as it varies from one type of party to another. However, Duverger provides a broad scheme that can be used to distinguish a party member from party supporter.

In everyday language the concept of 'member' of a party coincides with that of adherent – in Europe at least. The latter is distinguished from 'supporter', who declares his/her agreement with the doctrine of the party and sometimes lends it his/her support but who remains outside its organization and the community it forms; the supporter is not, properly speaking, a member of the party. (Duverger 1954: 62)

Article 3 of the UNP constitution and articles 22–27 of the SLFP constitution describe qualifications, rules and procedures, and conditions of
membership. For the UNP, anyone above the age of 15 and for the SLFP
above the age of 18 can obtain party membership by paying the membership fee. According to both constitutions, members should accept the
principles, policies and codes of conduct of the party. From time to time,
both parties have initiated membership recruitment drives. However,
neither party has maintained any such systematic recruitment campaign.
There has not been a formal recruitment process even at the electorate
level, and therefore, recruitment is very much at the discretion of the electorate organizer who initiates recruitment campaigns from time to time,
for various reasons. When a new electorate leader is appointed, it is quite
normal to follow that appointment with some sort of recruitment drive as
he/she often wishes to demonstrate his/her popularity in the electorate to
party headquarters. As one former UNP party secretary indicated, often
politicians purchase large quantities of membership cards purportedly for
their new membership in order to indicate electoral strength and impress
the party leader.

However, according to this former secretary, it has often been found
that the politician does not even take those membership cards to his/her
electorate but throws away them on the way home.[36] On the one hand,
becoming a member of these parties does not mean much, as parties
do not have a mechanism to manage membership, thus leaving matters
of party membership in the hands of the electorate organizer. On the
other, supporters of these parties accept membership mainly as a symbolic
expression of their allegiance to the electorate organizer, rather than to
the party. Therefore, party membership does not by any means indicate
that members are convinced and want to adhere to the policies of that
party. Neither the UNP nor SLFP has a formal and systematic mechanism
to educate its membership or even their rank-and-file members on party
policies. Consequently, there is no marked difference between members
and supporters of the two parties in terms of their ideological and policy
positions.

The nature of participation of members of the two parties is not
remarkably different from the nature of participation of their supporters.
In this context, leaders and village political actors have more clout in the
party organization than the few who hold membership cards. Neither
party depends on its membership to raise party funds. Hence, they pay
no attention to the collection of membership fees. For example, 40 years

ago, members of the UNP purchased membership by paying Rs. 2, and today one needs to pay only Rs. 10. This is clearly illustrative of the attitude of these parties towards membership subscriptions. Both parties adhere to a policy of raising funds from wealthy capitalists to finance election campaigns. Campaigns have become so expensive that using funds raised from their own members is unrealistic. At the outset, the parties would approach prominent private donors, industrialists, bankers or even local-level businessmen to raise funds for their election campaigns. In this context, the role of party membership has only limited symbolic representation.

ANCILLARY ORGANIZATIONS

Traditionally, as Duverger (1954: 106) termed it, ancillary organizations refer to various bodies created by the party and controlled by its constitution, or bodies that provide wider or greater participation. Duverger's conceptualization of ancillary organizations is that they are a democratic institution within a party that allows members and supporters to compete for political power on familial, social and cultural grounds. In this context, youth associations, women's clubs, sports clubs, past-pupils societies, intellectual or literary clubs, trade unions, cooperative societies and even associations such as housewives' societies often serve as ancillary organizations for the parties, as they provide party members the space for greater engagement and participation. The UNP and SLFP also maintain ancillary organizations. For example, the *Sri Lanka Nidahas Vurthiya Samithi Sammelanaya*, *Sri Lankan Nidahas Guru Sangamaya* and *Heda Sangamaya* (Sri Lanka Freedom Workers' Federation, Sri Lanka Freedom Teachers' Union, Nurses' Union) are some of the ancillaries of the SLFP. The National Workers' Union and National Estate Workers' Union are the trade union arms of the UNP, while the *Lak Vanitha* and *Jathika Yowun Peramuna* function as its women and youth wings, respectively. In addition to these standard ancillaries, there are many other organizations that function as ancillaries for the two parties—some at the national and others at the local-electorate level. However, these organizations mainly aim to strengthen party mobilization, rather than increasing participation, as Duverger described. Most of these ancillary organizations are highly dependent on leadership personalities on various levels. At the national level, organizations such as the *Jana Vegaya* project designed by Kumar Rupasinghe, Mrs. Bandaranaike's ex-son-in-law, in the early 1970s, the

Sucharitha project of then President R. Premadasa and *Tharunyayata Hetak* and *Nil Balakaya* of President Mahinda Rajapaksa's son Namal Rajapaksa are examples.

Based on the field evidence gathered for this research, one could say that it is possible to broaden the scope of ancillary organizations to be included in the party organization in the electorate. At the electorate level, youth and women's organizations clearly stand out as ancillary organizations, as do members and supporters of the parties, as they are involved in these organizations and technically linked to the national youth and women's wings of the party. However, although these ancillary organizations technically function independently, they are often subject to the control of the party organizer. The degree of control over these ancillaries depends on the capacity of the electorate organizer.

In addition to formal ancillary organizations, party organizers at the local level often utilize other formal and informal organizations in the electorate as ancillaries. Temples and their *dayaka sabhawas* (patron associations), funeral associations and other local associations such as sports clubs, fitness clubs and associations based on certain caste groups often function as ancillaries of the two main parties in the village during elections. The general membership of the party remains a very fluid element with office bearers not openly claiming that they are functioning on behalf of a particular party. Yet, very often village political actors who represent one or the other of the political parties also hold key positions in these organizations. Hence, during elections, these organizations provide excellent grounds for electorate organizers to mobilize their election campaign. These organizations, like any other ancillary organization, are weak in their capacity to be articulate within the party organization even at the electorate level. Instead, they enjoy the patronage of the electorate organizer, which is the essential reason for them to exist in the village. For example, the chief monk of one of the main temples in Dedigama recalled how he managed to obtain the assistance of Dudley Senanayake and Nissanka Wijeratne to get the village roads tarred, provide bus transportation and obtain electricity for the villagers.[37] He also described the role of his temple in garnering electoral support of the villagers for those two UNP leaders. Another example is the Fisheries Association in Weligama which was an active ancillary to Montague Jayewickrema. He had his men in certain positions in those organizations. Trade unions, however, are not meaningful ancillaries at the local-electorate level. This is especially so in agrarian villages. Despite the existence of several formal professions at the local level, the teachers union often appears to be the most active and effective ancillary in the electorate. This is perhaps due to the fact that on the one hand, teachers are well respected and regarded as knowledgeable (higher degree of cultural capital) in village society, while on the other hand they are available in numbers and spend more time in the village as compared to other salaried professions. The emerging trend amongst politicians is to start a 'Foundation' (*padanama*), which is somewhat similar to a Trust. They open Foundations claiming to help the poor or those in need in the village, electorate or country at large. Some Foundations were formed to commemorate the legacies of past politicians or notables or simply for the sake of the welfare of the community. At present, many politicians have their own Foundations and serve as Directors in them. The work and external appearance of the Foundations suggest that they are apolitical bodies, set up for the good of those who are in need. However, almost all Foundations turn into gold mines during election time. They are useful to collect funds for the election campaign and to approach poor voters with financially appealing and yet inexpensive clientelistic goods, such as eye spectacles, schoolbooks, medicine, vegetables, dry goods, self-employment equipment and career training for self-employment.

These organizations are utilized as ancillary organizations of parties and especially of individual politicians at elections. In between elections, most of these organizations and Foundations function independently of politics despite their ability to become a political machine at any given time. Irrespective of the type and size of the ancillary organization, they hardly enjoy articulation and participation within the party other than functioning as voter mobilizing machines.

The party organizational structure, then, draws on a variety of relationships, networks and capital to keep the party machinery well oiled at the level of the electorate. Parties draw their rank-and-file members as well as their village-level leadership from local political actors who also play key roles in the cultural and economic life of the village. In the past, these local political actors were the local elites who drew on their cultural and economic capital to organize the party in the electorate. However, today the legitimacy of the local political actor rests more on his/her social capital than on the cultural and economic capital that the traditional elites relied on in the past.

The guiding motivation for the party organization of both the SLFP and UNP at the local level appears to focus more on attracting votes than on building a strong party membership. As such, the feeble nature of the party organization continues to be reproduced at the level of the electorate. The main focus of both the SLFP and UNP seems to have shifted away from the establishment of a strong party organizational structure to an emphasis on party mobilization at the local level.

CONCLUSION

This chapter has explored the organizational structure of the UNP and SLFP at the level of the electorate. The information and analysis were informed by my fieldwork in the three electorates as well as discussions I had with current and former politicians who have represented the two parties at the national level. The findings of this chapter represent one of the first systematic attempts to map and understand the organizational structure of Sri Lanka's two main political parties at the electorate level.

The research in this chapter found that party structure at the electorate level is extremely feeble and, at best, rather loosely organized. As a result, the organizational structure of the UNP and SLFP contradicts the traditional understanding of party organization, which is thought to be built on an institutionalized and formal party hierarchy. Furthermore, this chapter has suggested that the party organizational structures of the UNP and SLFP remain largely dormant and are generally activated only as an election nears.

In the absence of a strong organizational structure, this chapter has argued that the electoral organizer is the cornerstone for the organization of parties at the level of the electorate. However, in spite of this, the chapter also found that the success of the electoral organizer is not dependent on his/her origin within the electorate. Therefore, this chapter affirmed the importance of the electoral organizer whose strategies and symbolic capital ensure the success of the party organization at the level of the electorate.

Therefore, the party organizational structure draws on a variety of relationships, networks and capital to keep the party machinery well oiled at the level of the electorate. In examining these relationships, this chapter has argued that these parties draw their rank-and-file members as well as their village-level leadership from the local political actors who also play key roles in the cultural and economic life of the village. In the past, these local political actors were the local elites who drew on their cultural and economic capital to organize the party in the electorate. However, today, the legitimacy of the local political actor rests more on his/her social capital than on the cultural and economic capital that the traditional elites relied on in the past.

Furthermore, this chapter observed that the guiding motivation for the party organization of both the SLFP and UNP at the local level appears to focus more on attracting votes than on building a strong party membership. Therefore, this study suggested that the feeble nature of the party organization continues to be reproduced at the level of the electorate. In making this observation, this chapter argues that the main focus of both the SLFP and UNP has shifted away from the establishment of a strong party organizational structure to an emphasis on party mobilization at the local level.

NOTES

1. At focus group discussions held in Tholangamuwa, Dedigama and Kananke, Weligama Provincial Council members and local council members drew a hierarchical diagram to describe how their party is organized in the electorate. Their presentation is very similar to those of the politicians interviewed in this research study. As Jupp (1978) conceived, party organization is a well-structured hierarchical static entity.

2. The term capital refers to the Bourdieu's concept of forms of capital (Bourdieu 1986). Bourdieu argues that capital presents itself in three fundamental forms: economic capital (material wealth in the form of property, money, shares, etc.), social capital (social resources in the form of networks and contacts based on mutual recognition) and cultural capital (informational assets in the form of knowledge and skills acquired through socialization and education, etc.). These three capitals can produce a fourth form of capital: symbolic capital (legitimate authority in the form of prestige, honor, reputation, fame). In the field of politics, the legitimate right to speak on behalf of 'the people' is considered as political capital, and it is a kind of symbolic capital (Stokke 2002).

3. Sir Francis had his legal practice locally, was an outstanding politician and had family connections (with the Eknaligodas and Mahawelatennes, for example) with the leading *radala* families

in the area. He was married to Adeline Meedeniya, daughter of Meedeniya Adigar of Kegalle, whose other daughter was married to D.R. Wijewardene, founder of the Lake House publishing firm. Sir Francis was imprisoned following a testamentary case in which he was the beneficiary, and the Senanayake-Wijewardene combine moved to have Dudley elected. Sir Francis Molamure was unseated from his Dedigama seat that he had represented since 1931, as he lost his legal case on charges of contempt of court. In 1936, the party caucus put forward Dudley Senanayake to take the vacant Dedigama seat. For more details, refer to Jiggins (1974, 1994).

4. Interviews with Samarasinghe, Berty Gunapala and Jayalath Bandu, who were personally involved in Dudley Senanayake's politics in Dedigama. They provided an excellent account of how they organized the electorate under Dudley Senanayake's leadership.

5. Ibid.

6. Ibid.

7. Interview with the current chief incumbent of the Dedigama Vihare.

8. Interview with the current chief incumbent of the Dedigama Vihare and the chief incumbent of the Manikkadevera Vihare.

9. Interview with Siriwardane from Ragalakanda, Dedigama. He had personally witnessed an incident where S.W.R.D. Bandaranaike was harassed during the election campaign.

10. Interview with Siriwardane from Ragalakanda, Dedigama.

11. Interview with Siriwardane from Ragalakanda, Dedigama.

12. Interview with Siriwardane from Ragalakanda, Dedigama.

13. Interview with Siriwardane from Ragalakanda, Dedigama.

14. Interview with the current chief incumbent of the Dedigama Vihare.

15. Interviews with Gunarathne of Algama and Siriwardane in Ragalakanda, Dedigama electorate.

16. Jiggins describes the nature of the violent election as follows: "It is certain that the tacit influence of Government authority in the highly-charged political atmosphere prevailing in Lanka was potentially inhibiting to the faithful registration of opinion, but to what extent intimidation was both effective and wide-spread is impossible to ascertain. However, the police turned out in force at every public meeting, and party lawyers were kept busy bailing out arrested supporters. One of the more grievous charges was

of impersonation. A UNP agent in Dedigama village alleged that there were as many as two thousand SLFP impersonators. An SLFP agent in the same village denied categorically all such allegations, and accused the UNP of thuggery in the remoter low-caste areas. Others cited the high percentage poll as 'proof' of substantial impersonation".

17. Interview with Wepola, a former member of the Sabaragamuwa Provincial Council. His father was a village organizer during the 1973 by-election. In addition to Wepola, interviews with BertyWickremasinghe, Samarasinghe and Jayalath Bandura also confirmed this widespread belief that J.R. Jayewardene sidelined Rukman Senanayake due to family rivalry.

18. This percentage is based on the estimation made by most of the senior party officers of both the parties.

19. Montague Jayewickrema's decision to construct the new Galle-Matara road avoiding the railway crossing antagonized many families on the Weligama coastal line. Due to his road project, which people viewed as his personal project, many families along the coastal line were forced to move out. In this context, Montague himself felt the public displeasure and hence wanted to contest from Haputale at the 1970 election.

20. According to the results published on the website of the Sri Lanka election commission, http://www.slelections.gov.lk/pdf/Results_1989%20GENERAL%20ELECTION.PDF.

21. All his inner circle members indicate this point; however, there is no formal way to validate this claim. He and his family have been holding the incumbency of the Devundara *devalaya*, which is considered as the symbolic institution of the *karawa* community.

22. Interview with Asanga Abeyagoonasekera who is presently the executive director of the premiere national think tank in Sri Lanka, the Lakshman Kadirgamar Institute for International Relations and Strategic Studies, http://www.island.lk/index.php?page_cat=article-details&page=article-details&code_title=60628.

23. This fact was confirmed by many interviewees (Algama Gune, Kamal Gamanayake and Keerthi Gunapala, Rathna Gunapala).

24. Many interviewees confirmed this point (George Daluwana, Dayan, Kalyani).

25. Interview with D.P. Wijethilake, the personal secretary of Cyril Mathew from 1978 to 1984.

26. Interview with Berty Gunapala.
27. The common belief amongst the political elites in Weligama is that the *karawa* caste constitutes about 15% of the total Weligama population. However, there are no official statistics on the caste breakdown.
28. The militia is, according to Duverger (1954), a kind of private army whose members are enrolled on military lines, are subjected to the same discipline and training as soldiers, and like them wear uniforms and badges, march in step preceded by a band and flags, and meet the enemy with weapons in physical combat. But these members remain civilian; in general, they are not permanently mobilized nor maintained by the organization: they are simply obliged to meet and drill frequently (36).
29. Many interviewees share this view that Bandara was perceived as Montague's illegitimate son, and he was responsible for most of the violent acts committed against opposition parties during the early 1980s. Interviews with Ruwan Karunaratne, George Daluwana, Dayan, Garwin Weerakoon and many others confirmed this point.
30. Interview with Champika Premadasa at his Rambukkana home. He said that although he denounced violence, he could not help resorting to it for self-defence, as his campaign was severely disrupted by goons of the UPFA politician. He claimed that his supporters were beaten and his cutouts destroyed by government thugs. Champika Premadasa feels that unless he countered this violence with equally aggressive violence his supporters would leave him, and no one would turn up on election day to vote for him. Therefore, through his contacts, the fact that he managed to get two gunmen from Colombo shows his capacity to counter government violence.
31. Interviews with Saman Gamage. He was one of the coordinating secretaries to Matara District Organizer and Minister Mahinda Wijesekara.
32. Intermediate classes refer to those who possess wealth, status and power in the village under the landlords and feudal bureaucrats.
33. Even though I decided to present the stories of Siriwardane and Berty Gunapala in this chapter, their experiences were reflected in many other interviews that I had with grassroots leaders of the same age.

34. Interview with Siriwardane at Ragalakanda Vihare, 16 February 2010.
35. Interview with Berty Gunapala at his home in Waddeniya, Dedigama, 20 May 2009.
36. Interview with Charitha Ratwatte, former secretary of the UNP and secretary to the Ministry of Finance from 2002 to 2004.
37. Interview with the chief incumbent of Dedigama Raja Maha Viharaya, 25 May 2009.

REFERENCES

Bourdieu, Pierre. 1984. *Distinction: A Social Critique of the Judgment of Taste.* Cambridge, MA: Harvard University Press.

Coomaraswamy, Tara. 1988. *Parliamentarian Representation in Sri Lanka 1931–1986.* Unpublished PhD thesis, University of Sussex.

de Silva, K.M., and Howard Wriggins. 1988. *J.R. Jayewardene of Sri Lanka: A Political Biography, Volume One: 1906 to 1956.* Anthony Blond/Quartet.

Duverger, Maurice. 19540. *Political Parties, Their Organisation and Activity in the Modern State.* London: Methen & Co. Ltd; New York: Wiley.

Gunasekara, T. 1992. Democracy, Party Competition and Leadership: The Changing Power Structure in a Sinhalese Community. In *Agrarian Change in Sri Lanka*, ed. James Brow and Joe Weeramunda, 229–260. New Delhi and Newbury Park/London: Sage.

Hettige, S. 1984. *Wealth, Power and Prestige: Emerging Patterns of Social Inequality in a Peasant Context.* Colombo: Ministry of Higher Education.

Jayanntha, D. 1992. *Electoral Allegiance in Sri Lanka.* Cambridge: Cambridge University Press.

Jenkins, Richard. 2002. *Pierre Bourdieu.* Rev. London: Routledge.

Jiggins, J. 1974. Dedigama 1973: A Profile of a By-Election in Sri Lanka. *Asian Survey* 14 (11) (November): 1000–1013.

———. 1979. *Caste and the Family in the Politics of the Sinhalese 1947 to 1976.* London: Cambridge University Press.

Jupp, J. 1978. *Sri Lanka: Third World Democracy.* London: Cass.

Moore, M. 1985. *The State and Peasant Politics in Sri Lanka.* Cambridge: Cambridge University Press.

Roberts, M. 1997. Elite Formation and Elites: 1832–1931. In *Sri Lanka Collective Identities Revisited: Volume I*, ed. Micheal Roberts, 191–266. Colombo: Marga Institute.

Robinson, M.S. 1975. *Political Structure in a Changing Sinhalese Village.* Cambridge: Cambridge University Press.

Saravanamuttu, P. 2008. Electoral Violence and Dispute Resolution in Asia-Pacific Sri Lanka Case Study. In *The Electoral Reform Debate in Sri Lanka*, ed.

Rohan Edrisingha and Asanga Welikala, 52–86. Colombo: Centre for Policy Alternatives.

Silva, K.T. 1992. Capitalist Development, Rural Politics and Peasant Agriculture in Highland Sri Lanka: Structural Change in a Low Caste Village. In *Agrarian Change in Sri Lanka*, ed. James Brow and Joe Weeramunda, 63–94. New Delhi and Newbury Park/London: Sage.

Stokke, Kristian. 2002. *Habitus, Capital and Fields: Conceptualizing the Capacity of Actors in Local Politics*. Oslo: University of Oslo, Department of Sociology and Human Geography.

Weber, Max. 1958. Class, Status and Party. In *From Max Weber: Essays in Sociology*, ed. H.H. Gerth and C.W. Mills. New York: Oxford University Press.

Wilson, A.J. 1975. *Electoral Politics in an Emergent State: The Ceylon General Election of May 1970*. London: Cambridge University Press.

Woodward, Calvin A. 1969. *The Growth of a Political System in Ceylon*. Cambridge: Cambridge University Press.

Wriggins, W.H. 1960. *Ceylon: Dilemmas of a New Nation*. Princeton, NJ: Princeton University Press.

CHAPTER 3

From Party Organization to Party Mobilization

The discussion earlier demonstrated that the role of party organizer at the constituency level is an intimately personal affair. In an electorate, the party organization is built as an informal and personalized network of professionals, businessmen and intermediaries (brokers) that stretches across the electorate. It is formed for the express purpose of winning elections. My field work in the three electorates and numerous discussions with rank-and-file members of the two parties indicated that party organization at the electorate level is surprisingly informal. It is far from being rigidly hierarchical, as is often presumed. Party organization at the electorate level is largely dependent on the discretion of the electorate organizer appointed by party leadership at the centre.

This chapter takes this analysis further by examining how party organization interacts with party mobilization, and how these strategies have been devised to contend with changes in the electoral system. To this end, specifying what I denote by the following concepts is important in clarifying the theoretical basis of this chapter.

I use the concept of *patronage* to refer to the relationship between the superior and inferior parties in a structure where the former enjoys more access to economic, social and cultural resources that the latter desires. The latter's access to such resources is facilitated through the former—either a feudal lord, or in the changed context of a more democratized

© The Author(s), under exclusive license to Springer Nature Singapore Pte Ltd. 2022
P. Peiris, *Catch-All Parties and Party-Voter Nexus in Sri Lanka*, Politics of South Asia,
https://doi.org/10.1007/978-981-16-4153-4_3

society, notable political actor at the village level. In exchange, the inferior party—the peasant or voter—extends their allegiance to the superior party, either in the form of continued service or casting their franchise for a candidate recommended by their patron. The two parties are identified as 'patron' and 'client', respectively.

Patronage is closely tied to the concepts of *clientelistic goods* and *club goods*, which denote the means by which benefits are accrued to clients in a patron-client relationship. *Clientelistic goods* are goods and services channelled to individuals for their personal benefit. These could be jobs, contracts, licenses, etc., given out to individuals who bring in votes during times of election. *Club goods,* on the other hand, target communities rather than individuals. While distributing more or less the same goods and services as in clientilistic goods, the focus is on rewarding an entire community such as a caste or an ethnic group that a given politician/important local level political actor represents. In the case of club goods, recipients of benefits enjoy far greater autonomy from the party organization than in the case of clientelistic goods recipients. While I have borrowed these concepts from Kitschelt and Wilkinson (2007), for easier comprehensibility, I will substitute the terminology used with the following phrases: 'Individual benefits' to denote clientelistic goods and 'community benefits' to denote club goods.

Network refers to a constellation of locally influential personalities such as village elites, community leaders and businesspeople amongst others. Parties rely on these constellations to reach out to different socioeconomic groups within electorates, which are mobilized through the distribution of individual and community benefits mentioned above.

In a related vein, *cleavages* play an important role in determining how an electorate is socially organized, and thereby the networks that parties can tap into. A cleavage here refers to a social division based on ethnicity, caste, religion and such other identity markers. Depending on how extensive a network based on a given cleavage is, parties can decide which fault line to appeal to, in order to secure the maximum amount of votes. However, this does not mean that parties limit their appeal to one or a few cleavage, but rather lubricate all possible networks through patronage, given their catch-all nature.

Transformation in the discussion refers to the changes undergone by party organizational structures and strategies in response to electoral reforms introduced in the country. *Oscillation* is taken to mean the active or inactive role assumed by the party organizational networks at the local

level, depending on whether the party is in power or not. Though transformation and oscillation are conceptually independent from each other,
in that the type of electoral system does not have a direct bearing on
whether a party is in power or not, it may be observed in relation to Sri
Lanka that after the introduction of the PR system the time taken for
one oscillation is much longer as compared to the oscillations during the
previous electoral system.

Within the parameters set by this theoretical framework, I first turn
my attention to examining the organizational structures of the UNP and
SLFP at the electorate level. I then proceed to discuss how the party
organization structures and mobilization strategies vary depending on
whether the party is in the government or in opposition. Lastly, I explain
how these strategies have changed over the past few decades in response
to changes in the electoral system and other larger socio-economic
implications and influences.

Feeble Institutions of Party Organization in Electorates

While there is invariably a party office in each electorate, these office
buildings do not belong to the political party. Instead they belong
to the incumbent party organizer. The party organizer usually utilizes
his/her own building or one that belongs to someone closely known and
connected. A change of the party organizer results in a change of the party
office as well. For example, Parliamentarian Champika Premadasa, the
current UNP electorate organizer of Dedigama, uses his private property
in the Warakapola town as his party office, and his predecessor, Manoda
Wijeratne, used a property of one of his friends as his party office. The
former SLFP Kelaniya electorate organizer, Minister Mervyn Silva, uses
one of his close confidant's houses in Kelaniya as his office. Documents,
membership registers and minutes of meetings relevant to the party institution in the electorate are neither maintained properly nor transferred to
the successor in case of a change of the electorate organizer's post, unless
the succession of power remains within the family. Although each electorate organization provides details of its organizational structure to the
party headquarters, such information is often incomplete. This compels
most new organizers to start his/her own party organization from the
scratch. Nissanka Wijeratne, Chulapadmendra Dahanayake and Mahinda
Wijesekara are examples. They have had to exert considerable effort to

rebuild—or more correctly, build anew—the party organization in their respective electorates. The hierarchical structures of the parties at the national level do not percolate down to the local-level party organization. Instead of well-defined hierarchical structures and positions, the local party organization is a loosely connected web of personal contacts. Therefore, in the electorate, the role of the party institution is relatively weak in relation to the role of the electorate organizer. In that context, party organizers exercise a great deal of agency in designing and establishing such personal networks for the purpose of winning elections. Nevertheless, as often argued in the structure-agency debate, it would be misleading to completely ignore the effects of the socio-cultural setting and history of the party in the electorate in forming and shaping these networks. The electorate organizer is the main architect of the party's organizational network in an electorate. However, his performance and the structural design of his network are subject to party history and the socio-cultural conditions of the electorate.

PATRONAGE THAT FACILITATES SMOOTH NETWORKING

Although one could construe the practice of patronage and clientelism as antisocial and antidemocratic, in Sri Lanka political parties and politicians offer patronage to their voters, while voters themselves demand that politicians and parties provide patronage in return for their support in the form of votes (Uyangoda 2010). Under long years of feudal rule, communities enjoyed patronage of the feudal masters (Hettige 1984), and this was also one of the main sources of living for a considerable proportion of village communities. Democratization has further reinforced this practice by providing some agency to the clients—voters—to influence their patron. Meanwhile, the ever-widening gap between the needs and aspirations of a majority of people and the opportunities available has rendered traditional wealth-based, personal, feudal patronage irrelevant. In this context, the increasing demands of clients could not be met with personal resources as in the past. Hence, the traditional feudal patronage system was transformed into an organized political patronage system.

In politics, as Kitschelt and Wilkinson (2007) elaborate, clientelism can be distributed amongst larger groups of communities (programming goods), a selected group of people (club goods) or amongst individuals (individual goods). At the electorate and party organization level what is most popular are 'club goods' and 'individual goods'.

Within an electorate, a party organizer can distribute patronage bene-fits in multiple ways. An individual can receive patronage either from one method or through a number of methods. As my field research interviews indicated, these methods can be summarized as follows:

i. Electorate organizer provides clientelistic goods such as government positions, jobs, contracts, various licences and status positions to grassroots elites who bring votes at elections. There is no effort to distribute these clientelistic goods to voters. I term these 'individual benefits'.

ii. Electorate organizer strengthens village elites and political actors financially by providing club goods such as various positions, contracts, licenses (liquor licenses, permits to transport various restricted natural resources, etc.) and status positions for them to provide patronage to the communities that they represent. In this case, voters receive patronage quite independent from the party and party organizer. In the remainder of the chapter, these are referred to as 'community benefits'.

iii. The most popular method is where the electorate organizer provides patronage to voters through grassroots elites. In this case it is clear to voters that they are receiving patronage from the party and the party organizer.

iv. There are instances where the electorate organizer provides patronage directly to voters without going through any interme-diaries.

In the first method, grassroots elites and political actors are the clients, as the benefits are mainly directed at them. Religious leaders, certain caste leaders and notables in villages who anyway possess great volumes of social and economic capital are the potential beneficiaries of these types of patronage distribution. As they possess significant influence over a sizeable voter base in the electorate, party organizers find it cheaper and more effi-cient to provide patronage to these elites or political actors than to their communities. In his work, Jayanntha (1992) describes how old village notables such as *korales*, *vel vidanes* and even the rich fish *mudalalies* (rich businessmen in the fisheries industry who usually owned trawlers and other expensive fishing gear) enjoyed the benefits of Blueville during the 1940s. Jiggins describes the existence of such situations similar to the 'pocket borough' in Sinhalese electorates in the early days of democracy, when patrons such as landlords and fish *mudalalies* played a key influential role in mobilizing support for parties or candidates at elections.

During the early stage of democratization, what was largely prevalent was community benefits. Here, grassroots elites and village political actors negotiated with national elites—who contested for the State Council and later Parliament—on behalf of the community, to have facilities such as transportation to a particular village, public wells, electricity or schools for village children. During this period, while grassroots elites enjoyed individual benefits, the electorates were often provided with community benefits. However, later, perhaps due to national-level economic transformation, voters preferred to have individual benefits, such as government jobs, promotions, houses and land deeds, rather than community benefits. In this context, those grassroots political actors who represented certain communities became effective vote collectors as long as they (grassroots leaders) could convince voters that they could address those individual needs following the election. Once the grassroots leaders began to emerge from non-traditional rich classes, parties felt the need to strengthen their local leaders with various kinds of patronage benefits. If the party is in power, those grassroots leaders were granted positions such as cooperative shop managers and other executive posts, and executive positions in government departments and corporations. In addition, these grassroots leaders were granted various honorary positions in the villages (i.e. Justice of the Peace and higher ranks and positions for monks, etc.) and promotions in their current occupations. Businessmen who would be a great source of financial support at elections were given opportunities to economically prosper with government contracts or other patronage. These patronage opportunities were meant to spill over to voters in the villages that these leaders represented, as these village elites became able individuals with the capacity to address the dire needs of the communities they represent. Villagers visit these village notables and political actors seeking their patronage for jobs, promotions, school admissions and various government permits, as for many that is the only method available to fulfil those needs. In addition, villagers are generally hesitant to visit government offices like the police and *kachcheri* alone, and hence they approach these village political actors either to appear on their behalf or to accompany them. In certain instances, electorate organizers extend patronage directly by circumventing the network structure. Although this type of patronage distribution is both rare and less efficient, politicians resort to this method of distributing individual benefits on the basis of caste and kinship; this is confined to a small group of people within the electorate.

In addition to the various forms of patronage given to grassroots political actors, both parties surveyed in this study granted a certain degree of state power to their party officials at the village level when their party held the reins of power. J. R. Jayewardene specifically emphasized that his village-level party representatives should be empowered in order for them to attract and command respect within the village.[1] In the early 1980s, UNP village elites were given various posts in government offices, and special positions such as 'Special Officer' were created for each village in order to strengthen UNP grassroots elites with wider powers at the village level. In the context of growing criticism for this ambiguous 'special officer' post, the then government decided to absorb them into the *Grama Sevaka* (GN) cadres. However, since then, all successive governments continued this practice by introducing various posts such as Janasaviya Niladhari and at present the Samurdhi officer. Currently, there are over 1.6 million households (Central Bank Annual Report **2008**) that are under the direct supervision of these Samurdhi development officers who are appointed by the party in government despite the officers representing a state welfare scheme. These officers enjoy substantial discretionary powers over Samurdhi beneficiaries and are often accused of biases and loyalties in selecting and managing beneficiaries.[2] The role of these government officers is somewhat different to the grassroots elites who enjoy the respect of the villagers and who can only passively influence the decision of voters. On the contrary, welfare officers from the community and various other officers such as agricultural officers exercise power over not only those who come under their direct purview, but also their relatives and those who expect benefits in the future. They often influence voters to take part in the electoral campaign of the ruling party, and sometimes they use passive coercion to bring voters to vote for their party. These officers allegedly go to extremes in wielding power to ensure the victory of the ruling party. Understandably, in the event of a regime change they would be the first political victims of the new regime.

Since competition amongst grassroots political leaders was intense, the electorate organizer always had the opportunity to renew his/her party network by enlisting people to improve and maximize the efficiency of the voter mobilizing mechanism. Organizers such as Mahinda Wijesekara in Weligama and Cyril Mathew in Kelaniya, who exhibited a great deal of sophistication in their party organization, in fact advocated for many village-level branch offices to represent various caste groups in the electorate. It was quite common to have more than one branch office in a village, as different caste groups preferred their own party branch, which in the case of subordinate caste communities allowed them to feel that they were equal with the hierarchically superior caste groups in the village. With their own party office, they could elect their own leaders and more importantly claim the same volume of patronage benefits that other groups received through the clientelistic elite network.

As the above discussion shows, political parties, especially the UNP and SLFP, organize themselves as networks of village elites, community leaders, businessmen and other influential personalities. The parties appropriate existing influential personalities in the electorates into their networks in order to reach out to the entire electorate. Each actor in these networks represents a particular socio-economic group in the electorate, and they mediate their community and state authority for votes. The electorate organizers of the two parties distribute individual benefits and services through these networks to maximize votes at elections. Hence, electorate organizers make use of social cleavages such as ethnicity, religion and caste as the territorial boundaries for political actors in the network, while lubricating the network-based election-engineering process through the accruing of individual benefits.

INSTITUTIONALLY WEAK BUT SOPHISTICATED IN PERSONAL NETWORKING

Electorate organizers always maintain two groups of people in the party organization: i) an inner circle comprising experts and trusted allies, and ii) a wider network of local (village) political actors who represent various social groups in the diversified electorate. The previous chapter discussed the role of the inner circle as well as how 'grassroots political actors' are formed in an electorate. However, what is most important in the party organization at the electorate level is how an electorate organizer establishes and maintains his/her elite network in order to maximize votes at elections. The following diagram illustrates how party organizations organize their networks of village political actors in electorates. In this diagram, the party organization is depicted as a network of relationships, rather than a hierarchical structure, which means that individuals are connected on the basis of some form of relationship, and that those relationships are always two-way processes.

The party organizational networks in the three electorates can be depicted using the above diagram. Neither the UNP nor the SLFP attempts to represent a special group of voters exclusively based on their caste, class, ethnicity or religion in their electoral campaign (this point will be elaborated on later). Instead, organizers of the two parties always strive to maximize their votes by approaching everyone in the electorate. In the above diagram, voters are symbolized by the thick stripe at the bottom. In between the thick layer of voters and the electoral organizer there are many individuals (depicted in various sizes of dots) who form a complex but informal network that is eventually linked to the party organizer in a particular electorate. In that network, village political actors/leaders in the electorate represent various groups of caste, class or religious communities in villages who help to connect the voters in those villages to this network. Some community leaders represent more voters than others, as they possess more status and power than other community leaders in the electorate. Those who possess a comparatively higher volume of various capitals always attract the respect and support of more villagers. Hence, they acquire higher status and power in the network of local political actors. The different sizes of the circles at the bottom of Fig. 3.1 indicate the varying degrees of power exercised by village-level elites, political actors and grassroots leaders.

However, the power these individuals possess is extremely fragile, as they themselves compete for recognition by acquiring more powers. Some of them rise to the second layer of the network where personnel with a comparatively higher volume of capital reside. Unlike village-level community leaders, those in the second layer of power can draw support from and exert influence beyond their home village. In order to extend their influence beyond their home village, they also have to establish and maintain a network of community leaders. Often these relationships are established on the basis of patronage, either with the personal wealth of the elite or on the basis of their personal capacity to access state resources. These political elites extend patronage to lesser village political actors in the electorate either through their own resources or authoritative powers. However, these relationships are also not static. They continuously negotiate and redefine the terms of the relationship due to the highly competitive nature of elite competition, where competing political elites and village-level political actors struggle to maximize their power

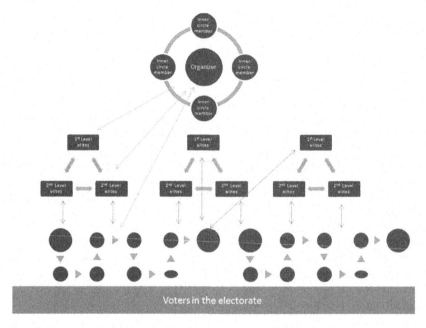

Fig. 3.1 Networks of local political actors in an electorate

through various strategies. Usually these second-level political leaders hold positions of various political and social institutions in the electorate. They contest for local government bodies such as Provincial Councils, Municipalities, Urban Councils and *Pradeshiya Sabhas*. In addition, they also contest for positions as office bearers in various state and non-state organizations in the electorate. These political elites possess more power than community-level elites, and some maintain direct contacts with certain groups of village communities. In any electorate there are a few elites who enjoy the allegiance of many second-level political actors and community leaders in addition to the direct links with the communities they have established on the basis of either cleavage representation or through the distribution of various individual benefits. They often contest local government bodies. After the introduction of Provincial Councils, many have contested for positions in the Provincial Councils instead of local government bodies.

In Fig. 3.1, second-level political actors are placed right below the electorate organizer, as they coordinate the other political actors in the electorate while maintaining direct contact with the electorate organizer. However, it needs to be mentioned that they acquire this position not because of their long years in the party organization, but due to their influential capacity to accumulate various forms of capital, such as wealth through successful business, popularity due to social service, and having many links with powerful politicians, bureaucrats and community leaders in the electorate. Leaders at all levels maintain relationships with various communities either directly or through other community leaders. These relationships are formed on various grounds such as kinship, caste, religion, ethnicity and most popularly patron-client relationships.

ROLE OF POLITICAL ACTORS IN MEDIATING STATE INSTITUTIONS AND THE CITIZEN

> In a society like ours, from birth to death, citizens, especially the poor and marginalized ones, have to rely on various political actors. (Kulasiri, a middle-aged, disabled voter from Dedigama)[3]

The above statement is not just an isolated, frustrated remark by a random individual. This statement alludes to the reality of the state-society relationship in our society and the role of political actors as mediators. Sri Lanka's experience with the formation of the nation-state is different from the formation of most western nation-states. The nature of the nation-state that colonial legacy produced in colonial societies—including most of the British South Asian colonies—is far from the ideal 'Weberian' type of state: "a goal oriented, unitary institute discrete from society with undisputed sovereignty in its sphere of jurisdiction" (Migdal 2001: 13–15), and with a "clear separation of powers between a judiciary, legislative and executive branches of government" (Berenschot 2009: 113). Especially since the 1972 constitution, successive state reforms (i.e. 1978 constitution, 18th Amendment, etc.), irrespective of whether by the SLFP or UNP, brought the bureaucracy under the control of politicians, inflicting lethal damage to state authority. "The hold of politicians over the daily operations of bureaucracy makes it difficult to see the state as an actor detached from society, as it is through them that the political mediators and societal elements penetrate the state from all sides" (Fuller and

Harris 2001: 22). Hence, the phenomenon of political actors functioning as the link between the citizen and state institutions is no great surprise.

Ward Berenschot (2009), in his research on communal violence in Gujarat, India, describes three types of mediation that a particular Municipal Councilor does on an average day. These are helpful to explain the role of political actors in the field locations of the study.

  i. Brokerage: Facilitation of the flow of information between state institutions and citizens
 ii. Patronage: Exchanging access to state resources for political support and
iii. Particularization: Undermining the uniform application of law and legislation to the advantage of private interests

Citizens often believe that they will receive sufficient or proper attention, if not extra attention, if they approach state or non-state institutions through someone relatively more influential or powerful than themselves. Before visiting state institutions such as the police, office of the Government Agent, public utility officers—electricity or water—and even a hospital or a school, the citizen, especially in villages, informs political actors to enlist their assistance. As Gunasekara (1992) also argues, villagers need the assistance of grassroots political leaders for a variety of reasons that are pivotal to their lives. Receiving government rations for the poor, obtaining a license or deed for land they have encroached on from a forest reservation, getting a job for an offspring, receiving fertilizer rations on time, receiving water for cultivation on time, seeking admission to a school in the town for children or grandchildren, seeking justice from village arbitrators for neighbourhood disputes, meeting government officials to seek efficient services and having a peaceful life without fear of goons and arbitrary arrest by the police are all such events in their lives. Therefore, these needs create a space for intervention by grassroots political actors. Not all of these grassroots leaders are identified with a particular political party. Even the ones who are identified with a particular party do not limit their association and assistance exclusively to supporters of the political party. As in Gujarat (Berenschot 2009: 114), in the electorates I chose also, political actors have so much say in the daily functioning of the bureaucracy and the state as to leave the citizen heavily dependent on them. Therefore, as Kulasiri said, these community leaders or political actors have become indispensible to the lives of the majority of citizens in villages. The role of the party organizer in the electorate is to establish the best and most comprehensive network of such political actors. The goal of the party organizer is to design this network by connecting with the most efficient community leaders while covering a majority of the social and political geography of the electorate.

ROLE OF NETWORKS IN COORDINATING THE MEDIATION OF CITIZEN AND POLITICAL ACTORS

In this model of networks of village political actors, citizens present their needs and grievances to their village-level community leaders and expect them to represent their interests before the more powerful actors, including the electorate organizer, who have the capacity to address those issues. Not all political actors have the same capacity to meet the interests of citizens. They have different levels of access to resources and ability to control state resources. Therefore, citizens will have limited opportunities if they limit their access to one such actor. In this context the networks of village political actors provide the solution where the citizen can reach out to any political actor desired.

Often, petty issues are resolved at the intermediary levels of the network by actors in the neighbourhood or village with lesser resources and powers. As for serious issues that the intermediary is unable to address, citizens approach powerful actors through their network of local political actors. If a particular party is in government, often the electorate organizer holds regular public meetings at his office along with his grassroots leaders to address issues of the constituency. This gives an opportunity for the community leaders and local political actors to represent the concerns of their community. Often, if not always, these discussions are limited to the distribution of various individual benefits and services that the community expects from the party hierarchy. Rarely do they discuss party policies.[4] It should also be noted that people do not always follow a set path in approaching the party organizer or another political actor in or outside the electorate to resolve their issues. As depicted in Fig. 3.1 there are multiple links amongst members of the network at multiple levels. Citizens make decisions according to their instincts in order to arrive at the best approach to resolve their needs. The most fascinating feature of these networks of local political actors is that except during election time, they do not explicitly operate with a particular party identity. Hence, citizens across party lines are free to approach and associate with them. These networks have thereby become legitimate structures of villages in non-party matters such as funerals, religious and other festivals, and communitarian work.

TURNING NETWORKS INTO THE PARTY ORGANIZATION STRUCTURE

Once elections are announced, these networks become the party organization structure in the electorate. Party leaders in the electorate appropriate the networks of village political actors and turn them into party networks in the electorate until the election is effectively over. Election campaigns are often carried out using networks where actors at various levels represent their communities within the electorate. These network actors mobilize their communities in support of the party and for the electorate organizer, who is usually the Parliamentary candidate. Often village-level political actors take their own initiatives and sometimes use their own wealth to campaign at the election. Members of the party organizer's inner circle provide administrative assistance and take the responsibility of fundraising for campaign activities. Even between two elections, if the party headquarters wishes to summon party members to the capital city, the party organizer uses these networks to supply the necessary numbers to the party head office. It is often the responsibility of the members of the inner circle—often the office staff of the party organizer—to provide the necessary support, such as buses, food, liquor, and in some cases, T-shirts indicating the electorate and party organizer's name for party-centric activities. Amongst members of these networks, often there are individuals with the capacity to either initiate or counter violence. The party organizer mobilizes them whenever their service is needed in the highly competitive and often violent electoral politics.

So far, the discussion on the 'networks of local grassroots leaders' has been limited to an introduction on how the networks are organized. These actors and their networks are not entirely a product of the structural conditions of the electorate. They can to some extent be considered as products of the politics in and outside the electorate. Since all actors in the networks are engaged in some form of competition, party organizers have the opportunity to choose the actors that he/she thinks are most efficient in collecting votes while being loyal to his/her leadership. Citizens also accept them and approach them not solely for their material needs but also for purposes concerning their identity-related interests.

Cleavages as Territorial
Boundaries for Political Actors

As repeatedly shown in this discussion, the objective of the party organization of the UNP and SLFP is to maximize votes. They strive to further the interests of particular social groups instead of pursuing the aggregate of voters. Hence, the party organization network is mainly established by individuals who exhibit the highest capacity to draw more votes, rather than ones who attempt to represent various interests of society. This is to say that even if a particular individual represents a certain interest of a particular group, the party organizer would not be interested in that person unless he/she has the capacity to gather votes. This explains why during the early days of the UNP, the party organization mainly rested on rich landlords in the electorate. The SLFP also followed the same tradition more or less despite its popular rhetoric of being a party of the poor and socially marginalized (Jupp 1978). Although the SLFP drew great support from the poor and the subordinate classes, even during the early days of the party, the grassroots leadership was drawn from the intermediate classes and not from the poor and marginalized (Wilson 1975; Jupp 1978; Jayasuriya 2000). In parallel to the expansion of democracy, the UNP and SLFP also extended the boundaries by reaching out to grassroots-level leadership beyond their traditional leadership bases. These expansions of party boundaries can be seen as a result of interparty competition of the UNP and SLFP, as well as class struggles within each party. At the initial stages of the two-party competition between the UNP and SLFP, the main strategy was to expand their outreach (Jupp 1978; Wilson 1975; Jiggins 1979). In this context, the two parties had to search for new grassroots leaders beyond their traditional group who could provide them with comparative advantages in maximizing votes. Hence, instead of focusing on elites who possessed economic capital, the UNP and SLFP began to look for individuals who enjoyed a higher degree of status amongst various social groups to reach out beyond the traditional boundaries. In this context, parties and their organizers singled out local political actors and community leaders who were perceived to represent the many social cleavages within the electorate. These cleavages included religion, ethnicity, social class and more importantly caste.

Caste as a Territorial Boundary

No social scientist has missed the category of caste in the analysis of Sri Lankan society. As Jiggins states, caste is considered a "very important" phenomenon amongst scholars as well as amongst Sinhalese themselves (Jiggins 1979: 7). However, the Sri Lankan caste system differs from the Indian caste system. As Gunasinghe points out: "in the absence of the priestly role of the brahmin caste, though ritual presentations and avoidance were practiced amongst different castes, the entire caste system acquired a certain degree of secularization" (Gunasinghe 1990: 33). Due to the lack of the "supremacy of priest," Dumont argues that the Sri Lankan caste system is more "quasi-caste than caste proper" (Dumont 1999: 216). Nevertheless, to date, caste has been considered a powerful denominator of cultural, political and economic influence by scholars of Sri Lankan politics and society (Jiggins 1979; Hettige 1984; Gunasinghe 1990; Gunasekara 1994; Dewasiri 2008). Another way they summarize the scholarly commentary on caste is 'caste as social stratification' and 'caste as an ideology.'[5] The former recognizes caste as an 'objective' category while the latter considers caste as a 'subjective' category. However, most scholars recognize the existence of caste in both objective and subjective spheres (Gunasekara 1994; Dewasiri 2008).

In the Sinhalese electorates studied for this research, caste represents a very important cleavage, which has been recognized by many scholars on Sri Lankan electoral politics (Jupp 1978; Wilson 1975; Jiggins 1979; Jayanntha 1992). Unlike social stratifications such as class, ethnicity, religion or education, caste is a taboo subject in Sinhalese society (Jiggins 1979; Spencer 1990). Jonathan Spencer attempted to illustrate the strange phenomenon of caste in Sinhalese society as follows: "Caste, rather like drink or enmity, is always present but almost never seen. It lies just beneath the surface of daily life, threatening to intrude or upset at any moment" (Spencer 1990: 191).

Caste was used to organize the Sinhalese community on a hierarchical order under the feudal system in the past, and it remains a potential source of 'pride' or 'enmity' amongst social groups (Spencer 1990; Gunasinghe 1990; Gunasekara 1994). Therefore, I treat caste as a 'potential source' instead of a given 'reality,' because it often becomes a source of 'pride' or 'enmity' depending on how it is constructed in a particular society. Therefore, caste only becomes politically effective as long as it is politically constructed by politicians for their own benefit. This explains how politicians sometimes manage to infiltrate across different caste groups using individual benefits. However, in Sinhalese politics, caste is not mentioned overtly. Nevertheless, caste is widely apparent in the Sinhalese political discourse, in the past as well as at present, through a vocabulary that does not imply anything other than caste. Caste is popularly referred to as a cultural factor (*sanskruthika sädaka*) by politicians in public speeches.[6] However, they do not hesitate to use even derogatory references to caste when the audience is from their own caste community. For example, during the 2010 Parliamentary election campaign, two Kandyan ruling party Parliamentarians requested *goigama* voters across the district not to vote for the *padda* (a derogatory reference to individuals from the *bathgama* caste), referring to another Parliamentarian from the same party who is from the *bathgama* (*padu*) caste. Meanwhile, this particular *bathgama* Parliamentarian campaigned saying that he is a *padda*, and therefore the entire *bathgama* community in the district should vote for him.[7] Caste hostility is not only limited to inter-caste conflict, because in some instances people identify further hierarchical fractions within a caste.[8] For example the *goigama* caste is further divided into *radala*, *govi* and *patti*. The *durawe* community is further divided as *heen durawe* and *maha durawe*. However, as already stressed, caste becomes an effective political cleavage amongst the Sinhalese electorate only when it is politically constructed.

Caste was one of the main categories that parties attempted to appeal to during the expansion of representation of grassroots leadership in the wake of the two-party competition that began in 1956. By the 1970s both the UNP and SLFP in the electorates of Dedigama, Weligama and Kelaniya had included grassroots leaders from respective caste groups or found leaders even from different caste groups (if there were individuals with the capacity to play a leadership role) to represent those communities in their party organization network. This inclusion of grassroots leaders from each prominent caste group was not intended by the party organization to reflect the interests of those caste communities, but rather to provide the assurance that they too were equal with other caste groups (hierarchically superior) in an electorate, in terms of receiving patronage that the party organizer distributes. Grassroots leaders of a particular caste group in a village become the intermediary between their own caste community and the electorate organizer, where voters surrender their votes in return for patronage.

Ethnicity, Religion and Class as Territorial Boundaries.

In the words of Uyangoda, "ethnic appeal has been an essential practice in electoral democracy amongst the mainstream political parties"
(Uyangoda 2010: 42). He argues that except for the Left, all political
parties in Sri Lanka have promoted ethnicized political visions since their
inception. Despite their political differences, the UNP and SLFP find
themselves in total accord on themes of language and religion, especially
Buddhism (Wilson 1984: 11). Hence, Wilson suggests that both parties
have produced a common oppositional front to the Ceylonese Tamils
(ibid.). The intensification of the ethnic conflict in the early 1980s and
thereafter provided a reason for political parties to be not only ethnic,
but also to be ethnic exclusivists (Uyangoda 2010: 42). However, as the
field work suggests, the ethnic factor does not play a significant role in
party-voter relations in the ethnically homogeneous Sinhalese electorates
as it does in national politics.

In the case of Dedigama, Weligama and Kelaniya, where there is a
sizable Muslim community, electorate organizers always accommodate
community leaders from the Muslim community in their party network to
reach out to that community. These grassroots leaders represent Muslims
across the electorate, thereby providing an important channel to the party
organizer to win the support of these communities at elections whenever
their support is needed.

Religion is another important cleavage in Kelaniya, where the Roman
Catholic community constitutes a good portion of the constituency. With
the help of temples in the electorate, J. R. Jayewardene successfully mobilized Buddhist votes against his Catholic opponent E.W. Perera at the
1943 interim election. S.W.R.D. Bandaranaike too approached Buddhist
temples—especially the Kelani Vihare—to mobilize votes against J. R.
Jayewardene at the 1956 election.[9] In addition to caste, ethnicity and religion, elite networks represent communities stratified by the locality, such
as urban and rural. Especially in the case of Kelaniya, there are communities who live in the urban up-market neighbourhood as well as in the
low-income shanty dwellings that need to be represented in the party
organization network. The following tables present caste and religious
backgrounds of the local community leaders of the two political parties
in selected areas in the electorate.

The above Table 3.1 confirms that the local community leadership of
the UNP and SLFP often represented the majority caste and religious

Table 3.1 Local political actors of the UNP and the SLFP in selected areas in the Kelaniya electorate during 1977–1980 (H: *hunu*, W: *wahumpura*, G: *goigama*, N: *nawandanna*, K: *kumbal*)

Ward Name	UNP	SLFP
Hunupitiya	Daya Pieries (H) Ramya Fernando (H)	Wijaya Dharmadasa (H) Rexi Nithyananda (H)
Iriyawatiya	Lionel Michel (W)	Regi Ranasinghe (W)
Dalugama	D.A. Piyadasa (N)	H.A. Gunadasa (G)
Wanawasala	Sirisoma Jayaweera (W) Lilarathne Senadheera (W)	Sirisoma Jayaweera (W) Lilarathne Senadheera (W)
Galborella	Dr. Sarath Rodrigo (K)	Wilmert Rodrigo (K)
Sinharamulla	K. Samarathunge (G) D.M. Amarasinghe (G) K.D. Somasiri (G) Sugathadasa Paranawithana (K)	Lusion Perera (G) D.S. Weerakkodi (G) Sisil Wickramasinghe (G) Deleen Rodrigo (K)

group in the community. For example, in Hunupitiya where the majority community belongs to the *hunu* caste, the two parties also had political actors from the same caste group. Similarly, in the areas of Iriyawetiya and Wanawasala, the parties had community leaders from *wahumpura* caste groups, which constitute the majority community in those areas (Tables 3.2 and 3.3).

This shows that these local political actors are not just representatives of a community living in a particular geographical space but instead represent the social characteristics of the community. Therefore, social cleavages provide imaginary territories to village elites and political actors to rise and compete for political power. In the same way, these cleavages assist party organizers to achieve sophistication in designing an efficient party network to maximize their ability to amass votes at elections. In addition, these imaginary territories provide the basis for any electorate organizer to distribute patronage benefits in order to maximize the chances of winning future elections. However, not all party organizers exhibit the capacity to identify cleavage-based territories in their

Table 3.2 Local political actors of the UNP and SLFP in selected areas in the dedigama electorate during 1977–1994 (B: *bathgama*, W: *wahumpura*, G: *goigama*, K: *karawa*)

Ward Name	UNP	SLFP
Algama	W.A. Tikiribanda (G)	W.A Dasanayake (G)
	L.M. Karunasekara (G)	I.P. Jayathissa (B)
Dedigama	I.R. Sumanadasa (G)	S.P. Perera (K)[a] Nimal
	M.A. Mapa (G)	Ranathunge (G)
Thambawila	G.R. Ukkubanda (G)	M.A. Somadasa (G)
	R.W. Jemis (W)	J.A. Amarasinghe
	R.K. Sisira (G)	Banda (G)
	N.A. Gunadasa (G)	Dayananda Balasooriya (G)
Weniwellakaduwa	K. Senavirathne (B)	A. Martin (B)
	T.M. Mallawabandara (G)	K.R. Dharmasena (B)
	A. Piyasena (B)	N.M. Simion (G)
	H.P. Wanasooriya (B)	

[a]He is originally from the south and had come there for business. Later he settled in Dedigama

Table 3.3 Local political actors of the UNP and SLFP in selected areas in the weligama electorate during 2004 (D: *durawa*, G: *goigama*, K: *karawa*, M: Muslim)

Ward Name	UNP	SLFP
Kanake	Sunil Edirisinghe (G)	Robin Sanke (G)
Mirissa	K.H. Padmadasa (K)	Donald Wirasekara (K)
Kamburugamuwa	Nandapala (D)	Kulaweera (D)
Midigama	C. Jayawardena (G)	Omila Jayawardena (G)
Welima Town	Lorezohewa Dhanmasiri (K)	Hemal Gunasekara (G) L.A. Cader (M)

electorate and design of their party network. As the research indicates, most of the successful electorate organizers in Dedigama, Weligama and

Kelaniya exhibited tremendous skills not only in recognizing the diversified social cleavages in their electorates, but also making connections with the most efficient actors in those communities.

Oscillation and Transformation in Party Organization

The discussion thus far hinted at the transformation party organizations have experienced as a consequence of the transformation of the basic elements of party organization. Those basic elements of party organization have undergone various shifts and turns over the past several decades consequent to the changes in the socio-economic landscape of the country. I would now like to focus on the following two main factors that have played, and are playing, a major role in reshaping party organizational dynamics in the electorate.

i. The ways in which change of the electoral system from first-past-the-post (FPTP) to the proportional representation (PR) electoral system reshaped and transformed party organizing dynamics in the electorate ('transformation').

ii. Shift of party organizational dynamics at the electorate level from being an active and enlarged organizing body while in power, to an inactive and deflated informal group when the party loses its power at the centre ('oscillation').

This 'transformation' of and 'oscillation' in party organization take place somewhat independently of each other. Parties have experienced oscillation irrespective of the electoral system. However, after the introduction of the PR system the time taken for one oscillation is much longer as compared to the oscillations during the previous electoral system. For example, from 1956 to 1970 every general election produced a change of regime, but this pattern was transformed after the introduction of the PR system in 1978. The following section will examine in detail the transformation and oscillation of party organizational dynamics in the electorate.

Transformation

Under the Donoughmore, Soulbury and first Republican constitutions, from 1931 to 1978, elections were held on the constituency-based, simple plurality, first-past-the-post system. Electoral competition under this system was less complicated, as parties and politicians competed for geographically small constituencies. Except for a few multimember constituencies such as Ambalangoda-Balapitiya, Colombo-Central, Colombo-South, Nuwara Eliya-Maskeliya and Balangoda, most of the constituencies were single-member seats. Party organization and electoral competition under this system was relatively simple. To win the electorate the candidate needed to score the highest number of votes amongst all candidates who contested. Under this pluralist electoral system, parties often appointed only one organizer for each constituency, and the same person was also the party's candidate at the Parliamentary election. For example, in the electorates of Dedigama, Weligama and Kelaniya Dudley Senanayake, Montague Jayewickrema and J. R. Jayewardene (until March 1960) represented the UNP, while Dharmasiri Senanayake, Panini Illangakoon and R.S. Perera represented the SLFP for many years, respectively. Therefore, when the voter decided on the party, he/she invariably chose the candidate as well.

However, under this pluralist electoral system, the politician, irrespective of his antecedents in the same electorate as an insider or outsider, had to be accountable to his electorate. The relationship between the voter, party and politician was simple and straightforward. At any given time, the support base of the party and the support base of the electoral organizer remained almost identical. In this sense, the electoral organizer usually enjoyed the support of party loyalists as well as his or her own personal loyalists. Those who wished to vote against either a party or electoral organizer did not have the option to support one while opposing the other.

On the other hand, under the FPTP electoral system, parties had to endow their support bases in an electorate on an individual whom they selected as the electorate organizer. Therefore, the party leadership had to make serious calculations in appointing electoral organizers. That individual had to be in the most advantageous position to garner the most number of votes in the electorate. Hence the parties paid much attention to the caste and family of the politician when appointing electorate organizers, as argued by Jiggins (Jiggins 1979). In the early elections in Sri

Lanka, political parties, and especially the UNP and SLFP, relied on the caste factor to attract votes. They used the resources of the family network in the electorate to influence voters at elections. This trend was observed by two scholars, Jiggins (1979) and Jayanntha (1992), who studied voter behaviour in Sri Lanka. However, after 1956 access to state capital became a more powerful alternative to the private capital of politicians in their distribution of patronage (Jayanntha 1992: 53). Hence, the importance of family resources as a factor in influencing voter decisions was drastically reduced. In this context, the SLFP and UNP increasingly relied on and appointed politicians outside the traditional wealthy classes.

Under the FPTP system, electoral organizers commanded more powers in the party-politician relationship. In that sense, parties were somewhat obliged to appoint the 'right' or 'most suitable' candidate in the electorate in order to win the seat. In instances when parties ignored the most suitable personality, often that particular individual decided to contest as an independent candidate, which could prove disadvantageous to the party's campaign in that specific electorate. It is assumed that pluralist electoral systems lead to constituency-based (local) politics and thus decentralized parties, whereas the PR system upholds a centralized politics and stronger parties (Sartori 2000; Bastian 2010). Under the pluralist electoral system, politicians enjoyed an edge over their party leadership as parties had to depend on the performance of the politician, who was expected to wield a great deal of political authority in the electorate. Therefore, in the FPTP electoral system, parties relied on politicians who had or were capable of having a successful network of local community leaders on the basis of cleavage and patronage. In this context, Jiggins' (1979) *Caste and Family*, and Jayanntha's (1992) *Patronage Networks*, held great significance in explaining the appointment of electoral leadership.

Electorates are hardly homogeneous. Of course some electorates are homogeneous in terms of ethnicity or religion. However, in the case of caste composition, even those electorates are highly diversified. Therefore, under FPTP the electoral organizer paid special attention to gestures that paid symbolic attention to all communities in the electorate irrespective of his/her own ethnic, religious or caste identity. Often party organizers formed their inner circles and their second-tier leadership in the network of local political actors by allowing representation for caste and religious diversity in the electorate. In the case of Dedigama, the UNP and SLFP both fielded *Goigama* electorate organizers under the FPTP system. Nevertheless, in their party organization networks, both parties included local grassroots leaders from the *Bathgama* and *Wahumpura* castes, which constituted the second and third largest caste groups in the electorates. Montague Jayewickrema was a *Karawa* politician representing the UNP in Weligama, where a majority of the community was from the *Goigama* caste. Nevertheless, he maintained strong links to the *Goigama* caste group through his own brother (Eral Jayewickrema) who was married to a Kandyan *Goigama* woman.[10] The estates belonging to his family that employed a large percentage of the *Goigama* community in the electorate allowed him to provide this symbolic recognition to the *Goigama* caste while being a *Karawa* elite. Panini Illangakoon, being a *Goigama* elite, could not enjoy the exclusive support of *Goigama* caste voters and had to depend on other communities such as the *Durawa* community in the Weligama electorate. Due to the traditional caste rivalry between *karawa* and *durawa* communities in the Weligama electorate, the *durawa* and *goigama* clans preferred electoral alliances against the *karawa* community.

In addition, both the UNP and SLFP maintained links to the numerically small Muslim community in the electorate. In comparison with Dedigama and Weligama, Kelaniya was somewhat complex due to the religious diversity within the electorate. Party organizers had to contend with not only caste and ethnic diversity but also religious diversity due to the substantial Roman Catholic community. It is widely believed that the reason J. R. Jayewardene left the Kelaniya electorate after the March 1960 election victory was that he realized it was not easy for a *Goigama* UNPer to harness the support of the *Wahumpura* and other hierarchically lower and numerically smaller caste groups in the electorate.[11] The factor that is emphasized in this study is that under FPTP, party organizers had to face the difficult challenge of convincing other caste groups that they too would receive adequate recognition and representation under the leadership of that particular electorate organizer.

Recognition and representation of cultural differences here could not be limited to a mere descriptive representation, where representatives often resemble those they represent. Representation warrants substantive representation—where actions taken should represent the interests of the voters. This is to say that electoral organizers had to show that they served all groups in the electorate in a manner that reassured that no group was discriminated against. In the case of the distribution of individual benefits to the electorate, the party organizer needs to be careful; otherwise patronage could be counterproductive to his electoral

competition. However, under FPTP the distribution of individual benefits was much simpler and relatively less challenging, as the electorate
organizer represented a comparatively small geographical area and voter
population.[12]

It did not require a huge amount of resources and individual benefits,
under the FPTP system, to satisfy the village leadership who brokered
the allegiance of the people to the electoral organizer. Since the electoral competition was limited to interparty dynamics, the support of party
loyalists and contributors of funds was only directed at the party organizer. Under FPTP, the party organizer met with fewer challengers within
his own party as he enjoyed a firm grip on his own party organization.
Even if there was village-level discontent with the electorate organizer,
serious damage could not be inflicted on him/her. The only option available to dissidents under FPTP was to campaign for another party, which
was not an easy alternative. In such a situation, the party organizer had
enough options to replace village political actors with new substitutes
to minimize damage to the electoral campaign. Therefore, under FPTP,
once the party network was set up by an electorate organizer, the network
survived with minimum changes throughout the tenure of the party organizer in that electorate. In the same fashion, competition at the village
level to represent the party was also less intense and dynamic. Under the
pluralist electoral system, traditional village political actors retained their
political capital for many years, representing their village or caste community. The bond between the village political actor who occupied various
positions in the network of political actors and the electorate organizer
was also relatively stronger, either due to the authority enjoyed by the
organizer or the lack of an alternative party leadership within the electorate. The distribution of patronage, providing party tickets to contest
for local authorities or appointments to various state positions within the
electorate was largely at the discretion of the electorate organizer under
the FPTP system. Therefore, in essence, before the introduction of the
PR system the party organization in electorates constituted of:

  i. Strong electoral leadership
 ii. A coherent network of local elites in the party organizing strategy
     and
iii. A clear and simple relationship between the voter and the electorate
     organizer

The FPTP electoral system was also blamed for many ills. Features such as massive electoral victories that provided the winning party with a numerical majority disproportionate to the popular vote in Parliament, and the underrepresentation of small parties in the legislature, came under severe criticism and prompted demands for reform (Welikala 2008; Uyangoda 2012). In this background, in the new constitution that the UNP drafted following its massive electoral victory in 1977 the electoral system was changed to PR. Under the PR system parties contest for larger districts composed of several electorates, and Members of Parliament are chosen on the basis of the preferential votes that each obtains from within his/her respective district.

Out of 225 seats, 29 are reserved for national list MPs. These 29 seats are allocated to the various parties based on the total votes polled at the national level. Any political party or independent group polling less than 5% (initially 12½%) of the total votes polled within a district is disqualified, and the balance valid votes are reckoned for allocation of seats on the basis of proportional computation. In each district, the political party or independent group securing the highest number of votes is entitled to have one member declared elected (the bonus seat). The balance number of members are declared elected on the basis of the proportion of votes obtained by each political party or independent group.[13]

Even though the PR system addressed some of the deficits in the pluralist electoral system, it triggered many new electoral deficits that contributed to a significant change in Sri Lankan politics (Bastian 2007: 92). In addition, this change in the electoral system had a far-reaching impact on party politics in general and party organization in the electorates in particular. As Bastian describes, because of the introduction of the PR system, patronage has been entrenched, and ministries and departments have proliferated in order to satisfy various functions in parties and coalition partners (Bastian 2007: 92). As my field research suggests, this new electoral system introduced a new set of rules to party organization strategies in the electorate, which in turn reconfigured the relationships of actors in the old networks in electorates. Let's examine how party organization and the dynamics of old political actor networks in the electorates changed as a result of the introduction of the PR electoral system, and how these new relationships of the networks of local leaders have influenced the voter-party relationship. Table 3.4 summarizes the knowledge elicited through field interviews on the relationship between the PR system and its impact on party organization at the electorate level.

Table 3.4 Effects on party organization in the electorate as a result of changes in the electoral system

Under FPTP	Under PR system
Higher degree of accountability towards the constituency	Relatively less accountability towards the constituency
Parties need to carefully select their electorate organizer	Parties are provided many choices when selecting the electorate organizer
Electorate organizer possesses relatively higher agency than the party	Party leadership possesses relatively higher agency than the electorate organizer
Electoral competition within the electorate is an interparty one	Electoral competition within the electorate is interparty as well as intraparty
Relationship between the electorate organizer and village political actors is usually one-to-many	Relationship between the electorate organizer and village political actors can be many-to-many
Grassroots political actor competition is relatively less as there is one base with the same party	Grassroots political actor competition is relatively high as there are many bases within the same party

Table 3.5 Electoral statistics of selected electorates

Under FPTP[a]		Under PR[b]				
Electorate	Registered Voters	Electoral District	Registered Voters	Number of electorates in the district	Total number of candidates that UNP fielded	Total number of candidates that SLFP fielded
Dedigama	83,554	Kegalle	613,938	9	12	12
Weligama	86,711	Matara	578,858	7	11	11
Kelaniya	83,105	Gampaha	1,474,464	18	21	21

[a]1977 election, Department of Elections Commissioner
[b]2010 election, Department of Elections Commissioner

Under the PR system, electoral competition is no longer on the basis of geographically small electorates; instead, politicians have to compete in electoral districts that are larger than the electoral divisions, geographically and population-wise. This has triggered numerous new challenges that have resulted in dramatic changes in electorate-level party organization.

As shown in the Table 3.5, under the PR system Parliamentary candidates have to compete in large district electorates with more than 7 to 10 times the voter population than under the previous electoral system. In addition, a particular candidate has to compete with candidates from other political parties as well as with candidates from his/her own party. Voters are given more options in selecting their candidates within a particular party by allowing them to cast three preferential votes, instead of the single ballot practiced under the FPTP electoral system. Therefore, under the PR system a party can win a seat (in a particular electorate) while the respective candidate can fail to be elected to Parliament. These new conditions of electoral competition resulted in the readjustment of earlier party organizational strategies of electorate organizers. For example, in the 1989 Parliamentary election, U.S. Perera, the UNP's Kelaniya candidate, won his electorate but failed to be elected to Parliament; he could not score enough preferential votes. There are numerous such examples that can be cited to illustrate this aspect of the PR system.

Under the PR system, the electorate organizer can no longer restrict the electoral campaign to his/her own electorate, as there are no boundaries within the district for those who contest for Parliament and the Provincial Council (especially after 1987).As Jayasuriya observes, "this was a marked departure from traditional electoral practices that encouraged members of Parliament to become involved in local issues" (Jayasuriya 2000: 105). Under this system, voters also enjoy the opportunity to vote for leaders beyond their own electorate. Under the PR system, the electorate organizers of highly-populated electorates often enjoy comparative advantages over the organizers of less-populated electorates. For example, as U.S. Perera, the Kelaniya electorate organizer for the UNP, pointed out, he managed to win the electorate at the 1989 Parliamentary election even though he could not get enough votes from the district to get into Parliament.[14] Under the PR system, an electorate organizer has to face new challenges in party organization. Two such new challenges are the need to:

i. Infiltrate into other electorates while securing his/her own base in the home electorate from other infiltrators
ii. Face intraparty competition within the district electorate while campaigning against opposition candidates

In order to meet these new challenges, the electorate organizer has to reconfigure the networks of power on the basis of new strategies. However, village elites also adjusted themselves and reorganized in order to reach their own goals under the new political system. Let's examine how these interests have reconfigured the electorate-level organizing mechanism.

Under the PR system, the electorate organizer cannot afford to maintain the same close relationship with the constituency as under the FPTP system.[15] On the one hand, it is not practical given the size of the present electorate, and on the other hand it is not cost effective. Even though political parties appoint electoral organizers to each electorate, since they are elected to Parliament from the entire district, they cannot be held accountable for their respective electorates. Unlike the previous electoral system, under the PR system the electorate organizer does not invest too much in organizing the electorate's networks of village elites by accommodating all actors who were in the old networks of local elites. Instead, the organizer maintains a selected number of the most trusted and electorally effective local elites, community leaders, businessmen and other influential persons in the electorate in his/her party network, while approaching other trusted local elites in other electorates within the electoral district. As mentioned earlier, this village grassroots leadership emerged from societies demarcated by various cleavage boundaries, while their main goal was to acquire and retain power and status by establishing access to state capital through national elites.

Unlike the earlier system, under the PR system voters can vote for the party without voting for its electoral organizer. Therefore, a party can still amass votes irrespective of the capacity of the electorate organizer. The party has to field a good team of candidates in the district, and it needs to be popular at the national level. In the context of the PR system, the party leadership enjoys a great deal of flexibility (Jayasuriya 2000; Bastian 2007). It can field the most loyal cadres as electoral organizers. Even if they are not electorate organizers, fielding them as candidates at elections would not dent the electoral strength of the party in that electorate. In addition, it should be noted that the changes we observe under the PR system are not solely due to the change in the electoral system. One must not forget the tremendous effect of the executive presidency, which was introduced under the same constitution, on the political party system and the behaviour of political parties. So far no systematic study has been conducted on the effects of the executive presidency on the party system in Sri Lanka. Nevertheless, it needs little effort to observe how the executive presidency has changed the principal political parties into extreme oligarchies while weakening them as national-level institutions. The PR system requires the electorate organizer to maintain extremely close relations with the party leadership at the centre. Organizers are no longer an indispensable resource to the party leadership at the centre.

Under the PR system, electorate organizers need to possess a bigger resource pool than ever before due to the sheer size of the electorate (de Zoysa 2013). Due to the scarcity of resources, party organizers are compelled to expand their party networks instead of maximizing the performance of actors in the network. My field research shows that, unlike in the FPTP period, the PR system involves patronage distributions on the eve of elections. While politicians maintain some form of patron-client relationship throughout, they intensify their patronage distribution during the last days of the election campaign in order to ensure optimum returns.

In the run-up to elections, electorate organizers and members of their inner circles approach various elites. These include even those who are not part of the party's village political actor network and other political actors from outside the electorate. This is to gather the maximum number of votes in return for patronage. The party at the centre and the politicians in the district provide ideological material through popular media and campaign communications explaining why they should support that particular politician in the election. For example, Champika Premadasa, the Dedigama electorate organizer, received support from Dedigama UNPers as well as many other community groups scattered in the entire Kegalle District. He received substantial support from Rambukkana, his hometown where his businesses interests are based.[16] In addition, he secured the support of the *Wahumpura* caste communities spread across Kegalle District through his personal networks of community leaders. In this design he was aware that he did not receive the support of all UNPers in Dedigama, and especially some of the *Goigama* caste UNPers. They were hesitant to vote for Premadasa on the basis of caste, which they indicated through various means. On the other hand, Manoda Wijeratne, who crossed over to the UPFA in 2006, could not get elected to Parliament even though the UPFA won the Dedigama seat at the 2010 Parliamentary elections. A UPFA senior politician, Mahinda Yapa Abeywickrama, is the Weligama electorate organizer. However, he received more votes from other electorates in the Matara District than from his own electorate at the

2010 Parliamentary election. He maintains a stronger network of village political actors outside the Weligama electorate.[17] The former Provincial Councilor (now an MP from Matara District) Hemal Gunasekara, an SLFP local elite from the Weligama electorate, managed to garner more votes from Weligama although he is technically the electorate organizer of the adjoining Kamburupitiya electorate.

Village political actors also exercise some degree of agency by being part of the network of local political actors created by various electorate organizers. Unlike the FPTP system, under the PR system they exercise much flexibility to pick and choose their patrons who could provide a comparatively higher return on their votes. In this case, those electorate organizers who have great potential to win an election while being a member of the ruling party, or the potential to become a minister in the next government, or at least as long as that politician exhibits his/her capacity to tap into state resources through the ruling party, will be the higher priority of these local political actors when deciding the future networks they aspire to be associated with. For example, Saman Gamage, village political actor from Kananke, Weligama, said that he resigned from the chairmanship of the Weligama *Pradeshiya Sabha*, which was governed by the UNP, and joined Hemal Gunasekara as his coordinating secretary. Explaining his rationale, Sunil stated[18] that he believed that Hemal Gunasekara would receive a powerful and lucrative position under President Rajapakse's government due to his personal relationship with President Rajapaksa. Therefore, Sunil believed that working for Hemal Gunasekara would provide him access to state resources and positions that he can use to meet his personal ambitions as well as the needs of his supporters. On the other hand, when traditional village political actors who support the party either as rank and file or at least as strong supporters fall out with the current party organizer in the electorate, they can conveniently continue their support for the party while linking up with the network of another electorate organizer in the same district. Thereby they can still ensure the continuous flow of patronage to the community that they represent as well as for themselves. The story of Siriwardane of Ragalakanda in Dedigama provides a very good example of such village elites. Siriwardane is no longer a member of the Dedigama SLFP organizer's network of village political actors. Nevertheless he continued to maintain his influential status and party allegiance by linking up with other district politicians such as Athauda Seneviratne. Another example is Gunarathne of Lenagala, Dedigama is an old member of the UNP village political actor network in Dedigama.[19] He is also a former member of the Warakapola local council, although he does not play a role in Champika Premadasa's networks at present. Instead, he functions independently and supports other UNP politicians at elections. Therefore, despite his problems with the current UNP electorate organizer, he continued to play a village political actor role in his village for those who support the UNP.

During an election campaign these village political actors organize pocket meetings in their villages for the communities they represent and invite the politician who heads the network that the village elite belong to. There are instances where these meetings are attended by multiple candidates with some sort of consensus amongst the politicians about who are linked to particular village elites.[20] Of course in some instances those pocket meetings turn out to be a source of intraparty rivalry. Often village political actors who belong to two networks of the same political party (under two national politicians) do not share their campaign strategies despite their rhetoric that they all work for the betterment of the party. Today, most campaign work is contracted to professionals instead of voluntary political activists. Therefore, it is not unusual to see the same person pasting campaign posters and distributing the pamphlets and manifestos of rival candidates in the electorate.[21] Violence used to be unleashed only on opposition party members and their campaigns during the FPTP electoral system. After the introduction of the PR system, however, violence amongst party members and candidates is as bad as violence amongst opposition candidates. For example, at the 2010 Parliamentary election, the Election Commissioner had to annul some results in the Kandy District where the accuser and the accused were both from the SLFP-led UPFA coalition (*The Sunday Times*, 11 April 2010).

To summarize, the introduction of the PR electoral system has radically changed party organizing strategies in the electorate. The network of village political actors that previously existed as the main structure of the party organizational mechanism has been weakened. The bonds in that network are no longer as strong as they used to be under the FPTP electoral system. Electoral organizers as well as village political actors look for more beneficial relationships, as Anthony Downs (1957) argued in his rational choice theory, rather than maintaining the old village elite network of the party organization in the electorate. Under the PR system, positions of the village political actors in the electorate have become fragile. Nevertheless, they have the opportunity to exercise their 'influence' by developing new relationships beyond the electorate.

In this context, parties rapidly reduce dependence on individuals, and patronage continues to be the chief source of ensuring party allegiance. Certain social cleavages such as caste that have been substituted by the patronage network begin to gain new importance under the PR system (Uyangoda 2010; de Zoysa 2013). Making a similar observation, Uyangoda also argues that "the availability of preferential voting under the PR system has provided a new impetus for caste-based voting" (Uyangoda 2010a: 59). Under the PR system patronage distribution can systematically accommodate and address caste rivalries in the electoral districts. Hence, in general, regime change has become extremely difficult as parties in the opposition become very weak nationally. Even in the electorates, the party in government can always reconfigure its networks of village political actors by absorbing village elites across party lines with the aid of state resources.

Oscillation

Incumbency in office and thus political power has oscillated between the two parties since 1956 (Uyangoda 2012). Even when they could not form a government alone they were always the principal partner in the coalition that formed the government. As discussed in the previous chapter, oscillations were not at long intervals before the introduction of PR. In general, almost every six years the main opposition party managed to capture power and replace the national and local leadership with new faces. When a party formed a government, the village political actor network on which that party organization was founded became active with the state power and state capital they accessed when in power. However, when the same party moved into the opposition, the entire village elite network that had been active and powerful while in government suddenly became inactive or comparatively weak. Hence, the party organization of the UNP and SLFP have swayed between being active and powerful or inactive and weak, depending on whether they were in or out of power, which I term as 'oscillation'.

As discussed earlier, party branches are generally founded on village political actors who are part of the party organizer's village elite networks. They become political party branches only during the election campaign. During other times neither the party organizer nor the villagers make a serious effort to maintain these party branches. However, village political actors remain influential community leaders even when their party loses power in the electorate and at the centre. These village political actors continue to negotiate with other actors who are in power, as well as the bureaucracy and state officials on behalf of the communities they represent.[22] Hettige also recognizes how local party organization (which he refers to as 'local fractions') becomes empowered and influential when its party is in office and holds power at the centre, and when party organizers from the ruling party reflect their grit in the local region (Hettige 1984: 159). If the village political actor proves to be incapable of resolving issues of the community, that community begins to search for alternative political actors instead of waiting for another six years or more. However, if the community sees the potential of the village elite to solve their issues in the near future due to a potential power change at the centre, they continue to rally around him/her. No matter whether they are poor or uneducated, voters have their own rationale to maximize their life opportunities when building relationships with their village elites. Before the PR system was effectively implemented, these village elites managed to maintain their own segment of loyalists in the village uninterrupted, as even those who were in the opposition had great potential to be powerful power brokers, since regime changes did not take too long. However, after the PR system effectively came into practice, village political actors of parties in the opposition had to stay as members of the opposition village elite networks for a longer period and, quite unfortunately, under the PR system it is hard to even guess when an opposition can form a government. Therefore, village political actors of the opposition have to maintain some form of connection to the networks of the ruling party at least to maintain their influential status in the village. Nevertheless, when a party goes out of power, the village political actor network of that party becomes very inactive and weak, either due to a lack of resources and capacity to address the issues of their communities or because the communities themselves do not seek the assistance of these elites, under the presumption that they are incapable of addressing their issues. As Hettige observed, referring to the 1970 election, "even during the elections even though the parties fight on broader economic, social and political goals, at the electorate level they are translated largely to personal goals" (Hettige 1984: 161). Therefore, it is quite understandable for the village network of national parties such as the UNP and SLFP to become silent and inactive while they are in the opposition.

3 FROM PARTY ORGANIZATION TO PARTY MOBILIZATION   115

As this study shows, what is most disturbing for parties in the opposition with regard to party organization is the difficulty in attracting resources for election campaigns. Especially parties such as the UNP and SLFP, which largely depend on the business community for their electoral financing, instead of on membership fees collected as in cadre-based parties,[23] find it extremely difficult to conduct electoral campaigns that can match the party in government. During the 2010 Parliamentary election and the local council elections held in 2011, the electoral campaign material and strategies of UNP members (who had been in the opposition since 1994, except for two years) showed a marked difference to those of UPFA coalition members. Fewer posters, substandard printing of posters and smaller crowds at campaign rallies of the UNP were very apparent. A young UNP Urban Council member from the Weligama Urban Council, Chaminda Perera,[24] indicating his frustration said that it is difficult to find even 10 people to paste his posters and accompany him in his house-to-house campaign canvassing. He is sympathetic towards his friends and supporters who are now reluctant to participate in his campaign. According to him, if his friends and supporters get to know that he is supporting them, since he is an opposition member, they might not be able to approach the ruling politicians and village elites to get assistance in the future. Chaminda Perera is from a *Karawa* family that represented the community living along the coastal belt of Weligama for decades. However, now the ruling UPFA has also appointed one of his relatives as their village party agent for the same community. Therefore, Chaminda continued to lose his voter base, which was primarily based on family and caste. In the dearth of resources, many opposition village political actors and second-tier politicians approach local and national non-governmental organizations to initiate collaborative work in their respective villages in order to maintain their status as an 'influential one'.[25] However, the dynamics of the party organization change dramatically when the party manages to form a government at the centre. Even if the electorate organizers lose their electorates, the local party organization can behave as if they were in power as long as they hold power at the centre. Dharmasiri Senanayake, a popular SLFP organizer from Dedigama, could not win the seat from 1965 to 1994. However, the SLFP's village political actor in the electorate considered that they were in power whenever the SLFP formed a government.[26] This illustrates how members of the party organizer's village elite networks and the supporters of a party acted as if they were in power and embraced new duties and authority in the electorates. The party in government takes control of the administration of all departments and corporations that come under the purview of various ministries. Appointment to positions in the administration and positions ranging from security guard to senior-level manager also fall under the influence of ruling politicians. Since this has been the primary source of employment for rural youth in the form of government jobs, those connected to the ruling party assume great importance within the community. Every electoral victory is followed by massive recruitment campaigns.[27] The central political authority distributes a quota of jobs amongst its electoral organizers. These are further distributed amongst village political actors who hold positions in the party branches of the village.[28] In addition, while Dharmasiri Senanayake was the chairman of the Tourist Board under Prime Minister Sirimavo Bandaranaike (even after losing the seat), Siriwardane succeeded in distributing many individual benefits such as jobs, promotions and land to his community.[29] Siriwardane (as with other UNP and SLFP rank and file) claimed that even when government officers and bureaucracy were opposed to it, he managed to allocate state land to his community using his political power. Most electorate organizers of the ruling party conduct weekly meetings called 'public day'. Here they meet their constituency and address their issues. Usually people visit the party office of the ruling party organizer with their respective village elites. These public days function in a very formal office environment. There are paid professional staffs to serve the visitors with a registry to mark attendance. Temporary security IDs are issued to the visitors. There are different desks to assist visitors on the basis of their needs. The staffs in these party offices and the members of the village political actor network often have a more decisive role than government officials in the area. Hence, people find these places to be more efficient in obtaining redress to their problems.

In addition, most of the village-level state positions are also gradually filled by the member of the ruling party. Positions such as the *Grama Sevaka*, Agricultural Officer and Welfare Officer are filled by individuals who are attached to ruling party members in the electorate. The party organizer's village elite networks bring all these positions and in some places even senior government servants in the electorate, such as officers in the local government administration and the police, under their control to maintain effective party mechanisms in the electorate. In other words, when a party is in power, its organizing network not only comprises its own cadres and village elites, but also absorbs a good number of government officers into its organizing web in the electorate. National and local leadership of the party utilizes these powerful networks of village political actors to suppress grassroots leaders, party activists and those who openly support opposition parties. Therefore, electoral campaigns of ruling party members are always rich in campaign material such as banners, flags and posters, and they hardly have to worry about human resources for campaign activities. People either come in numbers expecting patronage in return, or they come due to the fear that if they avoid participating they would lose their welfare rations and other government benefits. This is very apparent in the village elections meetings that I observed. In a typical meeting of the ruling party, activists perform their duties as energetic and proud cadres. The audience sits in the middle of the meeting place or close to the stage where candidates and other officials are seated and thereby expect to get noticed. This is markedly different from the campaign rallies of the same party when it is in the opposition. When the party is in the opposition, it is extremely difficult to bring people to its campaign rallies, and even most of those who attend do not make an effort to indicate their presence, unlike at ruling party rallies. Often, the ruling party enjoys free services of the Municipal Council or local government. They benefit from the free labour of government servants, and free advertisements through state-owned institutions. Most of the village-level state officials often participate in active election campaigns. Even in the case of violation of electoral law, the police has often been accused of turning a blind eye to offenders from the ruling party while punishing similar offenders from the opposition. The following newspaper report, publishing figures on the 2010 Presidential and Parliamentary elections (January and April, respectively), provides a glimpse of the extent of abuse of state resources by the ruling political parties for electoral benefit.

> Dues amounting to millions of rupees are yet to be recovered by Sri Lanka Rupavahini Corporation (SLRC) from airtime for election campaigns, and once again the government is the main culprit behind the abuse of state resources. The dues to the SLRC from airtime for election campaigns stand at a staggering Rs. 42,640,586 (approximately Rs. 42 million) as at July 27, 2010. The airtime had been allocated to parties affiliated to the governing UPFA. (*The Sunday Leader*, 13 March 2011)[30]

The party/ies in power enjoys access to economic resources of the state through the exercise of control over the state apparatus and political patronage (Moore 1994). The party in power takes control of electorate-level state institutions and state officials in organizing its network. In spite of the vehemence of their rhetoric while in the opposition, both the UNP and SLFP pay less attention to broader policies and ideologies after being elected to office. Once in office, as the ruling party, the main attraction is the ability and capacity to distribute patronage benefits in the electorates. Access to larger resources of state capital allows political party(ies) in the government to manage and maintain extensive elite networks. However, when the party loses power and is reduced to an opposition party, it experiences major financial crises and challenges in managing the village network of political actors. Referring to the 1970–1977 period Hettige describes this phenomenon succinctly: "[E]ven in late 1976, at a time when many supporters of the SLFP had already become disillusioned with the party and its local leaders, the UNP leaders [in Nilthanna where he did his field research] remained highly inactive and supporters were dispersed and disorganized" (Hettige 1984: 160). Especially after the PR system began to function effectively, maintenance of the party organization has become even more difficult as prospects for regime change are very slim. Therefore, under the PR system, parties in the opposition experience a breakdown of their elite network at the electorate level, as many political actors join ruling party organizations for their own survival. This repeats itself in national-level politics also, and when either the UNP or SLFP become an opposition party, it experiences a series of internal conflicts and dissent that often results in opposition members crossing over to the ruling party. When in power, the two parties manage to consolidate their authority over their Members of Parliament, and even if there are rifts they hardly disturb the stability of the party.

In this context, party organizational dynamics at the local level, especially of national parties such as the UNP and SLFP, have transformed the party organization into different shapes in response to the changes in the electoral system. In the meantime, quite independent of the transformation, those party organizations have oscillated between an active and powerful organizing structure, and an inactive and weak one, depending on whether the party is in power or not.

CONCLUSION

The paradox about how, in spite of the feeble organizational structure of the party, both the SLFP and UNP have continued to receive the highest number votes amongst Sinhalese constituencies merits attention. Any analysis of this phenomenon needs to take into account the key role played by the electorate organizer to mobilize the party at the electorate level. These organizers reach out to actors within certain social groups and connect them to the party's network at the electorate level by facilitating access to state patronage. Furthermore, the legitimacy of the local political actor is dependent to a large extent on the symbolic capital that is and can be earned through facilitating voters within their groups to access these individual benefits. Through this a significant argument that has emerged is that the party organizer's main focus is to organize the local political actors rather than the voters in the electorate.

The key role played by local political actors in the everyday life and political activities of voters within these electorates is also important. Through patronage, brokerage and particularization these actors have emerged as important nodal points in the everyday life and political decisions of the local community. It is due to this role within the community that these actors also become attractive to parties as well as party organizers. This also works to strengthen the hand of both the organizer and the political actor. Therefore, local political actors are the key nodal points that mediate the relationship between state and society.

Additionally, the party mobilization strategy changes depending on whether a party is in power or not. When a party is in power, the political actor network tends to expand and become complex, and the expectations of individual benefits from this network also increases amongst the community. However, when the party is out of power, this network of political actors tends to shrink and the expectations of these actors from amongst the community also change. Therefore, the local political actor networks of the SLFP and UNP continue to survive irrespective of whether the party enjoys the benefits of incumbency.

Furthermore, the introduction of the PR electoral system has increased the complexity and fragility of the party mobilizing strategies of the UNP and SLFP. The relationship between the party organizer and the local political actor networks that existed under FPTP and have been characterized as being 'one-to-many' has changed to a 'many-to-many' relationship after the introduction of the PR and the preferential voting system. This has increased the options available to electorate organizers, local political actors and most importantly voters. Therefore, the introduction of PR has in fact intensified intraparty competition and conflict. The introduction of PR and the attendant importance of the electoral district has also benefitted these two parties, since it has opened up opportunities for them to mobilize numerically small social groups within the district. Therefore, that the intended benefits of the PR system have accrued to the UNP and SLFP, rather than to smaller parties within electorates.

Notes

1. Interview with Mr. Wijethilake, the coordinating secretary to former minister and Kelaniya UNP organizer Cyril Mathew.
2. R. Jayaweera (2010), "Better Targeting of Transfers: Samurdhi Programme," IPS, http://ipslk.blogspot. com/2010/07/better-targeting-of-transfers-samurdhi.html.
3. Interview with Kamal Gamanayake, Wathdeniya, Dedigama, 11 August 2010.
4. Interviews with local political actors such as Saman Gamage of Weligama, Keerthi Gunapala of Dedigama and Wijethilake of Kelaniya confirm that their discussions mainly focus on individual benefits distribution and solving the problems of their party supporters. They say that they hardly discuss the policies of the party or voice their concerns about national politics.
5. Newton Gunasinghe's (1990) work can be considered as an example of treating caste as an objective category, while the work of Gunasekara (1994) and Dewasiri (2008) are examples of caste viewed not only as an objective category but a subjective category as well.
6. My interviews with numerous politicians at various levels revealed that the term *sanskruthika saadaka* in their parlance was an indirect reference to 'caste' in their public meetings and speeches. However, in private, within the confines of their own caste groups and ilk, these politicians often do not hesitate to refer to other caste groups by name, and that too in their raw derogatory usage.
7. The number of informants interviewed from Kandy and Nawalapitiya bore witness to this incident that occurred between two ruling-party politicians in Kandy on the eve of the fiercely contested 2010

parliamentary election. This incident is reported in the unpublished Master's thesis of Prasanna Zoysa.

8. Interview with Kularathne, in Waddeniya, Dedigama, 12 August 2010.

9. Interview with Jayaraj Chandrasekara, the grandson of *mudaliyar* Samarakoon of Kelaniya, 23 June 2012.

10. Interview with Henry Daluwatta, 20 June 2009. Daluwatta had been a strongman in the inner circle of both Montague Jayewickrema and Panini Illangakoon.

11. Interview with Wijethilake, December 2009. Wijethilake was the coordinating secretary of Kelaniya UNP organizer Cyril Mathew, and his grandfather served in J. R. Jayewardene's election campaigns.

12. My discussion with former UNP and SLFP village organizers in Dedigama, Weligama and Kelaniya suggests that the distribution of individual benefits amongst supporters was much simpler under the FPTP electoral system than the PR system.

13. In terms of Sect. 99 (6) (a) of the Constitution.

14. Interview with U.S. Perera, former Kelaniya electorate organizer, 11 February 2011.

15. Interview with Hemal Gunasekara, 15 December 2010. Gunasekara is the Kamburupitiya electorate organizer for the SLFP. However, he lives and is politically active in Weligama. His views resonated in interviews that I had with Champika Premadasa, the Dedigama UNP electorate organizer, and U.S. Perera, the former UNP electorate organizer in Kelaniya.

16. Interview with parliamentarian Champika Premadasa, 12 August 2010.

17. Interview with SLFP parliamentarian, Hemal Gunasekara, 15 December 2010.

18. Interview with Saman Gamage, Kananke, Weligama, 10 December 2010.

19. Interview with Lenegala Gune, 10 January 2010.

20. Interviews with Saman Gamage, Chaminda Perera, Ruwan Karunaratne (Weligama), Keerthi Gunapala, Kamal Gamanayake, Sunimal Kumarage (Dedigama), Wijethilake, Jayaraj Chandrasekara, Kelum Manage (Kelaniya) and many others during my field work confirmed this.

21. Interview with my field interlocutors and party organizers in the three electorates confirmed this point.
22. While I was interviewing an SLFP village political actor, Rathnayake in Weligama, on the eve of the 2010 general election, Subasinghe, a former UNP village political actor, visited Rathnayake to exchange his family vote in return for a job for his daughter. Subasinghe wanted Rathnayake to communicate this to SLFP district leader Mahinda Yapa Abeywardana.
23. Cadre parties, as Duverger observes, maintain better organization and stricter registries and indexes. Cadre parties are essentially based on the subscription paid by members (Duverger 1954:163).
24. I had many interviews with Chaminda Perera, and he provided much assistance by introducing me to the UNP elite network. I spoke to him several weeks before the local council election held in March 2011, when he expressed his frustration about the election campaign.
25. For example, Kamal Gamanayake, Rathna Gunapala and G.M. Tikiribanda, the UNP village organizers in the Wathdeniya ward in Dedigama, wanted my assistance to link with NGOs to finds funds to initiate local programmes. During my field work, many politicians and village elites approached me seeking assistance to initiate programmes, as there are hardly any avenues to maintain their patronage network while in the opposition. This is not only limited to local-level elites but is popularly practiced even amongst national-level politicians.
26. Interview with Premaratne, Thulhiriya, 5 January 2010.
27. Perhaps the UNP's victory under Ranil Wickremasinghe in 2001 was an exception. However, it should be noted that even though the UNP managed to form the government it had to share the executive with UPFA President Chandrika Kumaratunga.
28. The individuals I interviewed as rank and file of the UNP and SLFP, such as U.S. Perera of Kelaniya, Premrathne of Weligama, Berty Gunapala and Siriwardane, had served as chairmen of the cooperative shops in their respective areas when their party was in power.
29. Interview with Siriwardane.
30. Mandana Ismail Abeywickrema, The Sunday Leader, 6 December 2012, http://www.thesundayleader.lk/2011/03/13/dues-to-slrc-amount-to-rs-42-million/.

BIBLIOGRAPHY

Bastian, Sunil. 2007. *Politics of Foreign Aid in Sri Lanka, Promoting Markets and Supporting Peace.* Colombo: International Centre for Ethnic Studies.

———. 2010. Politics and Power in the Market Economy. In *Power and Politics: In the Shadow of Sri Lanka's Armed Conflict*, ed. Camilla Orjuela, 101–125. Sida Studies No. 25. Sida.

Berenschot, W.J. 2009. Riot Politics: Communal Violence and State-Society Mediation in Gujarat, India. Unpublished PhD thesis, University of Amsterdam.

Central Bank of Sri Lanka. 2010. *Annual Report 2010.* Colombo: Central Bank.

Dewasiri, Nirmal Ranjth. 2008. *The Adaptable Peasant: Agrarian Society in Western Sri Lanka Under Dutch Rule, 1740–1800.* Leiden and Boston: IDC Publishers.

de Zoysa, K.P. 2013, Caste Matters: Democracy, Caste and Politics in Sri Lanka After the Promulgation of the 1978 Constitution: A Case Study of Sinhala Society. Unpublished MA thesis, University of Colombo.

Downs, Anthony. 1957. An Economic Theory of Political Action in a Democracy. *The Journal of Political Economy* 65 (2) (April): 135–150.

Dumont, L. 1999. *Homo Hierarchicus.* New Delhi: Oxford University Press.

Fuller, C.J., and J. Harris. 2001. For an Anthropology of the Modern Indian State. In *The Everyday State & Society in Modern India*, ed. C.J. Fuller and V. Benei. London: Hurst & Co.

Gunasekara, T. 1992. Democracy, Party Competition and Leadership: The Changing Power Structure in a Sinhalese Community. In *Agrarian Change in Sri Lanka*, ed. James Brow and Joe Weeramunda, 229–260. New Delhi, Newbury Park and London: Sage.

———. 1994, *Hierarchy and Egalitarianism: Caste, Class and Power in Sinhalese Pleasant Society.* London: Athlone Press.

Gunasinghe, N. 1990. *Changing Socio-Economic Relations in the Kandyan Cuntryside.* Colombo: Social Scientists' Association.

Hettige, S. 1984. *Wealth, Power and Prestige: Emerging Patterns of Social Inequality in a Peasant Context.* Colombo: Ministry of Higher Education.

Jayanntha, D. 1992. *Electoral Allegiance in Sri Lanka.* Cambridge: Cambridge University Press.

Jayasuriya, L. 2000. *Welfarism and Politics in Sri Lanka.* Perth: School of Social Work and Social Policy, University of Western Australia.

Jiggins, J. 1979. *Caste and the Family in the Politics of the Sinhalese 1947 to 1976.* London: Cambridge University Press.

Jupp, J. 1978. *Sri Lanka: Third World Democracy.* London: Cass.

Kitschelt, Herbert, and I. Steven Wilkinson, eds. 1997. *Patrons Clients and Policies.* Patterns of Democratic Accountability and Political Competitio. Cambridge: Cambridge University Press.

———. 2007. Citizen-Politician Linkage: An Introduction. In *Patrons Clients and Policies, Patterns of Democratic Accountability and Political Competition*, ed. Herbert Kitschelt and I. Steven Wilkinson. Cambridge: Cambridge University Press.

Migdal, J.S. 2001. *State in Society: Studying How States and Societies Transform and Constitute One Another*. Cambridge: Cambridge University Press.

Moore, M. 1994. Guided Democracy in Sri Lanka: The Electoral Dimension. *The Journal of Commonwealth & Comparative Politics* 32 (1): 1–30.

Sartori, Giovanni. 2000. The Party Effects of Electoral Systems. In *Political Parties and Democracy*, ed. Larry Diamond and Richard Gunther. Maryland: Johns Hopkins University Press.

Spencer, Jonathan. 1990. *A Sinhala Village in a Time of Trouble, Politics and Change in Rural Sri Lanka*. Delhi: Oxford University Press.

Uyangoda, Jayadeva. 2010. Politics of Political Reform—A Key Theme in the Contemporary Conflict. In *Power and Politics: In the Shadow of Sri Lanka's Armed Conflict*, ed. Camilla Orjuela, 29–78. Sida Studies No. 25. Sida.

———. 2012. The State in Post-Colonial Sri Lanka: Trajectories of Change. In *The Political Economy of Environment and Development in a Globalized World: Exploring Frontiers*, ed. D.J. Kjosavik and Paul Vedeld, 345–373. Colombo: Social Scientists' Association.

Welikala, Asanga. 2008. Representative Democracy, Proportional Representation and Plural Society in Sri Lanka. In *The Electoral Reform Debate in Sri Lanka*, ed. Edirisinha and Welikala, 11–15. Colombo: Centre for Policy Alternatives.

Wilson, A.J. 1975. *Electoral Politics in an Emergent State: The Ceylon General Election of May 1970*. London: Cambridge University Press.

———. 1984. *The Gaullist System in Asia, The Constitution of Sri Lanka, 1978*. Hong Kong: The Macmillan Press Ltd.

CHAPTER 4

Examining the Logic and Practice of Voting

Introduction

Representative democracy requires citizens to elect their representatives to the legislature, for a limited period. It is thus a system of government that allows citizens to govern themselves through elected representatives. The secret ballot cast at a free and fair election should theoretically ensure the autonomy of the citizen, since it allows citizens to choose their representatives according to their own free will. Therefore, in a democracy, as the *responsible government model* assumes, political parties and politicians appear before the citizens every five years (number of years varies from country to country) to seek re-election on the basis of their performance.[1] The citizens are presumed to elect their representatives after an appraisal of their earlier performance. However, the practice of democracy is far from perfect. It continues to take different shapes and forms as it traverses across time and space and frontiers across the globe. Hence, the logic of electoral choice varies from one democracy to another. It also differs from one competitive party system to another.

This section aims to critically explore the logic and practice of electoral decisions of Sri Lankan voters in relation to the UNP and SLFP. This chapter is organized as follows. It begins by examining the nature of state-society relations as practiced in Sri Lanka, which is crucial to unravel the nature of democracy in practice. It then examines the different dynamics

© The Author(s), under exclusive license to Springer Nature Singapore Pte Ltd. 2022
P. Peiris, *Catch-All Parties and Party-Voter Nexus in Sri Lanka*, Politics of South Asia, https://doi.org/10.1007/978-981-16-4153-4_4

125

of voting that illustrate the nature of the logic of voting of those who lent electoral support to the UNP and SLFP. In the process of examining the nature of the logic of voting, this chapter emphasizes: (i) the importance of distinguishing the rationale of a citizen from the rationale of a voter to understand electoral choice of an individual, (ii) the importance of recognizing the weak autonomy of the Sri Lankan voter when making his/her electoral choice, (iii) the influence of the family in the electoral choice of an individual and (iv) the role of the individual's interests (material and identity) in determining electoral choice. Then I offer a discussion on the level of dependency of citizens on political mediators, and how this shapes and forms the electoral choice of an individual. Finally, the section discusses how rational public cynicism about politicians and political parties are forced into irrationality within certain logics and practices of voting.

TRAJECTORY OF THE STATE-SOCIETY RELATIONSHIP

Since independence, reform of the Sri Lankan state has followed a trajectory that defines the character of the state and its relations with the citizen, which in turn has also defined our political vocabulary. As Indian scholars have cautioned, terms as 'civil society', 'political party', 'citizenship' and 'bureaucracy', which originated out of the Western experience of state formation, do little to clarify the actual interaction that takes place between the state and citizens (Chatterjee 2004; Berenschot 2009). Hence, our knowledge would also be incomplete if we are to understand terms such as 'electoral participation' and 'electoral choice of the citizen' in isolation and independently of the specificities of state-society relations in Sri Lanka. Therefore, an effort will be made to discuss the nature of state-society relations in post-independence Sri Lanka, within which democracy had to function and voting decisions were made.

Universal adult franchise was instituted in Sri Lanka in 1931, 17 years before independence. At independence in 1948, the colonial state was transformed to a liberal democracy with political parties, administrative agencies and mass participation in politics (Kearney 1973: 1). As in the case of most post-colonial states, in Sri Lanka too political transformation preceded social transformation (Woodward 1969). On the one hand, as K.M. de Silva observes, "the immediate post-colonial period, 1948–1956, saw the seemingly successful transplanting of Western style democratic institutions and organizations of civil society in Sri Lanka" (de Silva 1998:

21). On the other, the state was heavily burdened with an extensive and complex web of welfare measures that covered health, housing, education and some social security, in addition to provisions of jobs, farm benefits and other resources for making a living (Jayasuriya 2000; Shastri 1983; Warnapala and Woodsworth 1987). As Warnapala and Woodsworth observed:

> There has been a history of universal provision for survival, in the form of a free rice ration and price control on basic goods, but the universal program was discontinued in favour of needs-tested program of food stamps, and other forms of subsistence are at a very low level. (Warnapala and Woodsworth 1987: 13)

However, these heavy welfare programmes (re)produced conditions of inequality amongst the citizenry, as welfare allocations were often made through discriminatory processes (Warnapala and Woodsworth 1987: 13). Lower-level bureaucrats such as the village headman, later *Grama Niladari*, enjoyed greater discretionary power in the distribution of these benefits. As scholars observe, the key role they played in the delivery of social services and poverty alleviation benefits has contributed to widespread corruption amongst these lower-level officials (Jayasuriya 2000; Uyangoda 2010). In this way, patron-client relations already in practice on the basis of personal wealth in an agrarian society gradually transformed into a patronage system based on state resources. This welfare policy regime that emerged in the 1930s along with the expansion of representative government linked to universal adult franchise has contributed to the patron-client relations that exist now (Uyangoda 2010: 61).

Scholars of post-colonial politics in Sri Lanka have acknowledged the vital role of patron-client relations in Sri Lankan politics (Bastian 2010; Hettige 1984; Jayanntha 1992; Jiggins 1979; Jupp 1978; Moore 1985; Robinson 1975; Spencer 1990; Wilson 1975; Uyangoda 2010). The broadening of social bases of political leadership to intermediary classes and further into two-party competition since 1956, coupled with state reform, have contributed to the expansion of the role of patron-client relations in electoral politics with a markedly higher level of sophistication. Over the years, welfare programmes shifted attention from costly universal benefits such as price controls on staple foods or transport subsidiaries to less costly but more useful political instruments such as food stamps (Warnapala and Woodsworth 1987). Hettige, who observes this phenomenon, states that "the major political parties, which became the central focus of national politics after independence and whose strength became increasingly dependent on the support of the rural electorates, have consciously or unconsciously exploited this state of affairs (dependency on state patronage to fulfil their various needs) for their own advantage" (Hettige 1984: 158). Patron-client relations, while allowing access to welfare benefits, also provided access to unlimited state resources. As discussed previously, these patronage goods and services were distributed through the political network in the electorate or village by maximizing their potential for garnering votes. Political actors at various levels in the process possessed the capacity to control the bureaucracy, and thereby to fragment the authority of the state. This shaped the outcome of government policies according to local political needs, and undermined straightforward application of the law (Berenschot 2009).

The relatively autonomous and politically independent bureaucracy inherited by the country from its colonial government continued to lose its independent character under post-colonial state reforms. As many scholars point out, the bureaucracy is no longer an independent actor within the state, and it is institutionally subservient to the political leadership in power (Weerakoon 1997; Ranugge 2000; Uyangoda 2010). On the one hand, political and public perception of the state bureaucracy is that it is a quite inefficient and lethargic institution (Uyangoda 2010: 50). On the other, especially since the 1970s, the bureaucracy was brought under direct political and regime control (Weerakoon 1997; Uyangoda 2010). Researching on *Riot Politics* in India, Berenschot emphasizes the dialectic between the difficulties that citizens face when trying to deal with state institutions, and the strategies that politicians employ to win elections (Berenschot 2009: 114). He states that:

> State institutions offer valuable services to citizens, but lack the capacity to make these services easily accessible, especially the poor turn to politicians and their supporters to gain access to state services. This dependence generates a political arena in which political success is premised on the capacity to control the distribution of state resources. This reproduces the dependence of both citizen and state institutions on political mediation: the strategies that political actors adopt to win support make it more difficult for state agents and citizen to deal with each other without mediation of political actors (Ibid).

The citizen can technically approach the local council official directly to replace a street light, repair the drainage system or repair the damaged neighbourhood road. But people generally prefer to seek assistance and mediation of local politicians as their efficiency is proven, not only because bureaucrats are subservient to politicians, but they too are often beneficiaries of the patronage networks of the politicians. The lack of transparency in the procedures of state institutions and their rigid and less practical regulations motivate citizens, especially the poor and underprivileged, to seek mediation from political actors. Therefore, we can see these political actors intensely involved in the daily operations of various state institutions.

The ever-widening gap between the needs and aspirations of the majority of the population and the limited opportunities available to them triggered a demand for particularization. This resulted in citizens seeking intervention by political actors to manipulate laws and regulations for their own benefit. Dilesh Jayanntha (1992) gives an extensive account of how these political actors manipulate regulations and standard procedures for the benefit of supporters. Gunasinghe says that since the state is the major job giver in Sri Lanka and MPs often exercise influence in the selection of applicants, getting a job in the modern state sector is closely tied with local politics (Gunasinghe 1990: 141). Ruwan Karunaratne, then a young UNP village leader in Weligama, says that many nonqualified candidates were amongst those given teaching appointments following the 1977 electoral victory.[2] Later, amid widespread criticism, the then UNP government issued a circular to retain those nonqualified teachers as long as they agreed to obtain the minimum qualification of completing the ordinary level exam the following year.

The story of Siriwardane mentioned earlier provides an example of how political actors assist poor villagers to encroach crown land and later to acquire formal deeds to legitimize these illegal acquisitions. Similarly, people seek the intervention of political actors for illegal sand mining in rivers, maintaining illegal quarries and obtaining licenses for illegal contracts. No effective legal actions can be taken against these groups as long as political leaders in power provide them the necessary political cover.

As Berenschot describes, on the one hand, the development of the state's scope propelled citizens to turn to the state to improve the quality of their lives, while on the other hand, the limited strength of the state made it difficult for citizens to deal independently with the state (Beren-schot 2009: 115). Hence, the mediation of political actors has become a necessity in the everyday life of the average citizen. Describing this reality succinctly, Uyangoda says that "the institutionalization of patron-client relations has eventually created a vision amongst the citizens that the state is the supreme agency of welfare and benevolence and patron-client relations constituted something like a 'social contract' between the ruling elites and the citizens of the subordinate classes" (Uyangoda 2010: 61).

As emphasized previously, the majority of citizens in a village are subject to the direct or indirect influence of these political actors or their agents, as they have to depend on them in their everyday life. As in a mediated democracy, there are only a small number of voters who are autonomous.[3] This leaves the majority of voters dependent on mediation through patronage benefits. As Berenschot observes, in the context of mediated democracy, the poor village inhabitant often lacks social capital. This is of immense value to get a government institution to act favourably (Berenschot 2009: 114). The voting decision of the majority of voters in this context is subject to the influence of the actors of the political networks in the electorate.

Explaining the 'Logic of Voting'

As already noted, scholars have ventured into the discussion of party and electoral allegiance or voting on the basis of two opposing premises: The social cleavage model of Lipset and Rokkan (1967) and Dawn's (1957) rational choice theory. The first premise assumes the primacy of social structure while the latter assumes primacy of agency of the voter. However, a social practice such as voting can neither be under-stood as an exclusive product of social structures and mechanisms that result from external causes, nor as a matter of individual consciousness and the outcome of the intentions and rationality of the actors who aim to maximize profit.

Bourdieu's notion of habitus provides a way out of the structure-agency duality, and it helps us to understand social action as an outcome of both social structures and human agency.[4] Habitus is a cognitive property of social agency that regulates behaviour without being subject to rules (Maton 2008). Habitus is neither a result of free will, nor deter-mined by structures, but created by a kind of interplay between the two over time; dispositions that are both shaped by past events and structures, and that shape current practices and structures and also, importantly, that condition our very perceptions of these (Bourdieu 1984: 170). In this sense, habitus is created and reproduced unconsciously, "without any deliberate pursuit of coherence … without any conscious concentration" (Bourdieu 1984: 170). Habitus constitutes dispositions for practice as well as schemes for perceptions, classifications and evaluations (Bourdieu 1998). Habitus is individual, in the sense that it is embodied and internal to the person, and acquired through socialization and experiences. Therefore, it forms a tacit knowledge and a practical sense that generates an actor's practices (Bourdieu 1990). Habitus is also collective and shared, as it is a socially constituted system where individuals who are relatively close in social space tend to have similar dispositions for action and perceptions and thus observe each other and behave much in the same way (Bourdieu 1977: 82). Habitus is relatively durable, as it forms objective structures and consensuses that merge with subjective and internalized cognitive structures of individuals (Bourdieu 1977: 78). However, although this embodied, subconscious and unstated nature of habitus make it stable, it is also exposed to change; as an open system and the product of history, future experiences will shape it (Bourdieu 1977: 82). Habitus is not only a product of social conditions and practices, but is also the producer of strategies and practices in relation to conditions of the social world. Therefore, habitus makes that world feels natural and self-evident to actors (Bourdieu and Wacquant 1992). Habitus constitutes a common sense that is not reflected upon, but which makes certain actions and ways of thinking more probable and natural. Bourdieu uses the term doxa to refer to this established common sense (Bourdieu 1977: 167). It is implicit and unformulated and reflects how people most of the time take themselves, their perceptions and the social world they relate to for granted (Jenkins 2002). Hence, the actor adheres to certain practices without explicitly questioning them.

Bourdieu's concept of habitus provides us a powerful theoretical framework to analyse and comprehend the practice of voting. By avoiding the complete rejection of structure-based theories as well as agency-oriented approaches, habitus helps us to understand the logic of voting practices of Sri Lankan voters. The numerous interviews and observations conducted during this work can be used to inquire into the voting practices of those who vote for the UNP and SLFP. These field observations provide strong evidence that the voting decision is influenced by both the cognitive structures of the voter as well as the external structures of the social world within which the voting action occurs. Not only the conditions of the social world of the voter, but also the voter's common sense, or doxa, influence the practice of voting.

In addition to field observations and analysing documents, this study also employed phenomenological research methods to understand the rationales of voting by different social strata in the electorate.[5] As Bourdieu explained, those decisions may neither be completely rational nor completely irrational (Ritzer 1996: 541). Voters make their choice according to their own rationale. This chapter attempts to expose certain myths that exist in our perception of voting practices and thereby elaborates the actual nature of the 'social contract' that exists in Sri Lankan society. The term 'voters' in this research refers to those who have cast their votes either for the UNP or SLFP or those who are willing to consider one of these parties when casting their votes in future. While the term 'voter' captures the characteristics of an overwhelming majority of Sri Lankan voters, it may not fully reflect the characteristics of voter bases of small leftist, religious and ethnic parties.

Importance of Studying the 'Voter' Instead of the 'Citizen'

Recognition of the nuanced difference between a 'voter' and a 'citizen' allows us to understand the logic of voting decisions. In a democracy, all citizens eligible to vote at an election are considered voters. However, the application of different perspectives allows us to draw distinctions between the citizen and the voter. A citizen, eligible to participate in voting, becomes a voter only in the midst of the election campaign, not only by being eligible or qualified but also by reaching a special psychological capture or fascination. This is somewhat similar to a quiet blue- or white-collar worker becoming vocal and animated after stopping at a bar for a drink on his way home after a hard day's work. The logic of the action of this worker becomes somewhat different from his usual practice when he stops for a drink. The logic of the voting decision or the rationale behind the electoral choice of the voter could also be different during the period of elections and when elections are not due. Outside of election periods, people are less partisan, and even if they are those

biases are confined to certain spheres. Jonathan Spencer (1990) highlights this phenomenon in Thanna, a village in the Ratnapura District.
He describes how an otherwise peaceful village became violent once an
election was announced. Making similar observations in Nilthanne in
Anuradhapura District, Hettige states that "at the peak of the heated election campaign, the village was polarized in two broad fronts" (Hettige
1984: 152). People refer to this psychological state as *chanda unusuma*
(election heat).

Election campaign propaganda at the national and local levels is
intended to induce and stimulate a particular psychological environment within which voters are expected to make their electoral decision.
Activities such as canvassing, holding meetings, debates, decorations and
even the violence that party activists are responsible for in the electorate
stimulate a particular mood amongst voters. Once voters get into this
mood, their innermost feelings of affection or animosity for certain identities such as religion, caste, class and ideology are aroused. If I may
borrow the term of Lipset and Rokkan (1967), at the peak of election campaigns, parties are instrumental in crystallizing social cleavages
in society. Karunanayaka, a village political actor and former local council
member of the SLFP, explains this phenomenon by claiming that political parties through their propaganda arouse the inner feelings of the
voter (*bawaya avisseema*).[6] Under this momentary but highly charged
condition, parties and politicians succeed in arousing the constituency and
mobilizing their support. Mr. Dassanayake, a retired government servant
from Weligama, elaborates this phenomenon with his own experience.[7]

I am an SLFP supporter. However, at the last election, I decided to stay
away from politics as I did not think that what we have today is the
real SLFP politics. Before the last election [2010 parliamentary election] I
decided not to work for the party or get involved in any party activities. I
have even told people at home that if the party people came looking for
me to send them off by saying that I was not at home. During the first
few day of the party propaganda campaign I stayed inside the house and
listened to news and political discussions. When party supporters began
to canvass and decorate the neighbourhood, I could not resist my urge
and I started watching them from my window. After a few days, instead
of watching them from my window, I walked up to the gate and talked
to them. On the day before the election, I found myself inside the party
office of my area.

As Dassanayake describes it, the atmosphere and the election propaganda serve as a stimulus to arouse interest in politics. Under such conditions, not only the politically charged voters, but even those who are typically indifferent to politics, are inadvertently made partisan. Passive citizens become active when they are engulfed in the 'voter trance'. This suggests that the rationale and logic of a person as a voter may differ from his/her rationale as a citizen. Sometimes a person may find his/her decision as a voter to be not as rational as it was assumed when seen in retrospect, out of the context of the election period. Therefore, patterns of voting need to be understood in the context of the voter's point of view, and not necessarily as a rational choice of a citizen.

Voting is Far from Being an Individual Affair

In a representative democracy, it is assumed that the principle of 'one man one vote' means that every citizen of voting age has an equal opportunity to contribute to electing his or her own government at the election. However, often this is not so. In societies such as Sri Lanka where inequalities as well as social and political marginalization are still deep-rooted, there is no guarantee that every citizen will have an equal impact in electing their representatives. Even though the secret ballot ensures the procedural freedom of a voter's independent choice, there are many loopholes in practice in societies such as ours that hinder the autonomy of the voter. In fact, Kanchan Chandra illustrates several examples to argue that in patronage democracy, the 'secret ballot' may not be so secret (Chandra 2004: 52). This process of challenging the individual autonomy of the voting decision starts from the household itself. Often women exercise less autonomy as compared to men in terms of electoral choice. This was evident in the qualitative interviews as well as in the available survey data of electoral behaviour. However, this analysis exclusively focuses on and is limited to voter behaviour in Sinhalese society in relation to the two main political parties.

A survey that was conducted in 2011 (a year after the 2010 Parliamentary election) provides a macro view of the voting patterns of Sinhalese households.[8] The survey reveals an interesting voter behaviour pattern; the voting choices of an overwhelming majority of family members are identical. However, by no means is it claimed that this pattern is unique to the Sinhalese community. In order to find out how a husband and wife make their electoral choice, the respondents were asked how their

Table 4.1 How did your parents vote in the elections? Which of the following statements reflects their voting practice?

How did your parents vote in the elections?	Percentage
They both always voted for the same party	56.0
Most of the time they both voted for the same party	13.5
They both voted for a party of their own choice	17.3
I do not know	12.9
Base	890

Source Social Scientists' Association (2012)

parents voted at elections. Since it was a structured questionnaire, the answer categories were formulated to examine whether they voted for the same party or different parties. According to the survey results, over two-thirds of the Sinhalese voters said that their parents always or at least most of the time voted for the same party at elections (Table 4.1).

The data indicate that 12.9% claimed that they did not know how their parents voted. It is better to ask about their parent's voting pattern to avoid the risk of normative answers—indicative of the voting practices between husband and wife—than to question the respondents' own voting habits. The revelation that both husband and wife voted for the same party is important but not adequate to make sense of the voting habits of husband and wife. It is necessary to ascertain who influences the voting decision if they vote for the same party. Qualitative interviews offer help to address this important question as to who is most influential in a household when reaching the voting decision.

A village-level leader (an office bearer of the village *Govi Samithiya*) and a farmer, Weerasekara, has impressive knowledge of not only local politics, but also of national politics. He claims to have never forced his children or wife on their voting decisions.[9] However, he said that he discusses politics with his children and wife during the time of elections. When asked whether his children and wife also voted for the same party that he had voted for in past elections, he responded that he was aware that usually the family also voted for the party he voted for. He justified it by claiming that they (children and wife) followed him, as he was more politically knowledgeable and, more importantly, out of respect for him as the father. M.A. Victor of Kananke, Weligama, is a poor labourer of the *berawa* caste.[10] He is in his late 60s and still struggles for a living. His married son also works with him as a painter and lives in a separate part of the same house. Victor claimed that he is ignorant about politics and does not have any access to what was happening outside, other than what he sees on his small television, where he can only watch the government channels. Describing how his family made the voting decision at the last Parliamentary election (2010), he denied using any influence over the voting decision of his wife or son. Nevertheless, he claimed that he discussed the election with his wife before voting, and both voted for the same party. However, he was not sure how his son voted. He believed that the son too had voted for the same party. Not only did Victor think that his wife was ignorant about politics, but also said that she also admits it openly and says that she would allow him to tell her which party she should vote for. To Victor, voting together for the same party is a reflection of the unity or the bond within the family.

Dhanushka is a young office executive from Kelaniya, who said that he voted for the incumbent President at the Presidential election.[11] Dhanushka neither asked his father nor was he told. It was common sense for Dhanushka to vote for the candidate put forward by the SLFP-led coalition at the Presidential election of 2010, because his father was a staunch SLFP supporter. However, Dhanushka had later found that his father and mother had made a last-minute decision to vote for the opposition common candidate, Sarath Fonseka. These few selected stories illustrate how the husband or father makes the electoral decision not only for himself but also for the wife and sometimes for other family members. However, this influence is subtle and often resides in the 'universe of undiscussed', as Bourdieu explains in his concept of doxa[12] (Bourdieu 1977: 164). People often practice these habits without question. The interview with young Nalika provides some interesting insights into what women (wives) have to say on this subtle influence of men in their electoral choice.[13]

Nalika is a young mother of three children living in her parents' residence. Her father and mother claimed that they were supporters of the SLFP. They were both engaged in manual labour for their livelihood. Her husband, Priyantha, in his late 20s, is from the Galle District and lives with Nalika and her parents in Kananke, Weligama. Priyantha is currently unemployed and is struggling to find a job to support his family and his in-laws. In fact, his father-in-law had unsuccessfully approached a number of ruling SLFP MPs to find a job for his son-in-law. When asked which party she voted for at the last general election, Nalika said that she voted for the UNP despite her parents' loyalties to the SLFP. She justified her decision and said that her husband was a UNPer and that she, as wife, should also vote for the same party. Interestingly, her husband Priyantha and her parents, who were also present, agreed that the wife should follow the husband's electoral choice.

This framework of electoral attitude is not limited to the poor and uneducated. For example, Kalyani, the librarian of the Weligama municipal library, also expresses similar views on making electoral choices within the family. In fact, she stresses the influence of culture that has permeated the electoral practices of Sinhalese villages. This perhaps is applicable to other ethnic communities as well. Kalyani's spontaneous reaction was that a wife should vote for the same party as the husband, and that it was demonstrative of the virtues of a typical Sinhalese woman. This can be understood in the context of Bourdieu's concept of habitus where actors internalize the externality while externalizing the internality.[14] While there is no established rule as such, it is commonly agreed that in rural society, the husband and wife make the same electoral decision, and that it is 'virtuous' (*honda kanthawak thamange samiyage mathayata thana diyayuthuya*) for the wife to follow the husband.

Edwin Silva and his vice-principal wife represent an economically self-sufficient family in the Weligama town.[15] When asked how they reached the voting decision, Edwin repeatedly stressed the point that they made their decisions independently, while at the same time strongly emphasizing that there was no resentment between him and his wife. However, both of them indicated that despite their claims of making independent voting decisions, they had always voted for the same party. Since it was commonly assumed amongst villagers that the voting decision of an ideal couple should be the same, Edwin had to make an extra effort to emphasize their harmonious relations while practicing independent voting.

Of course, as is revealed in the survey data (Table 6.1), there are families where partners vote for different parties. Nevertheless, when they claim to have voted for the same party, as confirmed in the field interviews, the voting decision of the wife is almost always influenced by the decision of the husband. However, interestingly, in the case of voting, the man influences the woman's decision only as husband or father (or care giver), but not as a brother or a friend. Therefore, this influence of men over women's voting choice could be considered as a product of the 'values and virtues' regime of the Sinhalese family institution and not as a gender-related practice of society at large. Therefore, the concept of 'every voter has one vote' is far from being true even with regard to voting practices within the family, let alone other serious factors in a society such as Sri Lanka.

VOTING AND INTERESTS OF THE CITIZEN

In classical political party literature, it is assumed that political parties provide representation of the interests of citizens in the national legislature (Leiserson 1958: 70; Duverger 1954: xxiv; Woodward 1969: 12). Hence, people choose a party at elections that they presume to represent their interests best in the national legislature. The interests of voters can be categorized into two groups: (i) identity interests and (ii) material interests. This can be explained by the Marxist 'base and superstructure model' of institutional behaviour.[16] While identity interests can be considered as products of the superstructure, material interests can be considered as linked to economic and material interests. Some voters can be highly charged in terms of 'identity interest', while others can be deeply motivated by their 'material interests'. However, at any given moment, an average voter would seek to satisfy both kinds of interests. These identity and material interests are not completely mutually exclusive categories, and they are divided by a thin and fuzzy line. Therefore, certain interests of voters fall in the middle of this identity-material interest axis, where they can be treated as identity as well as material interests. Let's discuss how these interests explain the logic of voting practices of the Sinhalese electorate in terms of the two main parties.

Voting and Identity Interests

Oberschall and Kim define identity as the answer to:

> the basic existential questions, 'Who am I?' and 'With whom do I belong?' The categorization of a 'we' and a 'they' is a fundamental social psychological manifestation of human sociality. 'We' and 'they' are experienced and socially validated with we-feeling, approval seeking, attachment and conformity to group attitudes and norms, and a corresponding tendency to distancing, negative affect, and stereotyping of other groups and social categories, the 'they'. (Oberschall and Kim 1996: 64)

These tendencies towards categorization and stereotyping, in-group favouritism and out-group prejudice can enhance the capacity of inter-actants to act collectively in pursuit of common interests (Macy 1997: 429). In the social cleavage model of Lipset and Rokkan (1967), it is assumed that social groups (voting blocs) are formed on the basis of four basic cleavages: centre-periphery, state-church, owner-worker and land-industry. These cleavages mainly represent numerous interest groups based on social structures such as ethnicity, religion, region, language, caste, class and cultural values. Pradeep Chibber and Mariano Torcal (1997) observe the importance of political cleavages—such as with Pero-nist supporters in Argentina, or leftist supporters in Sri Lanka—in forming identities that in turn are used to mobilize voters into voting blocs. Iden-tity can be considered not only as an objective category but also as a subjective category. Identity can be recognized as objective external cate-gories such as ethnicity, religion and caste where the category exists independently of the preference or feeling of the person. At the same time, identity is also a cognitive and therefore a subjective category where the person believes that he/she belongs to a particular category and acts accordingly.

Unlike the states of Western Europe that Lipset and Rokkan studied to construct their theory, Sri Lanka never experienced a complete 'national revolution' or 'industrial revolution' to either create or trigger similar cleavages in society. However, independence from British colonial rule in 1948 and the state reforms that followed triggered social divisions within society on the basis of ethnicity, religion, region and ideology. The precolonial, feudal caste system, as Gunasinghe argued, has not only survived but also continued to influence post-colonial politics of the country (Gunasinghe 1990: 144).

Since the introduction of the franchise, the role of ethnicity in party allegiance has been clearly visible in Sri Lanka (DeVotta 2007; Jupp 1978; Sahadevan and DeVotta 2006; Wilson 1975; Uyangoda 2010). With the establishment of the All Ceylon Tamil Congress in 1944 under the leadership of G.G. Ponnambalam and later the Federal Party in 1948, a majority of Tamils extended their electoral support to Tamil political parties. In 1981, the Sri Lanka Muslim Congress was formed to repre-sent the interests of the Muslim minority community.[17] Later, in 2004, the Jathika Hela Urumaya (JHU) was formed to represent the inter-ests of the Sinhala Buddhists community (Uyangoda 2010). A number of Left parties, and their inevitable splinter groups due to ideological schisms, have emerged to provide representation to workers and the proletariat. However, an overwhelming majority of voters, especially the Sinhalese, gravitated towards the UNP and SLFP. These two parties strive to portray an inclusive national image and do not attempt, at least openly, to represent any particular interest group exclusively.

It is important to mention that the two parties attract votes from a wider spectrum of identities. Especially in the case of the Sinhalese community, the two parties tend to represent multiple and often conflicting identity interests. For example, the SLFP draws support simultaneously from the left and right, while the UNP attracts both Sinhalese extremist and liberal pluralists. In the three electorates where fieldwork was conducted, the political networks of both the UNP and SLFP are linked mainly with village temples. Politicians of the two parties dare not hurt the interests of the majority Sinhalese community either at the village or national level. Therefore, with such ambiguity and lack of distinction of their positions, it is largely the effectiveness of propaganda that triggers identity-based voting, based on considerations of ethnicity, religion, region and class.

Caste Interests

Caste continues to be one a powerful mode of stratification in Sinhalese villages. Hence, caste has continued to receive the attention of scholars of Sri Lankan politics, as it has always been an important factor in electoral politics (Jiggins 1979; Jayanntha 1992; Gunasekara 1992, 1994; Gunasinghe 1990; Kearney 1973; Spencer 1992; Uyangoda 1998). The intensity of caste differentiation in the community varies from one electorate to another. It depends on characteristics such as the pre-colonial and colonial history of the electorate, the present caste composition and present socio-economic conditions of that electorate. For example, out of the three field locations, caste constitutes a deeper stratification in Dedigama. This electorate is in the centre of a Kandyan district where feudal practices and the dominance of the *goigama* caste have existed for many years. It has remained so even after independence. People in Dedigama appeared to be comparatively more caste conscious than those in either Weligama or Kelaniya. Caste is, as already noted, a taboo subject in Sinhalese society. As became clear in the field study, caste still plays a crucial role in modern day democracy, though not as explicitly as Jiggins (1979) or Gunasinghe (1990) argued. In a similar vein to Jiggins (1979),

Gunasinghe says that "caste has become so important in parliamentary and local authority politics in Sri Lanka that no major party dares to put forward a candidate who is not a member of the numerically dominant caste in the area" (Gunasinghe 1990: 144). The fieldwork suggests that the role of caste in electoral politics still remains strong in substance but exists in a different form.

As Uyangoda states, "political parties, including Left parties, have traditionally tended to select their electoral candidates with caste constituency in mind" (Uyangoda 1998: 26). He further states that there is always the likelihood that members of the numerically strong caste will be considered in the selection of candidates. However, Jayanntha is critical of this oversimplified caste electoral politics relationship and argues that often it is the dominant caste groups that produce the leading 'patrons' of the area (Jayanntha 1992: 4). The field research of this study highlights the complex nature of the caste dynamic within electorates and shows how it functions in electoral mobilization within and outside of the electorate.

Despite its wide presence and importance, caste is a topic that is highly disconcerting and therefore not openly discussed in Dedigama, in comparison with the other two electorates. In some villages in Dedigama, there are two or more funeral societies that represent different caste groups in the village. I witnessed three New Year festivals (*Aluth Avurudu Uthsava*) in three adjoining villages in Wathdeniya, Dedigama, during April 2011. Tikiribanda, one of the field interlocutors, explained that due to conflicts caused by caste rivalry during the previous New Year celebrations, villagers had decided to organize separate functions for each caste group. However, nobody identifies these festivals as festivals of a particular caste group. Instead they are referred to as functions exclusive to a particular village. However, the name of the village is often indicative of the respective caste identity of the group. For example, the festival celebration of the *wahumpura* caste and the *bathgama* caste in that area are referred to as the festivals of the Waddeniya village and the Weniwellakaduwa village, respectively.

The account given by Appuhamy in Weniwellakaduwa, Dedigama, illustrates this point.[18] He belongs to the *bathgama* caste, as do all others in Weniwellakaduwa. Recalling politics in the days of his youth he said that his entire family decided to support the then SLFP candidate, Deshapriya Senanayake, purely because of S.W.R.D. Bandaranaike. Referring to politics in the 1960s, Appuhamy said that his family was very poor and innocent (*api duppath ahinsaka minussu*), as were most villagers in

Weniwellakaduwa. It was S.W.R.D. Bandaranaike who paved the way for these poor communities to achieve some social recognition. It was clear that what he meant by 'poor and innocent' was nothing but the oppressive caste discrimination that prevailed in Kandyan Sinhalese villages at that time.[19] The system kept them entrapped in the innocence of neglect and ignorance. He thinks that it was only after Bandaranaike that these villagers (referring to *bathgama* villagers) got an opportunity to benefit from education and share in the economic progress. Hence, their families continued to extend their loyalty to the SLFP. To cite another example, Kodikara in Weligama is a retired principal from the *Hinna* caste. He said that he got "goose bumps" (*hirigadu pipenawa*) when remembering Bandaranaike. He was explicit about his caste and the oppression suffered by his community at the hands of dominant caste groups during the 1960s. He associated the UNP with the *Goigama* caste and the oppressive forces in the village at the time of his youth. For example, he recalled the tyranny of a local landlord Arty Nilame, who used to cruelly exploit and abuse poor villagers with the power of his wealth and social status.

Jayasinghe Banda represents the other side of the relationship between caste and politics.[20] He is known and is addressed as 'Nilame', the title of a feudal worthy in his ancestral village Waddeniya that adjoins Weniwellakaduwa. His ancestors were the feudal lords in Otharapattuwa of Sathara Korale. Through the passage of time, his family has ceased to command the higher status they enjoyed a few decades ago. He says that his family was one of the strongest UNP loyalists in the village. He recalled that all UNP leaders who visited Waddeniya never failed to visit his residence to have tea or a meal. He thinks that it was his caste and class that the UNP represented in those days and it was their duty to support their party. However, he had promoted Berty Gunapala as the party leader of Waddeniya because he felt that it was necessary to get the support and the votes of the *Wahumpura* community that constituted a majority in the village. During my interviews, UNP supporters of the *Goigama* caste expressed their disappointment with the current organizer of the Dedigama electorate, as he did not have the skills or qualifications to be their electoral organizer. Instead, they had high praise for Kabir Hashim, a Muslim and the electorate organizer of Kegalle. Kabir Hashim is also the district leader of the UNP party organization. As he himself identifies, his main voter base is the Sinhalese in the Kegalle district.[21] Of course, Champika Premadasa is not a charismatic popular politician. His unpopularity, however, amongst the *Goigama* UNP supporters stems mainly from his *Wahumpura* caste origins and not due to any other reason. Some *Goigama* UNP supporters of Dedigama believe that their electorate organizer, Champika Premadasa, is partial towards the *Wahumpura* caste.

These examples at one level confirm the thesis of Jiggins (1979) that caste plays an important role in Sinhalese electoral politics. Nevertheless, as Jayanntha (1992) critiques Jiggins' thesis, we can also find enough evidence where electoral results do not match the caste composition of the electorate. However, one should replace/substitute the caste factor with the patron-client network, as Jayanntha (1992) argues, in explaining electoral allegiance. The fieldwork of this study does not suggest that patronage networks substitute the caste influence in electoral politics. Rather, the caste based political actor network made patronage a more efficient mechanism of collecting votes.

Ideological Interests

'Ideology' is a body of ideas reflecting the social needs and aspirations of an individual, group, class or culture.[22] The importance of ideology in determining the voting decision is recognized, both in the cleavage-based (Lipset and Rokkan 1967) and rational choice-based (Downs 1957; Chandra 2004) political party literature, although not with the same emphasis. Cleavage-based theorists argue ideology as a cleavage that divides voters along party lines (Lipset and Rokkan 1967; Chibber and Torcal 1997). As Chandra puts it, "Downs identifies ideology as the voter's principle shortcut: Ideology helps him/her focus attention on the differences between parties; therefore they can be used as sample of all the differentiating stands" (Chandra 2004: 35). In this context, all political parties like to show that they have unique policies, principles and programmes that address their constituency. However, Kirchheimer assumes that catch-all parties will adopt similar policy positions in the centre of the political spectrum and that they will emphasize similar issues (Kirchheimer 1966: 195).

In the case of the UNP and SLFP, their ideological differences have become rather fuzzy. Scholars commenting on the two parties in the 1970s classified the UNP as a centre-right party and the SLFP as a centre-left party (Jupp 1978; Kearny 1973; Wilson 1975). However, in response to the political context, especially due to the nature of electoral competition, the ideological position of the UNP and SLFP was transformed from their original positions. Commenting on party coalitions and the "bipolarized multiparty system in Sri Lanka", Uyangoda states that "the development of two coalition centres, along with a host of small parties, led to the outcome that required a great deal of ideological and personal adjustment" (Uyangoda 2012: 189). The UNP, a party considered to be a "non-sectarian Centre-Right party whose leadership comprised of the comprador elites that represented landed aristocracy, bureaucracy and big businesses" (Jayasuriya 2000: 97), experienced shifts in its ideology following the 1977 victory. The Sinhala Buddhist nationalist ideology of the state under the United Front coalition, led by the SLFP from 1970 to 1977, continued under the leadership of J.R. Jayewardene. Following the First Republican Constitution, the UNP regime also maintained the clause that grants Buddhism the 'foremost place' and stated that it is the duty of the state to protect and foster the *Buddha Sasana* (Constitution of Sri Lanka, 978, Article 9). Borrowing from Buddhist tradition, J.R. Jayewardene "tried to cloak himself as a 'righteous' (*dharmista*) ruler and promised a 'righteous society' (*dharmista samajaya*) under his leadership" (Richardson 2005: 342). Venugopal noted that the 1977 election manifesto of the UNP claimed that: "The UNP is not only a democratic party: it is also a socialist party ... Our policy is to ... terminate the exploitation of man by man" (Venugopal 2011: 91). As Jayasuriya observed, under the leadership of R. Premadasa, the UNP managed to appeal to the rural peasantry with its populist strategies and programmes such as the Mahaweli scheme and colonization of dry zone farming areas (Jayasuriya 2000: 106). Under the leadership of Chandrika Kumaratunga, the People's Alliance (PA) continued the UNP's free market economic policy, shifting from the SLFP's closed economic policy. The PA regime did not reject the market economy of the UNP, despite being severely critical while in the Opposition, and continued under the banner of "free market economy with a human face". In the 1990s, both the SLFP and UNP moved away from Sinhalese ethnic politics and began to make political appeals across ethnic identities (Uyangoda 2010: 42). The decision to abandon the Sinhalese ethno-nationalist ideology costs both the UNP and SLFP their Sinhala nationalist voter base, strengthening the JVP and the JHU (Uyangoda 2010: 42–43). Confirming the fact that party ideology is very much a product of party leadership, the SLFP shifted its ideological position back to the old Sinhala Buddhist nationalism following the change of leadership to Mahinda Rajapaksa in 2005. Hence, the ideologies of these two parties are far from being clear and stable.

The field interviews of this study indicate that voters had no objective understanding of the ideologies of either party. In addition, as will be discussed later, the UNP and SLFP do not attract voters exclusively from a particular ideological position. Therefore, the relationship between ideology and voting does not fall in line with the arguments adduced in the cleavage model or in rational choice theory. Nevertheless, some field interviews also suggest that ideology is not absent altogether in the voting decisions of those supporting the two parties.

For example, explaining why she cannot vote for the UNP, a lady principal from Weligama town said that the UNP did not represent "our values as Sinhalese" (*ape Sinhalakama UNP ya thula pennum karanawa adui*). Although she did not elaborate what she meant by 'our values', she claimed that the SLFP was much closer to our values (*ape kama*). Suchithra, who had benefited under the UNP administration during the 1980s, voted for Mahinda Rajapaksa at the 2010 presidential election.[23] Justifying her decision, she said that Ranil Wickremasinghe did not represent Sinhala values (*sinhalakama*) and was more westernized (*batahira widiha*) and lacked masculinity (*pirimikama*) as compared to Rajapaksa. Sarath,[24] a factory labourer, said that he did not vote for the SLFP as he feared that people would suffer under SLFP rule. While he had not experienced the bleak conditions of the 1970–1977 period, when people had to stand in long queues, Sarath felt that the SLFP generally tended to bring economic misery to the people. Hence, ideology was often found more useful for voters to reject parties and politicians than in choosing them. This is further elaborated by my interview with Saman Gamage, a local politician from Weligama.[25]

Over lunch at his house, Saman Gamage shared his experience as a local politician. He said that he did not have much regard for Buddhist monks and the temple in his area, because they always needed something. Asked whether he does not visit the temples or associate with the monks at all, Sunil promptly clarified his position:

> No ... no ... I always maintain my relationship with temples. Otherwise, you can't do politics in our villages. Even though you do not get any substantial support from them at elections, if you antagonize them they can be a serious hindrance to your politics. They can spread the word amongst their patrons that I am not a good Buddhist. That would certainly have a negative impact on my electoral campaigns.

Sunil makes an interesting observation. If a politician openly challenged the accepted ideals of Sinhalese society, he/she could be subject to a negative campaign by political rivals. Therefore, even though politicians may not attract more votes by observing those ideals, they can lose votes by challenging the same ideals of society. Edirimanna is an old Marxist who was involved in trade union activities in his youth. However, in later days, he turned his allegiance to the SLFP. He had served in the Weligama Urban Council as a Council member. He made an interesting analysis of the Sinhalese constituency. Although he did not believe in Buddhist rituals and traditions, he did not denounce or reject them overtly, as this could have drawn unnecessary attention from the people in the neighbourhood.

These ideals or cognitive structures are similar to what Bourdieu conceptualized as 'habitus' in shaping the electoral of practices of the voter. However, unlike caste, which can function both as an objective as well as a subjective category, these ideals hardly form objective categories to stratify the community. Even though people are conscious of the existence of these ideals in society, the practice of those ideals was often subjected to evaluation at the time of election.

Attention to these ideals is aroused at the time of elections in the context of election propaganda. The anecdotal narratives cited demonstrate the role of voter consciousness in formulating electoral decisions. The characteristics of voter consciousness would be less important in drawing votes as voters expect all their leaders to concur with those virtues. However, the inability of the politician to successfully communicate to voters that he/she upholds those virtues can cost him/her many votes. In Sri Lankan society, it is common to see politicians visiting temples irrespective of their own religion, observing traditional rituals although they do not subscribe to those traditions.[26] As Bastian observes:

> Nationalist ideologies helped to translate the emphasis on rural areas in general and paddy agriculture in particular articulated in policy discussions, to something much bigger. In the ideological constructions of Sinhala nationalism rural areas occupy a privileged position. The Sinhala peasant cultivating paddy and living in a village is considered the authentic representative of the Sinhalese. The other elements in this idyllic Sinhala milieu consist of the village tank and the Buddhist Vihara. This nationalist imagery is propagated through various means and by various actors including academic writings. It has a powerful hold on society, and politicians across the political spectrum uphold this ideology. (Bastian 2010: 4)

Voting and Material Interests

In addition to the identity interests of the voter, electoral decisions can be highly influenced by material interests. Scholars of patron-client relations accord importance to material interests of the voter as a factor determining electoral allegiance. As Kitschelt and Wilkinson argued:

> In many political systems citizen-politician linkages are based on direct material inducements targeted to individuals and small groups of citizens whom politicians know to be highly responsive to such side-payments and willing to surrender their vote for the right price. (Kitschelt and Wilkinson 2007: 2)

Kitschelt and Wilkinson observe the existence of clientelist politics in non-industrial nations as well as some industrial nations such as Belgium, Austria and Japan (Kitschelt and Wilkinson 2007: 3). Many scholars of Sri Lankan politics have also observed the practice of clientelism amongst electorates from the early days of electoral democracy (Jupp 1978; Wilson 1975; Jiggins 1979; Hettige 1984; Spencer 1990; and Jayanntha 1992). However, most of the Sri Lankan literature has overtly focused on the supply side of clientelism while paying less attention to the demand side of it. In Sri Lankan society, as noted in this chapter, patronage has been an essential avenue in meeting most of the basic needs in villages, especially in rural society.

Simon Dias is a local SLFP leader and a Justice of Peace from Kananke, Weligama. He says: "Always there is a scarcity of resources. Nevertheless, people have unlimited desires. Therefore, people have become slaves of greed".[27] This statement highlights important aspects of the material interests of voters. The scarcity of resources leads to many types of deprivation. These include the absence of a livelihood, inadequate shelter or other basic needs such as roads, water, electricity, health care and education. As Simon Dias said, fulfiling basic needs alone is not enough. People have unlimited desires. Fulfiling the need of an individual or family is not only about addressing material needs but also addressing the identity interests of the voter as well.

Jobs

Employment is a pressing need amongst voters. It provides a livelihood, security and social status. Above all, amongst those men and women with the required basic qualifications, it is also a launching pad for further advancement in life. The annual addition to the labour force is estimated at about 140,000,[28] and this is in addition to the thousands of already unemployed and underemployed men and women. Unemployment is three times higher amongst youth than adults, and 24.6% of women and 18.6% of men in the age group of 17–24 years were estimated to be unemployed in the second quarter of 2010 (Central Bank 2010). Unemployment amongst the educated is also high in Sri Lanka. The share of unemployed persons with educational attainments of GCE (A/L) and above was 10.8%. This is above the average unemployment rate for males (6.6%) in 2009 (Central Bank 2010). While we have an agrarian society, there is a severe scarcity of agricultural land in the villages. According to available data, over 85% of employment in the agriculture sector is informal. Amongst those in informal employment, a majority (65%) is male.[29] Most of the unemployed poor search for jobs such as carpentry, masonry and manual labour at construction sites in cities. Some are in search of non-agricultural occupations. This makes finding a government job one of the top priorities in their lives. A job in a government office gives job security and it usually ensures a pension after retirement. This offers them a degree of security in their lives and promises a social status much better than their lot in the agrarian sector. Those with a permanent job hold a higher status than farmers who may sometimes earn more. Free education provides a majority, a substantial level of education. It discourages them from reverting to the occupations of their parents. The desire then turns to some form of a formal job even if it is not a government job. Sri Lanka is characterized by a high level of underemployment. Amongst the rural population, underemployment is much higher than in the urban sector.[30] It is socially embarrassing and stressful for a youth to not have a job after completing school education. It is even worse for those who have pursued higher education. Those who obtain a proper job can always hope for advancement in later life. In the case of arranged marriages, those with good jobs can hope for better prospects of a partner with added advantages such as a dowry or other material benefits. In the case of an educated woman, it is important to have a good job unless her parents have sufficient wealth to offer a good dowry.

What are the avenues available for an individual to find a job? The standard method to obtain a government job is to apply for jobs advertised in the government gazette, sit for a competitive examination and get selected for appointment. In order to find a job in the private sector, candidates need to apply for jobs advertised in newspapers and be selected after an interview. However, the usual practice of filling government vacancies has been surrendered or subjected to the authority of the line minister of the government. The line minister distributes a certain percentage of jobs amongst his/her fellow MPs in the ruling party while the lion's share is allocated to his/her own electorate. These jobs are then distributed amongst village political actors connected to the politician through various social groups in the electorate. In distributing the job opportunities obtained from the national-level politician, village elites use their discretion. In order to institutionalize this process and to rectify malpractices in the process of distribution of jobs, the ruling parties have introduced a system called the 'job card'. These job cards are distributed amongst those seeking jobs in the electorate in order to collect information regarding job seekers. The political party and politicians use the 'job cards' to distribute any new job opportunities amongst the electorate. Often politicians boast of the number of jobs they have distributed.

A coordinating secretary of a former prominent minister in charge of the Port Authority boasted that her minister had given 12,000 jobs to his electorate by creating a new section in the Port Authority.[31] A son of a deputy minister in the same ministry under the SLFP boasted that his father had managed to provide 1,200 jobs within the brief period he served in that ministry.[32] Ruling politicians are expected to generate jobs. Susantha, a member of the Weligama Pradeshiya Sabha, spoke highly of his minister, Mahinda Wijesekara, and his ability to generate jobs for the electorate.[33] According to Susantha, Wijesekara, as the minister in charge of the Postal Department, had introduced a concept of setting up branches of the DFCC bank at each post office. The main objective, according to Susantha, was to create jobs for his electorate using a ministry where there was little opportunity to create jobs. In addition, the minister had allegedly cancelled the list compiled after a competitive examination to insert names of persons from his electorate. Susantha sees this as a very noble act of his minister to address a pressing problem of his electorate. The above evidence demonstrates 'politicization' of job creation on the ground.

Ruban Kuruppu was a young man when Montague Jayewickrema began to reorganize his electorate focusing on the 1977 election. As a youth, he had played a prominent role in Kananke, Weligama. He still recalls how he distributed so many job cards and he himself had received 12 jobs to choose from. He says that following the election victory,

over 1,200 teaching appointments had been given to the Weligama electorate alone. There had been individuals who did not possess even the
basic educational qualifications. Job creation was one of the main objectives of the UNP government at the time. Numerous mega-development
programmes initiated under the UNP government provided enough
opportunities to generate jobs. What mattered to citizens were jobs, not
whether it contributed to the economy. Mr. Wijethilake, coordinating
secretary of Industry minister Cyril Mathew of the J.R. Jayewardene
government, shared his experience at that time in the Kelaniya electorate.
One of the profitable corporations under the SLFP government had to be
closed down due to mass-scale job creation by a director who was a political actor in the minister's political network. While the particular director
became popular in his electorate the corporation had to be closed down
in a few years.

Kaushalya works at the Weligama Municipal Council library. She was
first posted to the job as a temporary library assistant. A UNP Local
Council member, Ajith Kumarasinghe (popularly known as Ajith Sir),
got her that position as she and her brother had worked for him despite
their family being hardcore SLFP supporters. She is very pleased with
the present Mayor under whom her position was made permanent after
years of waiting, although being a member of the ruling party. She said
that despite the Mayor being a Muslim, her whole family worked for the
Mayor's election campaign. She and her husband personally called their
relatives to garner votes for the Mayor. She admits that people insulted
her and her family for working for a non-Sinhalese. She had continued to
work for the Mayor's election campaign as he was an honest man. He had
proved that he delivered what he promised. She invites others to work for
the Mayor as they too could receive assistance from him.

Not everyone succeeds in obtaining a job through the pursuit of politicians. Nevertheless, rural youth continue to seek assistance of politicians
because they can see that others in the village have succeeded in obtaining
employment, while on the other hand, they see no other viable alternative. Chaminda Perera, a young Local Council member from Weligama
town, illustrates this phenomenon as follows[34]:

When a youth finishes his or her education they approach a politician
with an expectation of finding a job. Usually politicians promise jobs
for youth explicitly and implicitly and use their labour for election work.
If the politician gets a good portfolio in the government, those young

guys are lucky and most of them get jobs. Otherwise, the politician has to disappoint many except a few for whom he manages to assist using his personal contacts. Nevertheless, young voters continue to follow the politician expecting a job in the near future. After a few years, some leave the politician out of disappointment, but there are many to join the bandwagon. Those who leave one politician often join another politician expecting a job from the new politician. During this process, those who are lucky get something and those who are unlucky give up the process by the time they realize that they can no longer live on hope. They find some work available to them by their own in order to meet the rest of the challenges in their lives. However, a politician will never cease to have youth hanging around in his garden or at his office seeking jobs as every year thousands of youth enter into the job market.

Granting a job or the promise of a job does not mean the securing of only one vote. Usually, one job attracts the votes of the entire family and perhaps even the votes of relatives. In some instances, politicians are clever enough to win the votes of the entire community through one single job. This will be further elaborated later.

Land and Shelter
Land and shelter are the other most common material interests of the community. As the population grows, people invariably look for new land and housing. A majority of Sinhalese consider owning a house and land as a mark of stability and attaining a healthy family life. In a non-industrial society, those who own land possess wealth, power and status, and it is said that "Land is to rule". However, as the economy began to diversify, other economic opportunities opened up. In rural society, the signifi-cance of land has diminished. As the Centre for Poverty Analysis (CEPA) observes:

> Sri Lanka has begun this process of transition – land is not as significant today as it was 30 years ago. However, even today, despite the fact that only 16% of GDP comes from agriculture, over 35% of the population is directly or indirectly dependent on land. Therefore, until further economic diversification, land is an important determinant of poverty. Aside from agriculture, land is vital for housing, industry and recreational activities. (Melis et al. 2006)

Obtaining a land has always been a major priority for the average family. This is so not only for poor villagers but also for the majority of urban, middle-income groups. Parents usually distribute their wealth, especially lands, to their children when they leave home after marriage. However, government land distribution schemes have been the major avenue for a majority of rural communities. Be they Land Development Ordinance (LDO) permits, State Land Ordinance (SLO) permits or any other land distribution scheme, the politician commands a great deal of discretion in determining beneficiaries.

In addition to land, housing also has been a critical need of villagers. As the website of the National Housing Development Authority puts it, "Whatever talk in political arena, the problem for housing in Sri Lanka seriously worsened rapidly".[35] The same website claims that the total shortfall of houses in Sri Lankan at present is 1.2 million. Even though it is not clear how these estimates are arrived at or the real motives, like all previous governments, the present government too has given attention to the housing needs of communities. Successive governments have attempted to address this issue with various development projects such as the Udagam Viyaparaya, Nivasa Dasadahasa and the Jana Sevana national housing project of the Rajapaksa government. Even though these projects are portrayed as nationwide nonpartisan programmes, they are implemented by ruling politicians who turn the projects into a part of their patronage politics. As argued previously, government officials such as *Grama Sevakas*, Samurdi *niyamakas* and officials in Divisional Secretariats are made subservient to the authority of local politicians. Hence, the distribution of houses and land happens largely under the discretion of ruling party politicians. This type of large project is usually initiated by the central government and cabinet ministers. Therefore, they are not implemented according to the agendas of local politicians. However, local politicians of the ruling party have the capacity to bring the benefits of those projects to members of their network in the village. In addition to programmes aimed at addressing the land and housing requirements of communities, sometimes politicians distribute state lands sometimes illegally amongst their supporters or they encourage their clients to seize state lands in the village or in the district under their political cover. For example, a powerful government minister was accused of mobilizing his supporters to grab lands from a state-owned coconut estate. The following excerpt in the *Sunday Times* on that incident illustrates this point.

A Zimbabwean style land grabbing case with powerful political backing has led to the cutting down of more than 5,000 highly productive coconut trees with squatters moving into state land in the Negombo area ... A private plantation company claims to have suffered losses running into millions of rupees because its estates are being destroyed and encroached on by people in the area with alleged political backing ... During our visit we were made to understand that this episode had begun due to an election promise allegedly made by Minister of Plan Implementation, Parliamentary Affairs and MP for Negombo District, Jeyaraj Fernandopulle. However the Minister denied the allegations.

... A letter sent by the Katana AGA to the Ministry of Agriculture and Lands states that there are 6,800 homeless people in the Katana Divisional Secretariat, which included Katunayake, Seeduwa, Raddoluwa, Liyanagemulla, etc. It further states that Minister Fernandopulle had instructed the AGA in February 1999 to distribute these lands to reduce the number of homeless people in the area. (Fernando and Farook 2000)

Even though such illegal acts may temporarily solve the problem of ownership of those lands, it remains until they receive the legal deeds for those lands, which again requires a crucial role on the part of the politician. Siriwardane of Ragalakanda, Dedigama, recalled how he managed to get lands for poor low-caste villagers when he was a member of the Local Council. He said that with the help of Dharmasiri Senanayake he got the landless poor villagers to seize some of the unused state land in the electorate, and years later he had got them deeds under the Swarnabhoomi deed programme. He considers this as a noble act as it solved a pressing problem in his area.

Other Goods
In addition to jobs, land and shelter, ruling parties and politicians make their supporters happy with various other offers of assistance. These goods are distributed under various programmes initiated by the government. The government conducts various programmes under various ministries to assist communities with their livelihood needs, such as distributing agrarian equipment and fishing gear, and various types of loans for self-employed individuals to address the livelihood problems of poor communities. These programmes always appear to have justifiable, rational objectives, although they are intended to serve the voter bases of the party or a particular politician. Often these programmes and what is being provided are supply driven rather than demand-driven. This is

not to say that these goods are not beneficial to poor villagers. This can be useful supplementary assistance for the villagers although they do not address basic needs such as jobs, houses or land. Irrespective of the usefulness of the goods, people still value them for the simple fact that they get something for free.

Usually, political parties and politicians initiate various assistance schemes to distribute various benefits amongst the electorates targeting elections. Things such as toilet appliances, metal roofing sheets, water pumps for farmers, sewing machines are some of the popular items distributed. Even though these items do not induce lasting allegiance amongst voters towards the party or to a politician, because they are distributed on the eve of elections, those items can generate electoral support for the politician. As discussed earlier, distribution of these types of goods is important, especially in lubricating the network of village political actors that electoral organizers depend on for organizing electoral campaigns.

For the Community
In addition, people are in need of various services. Roads, public transport, electricity, pipe-borne water, schools and health and recreation facilities are important services that ordinary villagers require for an ordinary life. These services are usually for the consumption of the larger community instead of for one or two families. When a politician provides these types of services in return for votes, such services are called 'club goods' in the literature on clientelism. The chief monk of the Dedigama Raja Maha Viharaya recalled how he managed to widen the road that leads to the village temple and later got bus service through then Prime Minister and Dedigama electorate organizer Dudley Senanayake. In the early years after independence, villages lacked basic facilities such as roads, water and schools. Hence, villages and towns competed amongst themselves to attract the attention of bureaucrats and politicians to fulfil their needs. Although facilities have significantly improved in villages over the past several decades, communities continue to look for more services. The demand for more facilities never ceases. On the one hand, existing facilities need to be maintained and improved, while on the other hand, expectations also increase in terms of quality and quantity. Resource limitations always leave local authorities disabled in providing for even the most pressing needs of the villages. In this context, not only are villagers motivated to seek favours from the authorities, but even authorities see

favouritism as a convenient way of service delivery. Hence, favouritism becomes institutionalized in governance. In this context of exacerbated competition for resources and services, politicians turn out to be the best mediators in securing these services. Usually, when an election gets close, ruling politicians show interest in addressing these issues as it provides them an opportunity to show the electorate that they have done a great deal of work for it. Sometimes roads are carpeted overnight or, at least, granite chips needed for road construction are piled up along the road, before an election, to indicate that the road is soon to be completed. Sometimes, ironically, those raw materials disappear soon after the election as they were only meant to deceive the people.

Not having a good local school for children has become a serious problem for many. Similarly, electricity may have come to the village but getting an electrical connection to the home can be a problem. Sometimes getting the electricity connection is not possible due to the legal status of the house or if the house does not meet the regulations of the electricity board. Irrespective of eligibility of the house for electricity, people believe that the politician can get them the connection. All needs of the people are not always legitimate or just, and they need the assistance of politicians to meet their needs even if they are against the rule. Not only service recipients but service providers such as local electricity board branches impose unfriendly policies and discriminatory practices to legitimize the mediation of politicians in government service delivery.

Many approach government service providers through politicians to receive electricity connections, water connections, admission of children to a good school, undue transfers or promotions at work and even to get a bed in the overcrowded government hospital. When the police arrest a member of the community, irrespective of whether that person committed an offence or not, the community expects mediation of their politician. For example, as Susantha said, his community (fisher folk from Weligama town) terribly missed Mahinda Wijesekara, as now there was no one to intervene if someone was taken in by the police.[36]

It is an extremely difficult task to describe all the diverse forms of relations between material interests and voting due to the complex nature of the material interests of voters. What has been illustrated here is the simple straightforward material benefits that people often expect. There are many forms of material interests that are complex and remain publicly unstated. One example is what Karunaratne of Algama, Dedigama, expects in return for his support to politicians.[37] Karunaratne said that he threatened a principal (from the *Kumbal* caste) of an underdeveloped school in the village, saying that he would never allow the principal to get a post in the more prominent school in the area. Karunaratne is confident that due to his political connections with politicians of both the UNP and SLFP in Dedigama, he can obstruct any promotion offered to this principal of the *Kumbal* caste. So, his expectation from politicians (in return for votes he can mediate) at the moment is simple, but unconventional. During the fieldwork in Kelaniya, Dedigama and Weligama, there were many interviewees who described the unconventional and not openly discussed issues of how village political actors trade votes with politicians for jobs and other material benefits, which they in turn trade with women for sexual favours. However, the basic argument applies to any form of material interests that the 'vote' has increasingly made a common currency for citizens, especially the less affluent ones, in fulfiling various material needs.

STATE OF DEPENDENCY OF THE VOTER

We know from Jiggins (1979) and Jayanntha (1992) that both interests—identity and material—influence the electoral decision of the voter. However, what we do not know yet is how much each interest contributes to the voting decision in Sinhalese society. Do they equally influence the decision? Or does one interest play a more important role than the other? Or does this vary from person to person, contingent on a person's life experience? Social cleavage theory (Lipset and Rokkan 1967) argues the primacy of identity interests (cleavage group identity) in determining the electoral decision. On the other hand, patron-client theorists (Kitschelt and Wilkinson 2004) argue for the primacy of material interests in influencing the voting decision. However, contrary to both arguments, my field research suggests that both types of interests matter when making electoral decisions. Further, the question of how much each interest matters is contingent on the circumstances of the voter or his/her immediate family experience at election time. People have needs and certain capabilities to meet those needs either fully or partially. The needs and capabilities of a person change over time. Based on a person's needs and capabilities at a given time and space, that person can be at different 'stages of dependency', or, in Amartya Sen's (1999) terms, varying degrees of 'freedom'. For the convenience of analysis, I would like to introduce three loosely defined categories to represent a person's status on the basis of the deficit in his/her capabilities in fulfiling needs at a particular time. Those who have pressing needs that far exceed their existing capabilities can be described as 'strong dependents'. For some, even though they manage to fulfil their basic needs still there are unmet needs, and I would call them 'weak dependents'. The third group, who also have needs but are very capable in fulfiling them without external assistance can be called 'independents'. Therefore, depending on the deficit between the needs and capabilities of a person (his/her immediate family), he/she would fall into one of the three categories of dependency. The state of dependency that a person belongs to at any given time determines his/her vulnerability to prioritize material interests over identity concerns. It should be noted that the same person can fall into different stages of dependency at different times depending on his/her (or the immediate family's) life circumstances. Let's look closely into these three categories of dependency.

The **strongly dependent** stage is when a voter (his/her immediate family) is desperately looking for external assistance to fulfil basic needs ranging from livelihood and shelter to security. Those who are at this stage usually do not find a solution to their needs on their own. For them, fulfiling those critical needs are the top priority, and often they are willing to compromise identity interests for the sake of that particular material need. It should be noted that 'strong dependents' are not only motivated by material interest, but are also greatly dependent on members of the political network, especially of the ruling political party or coalition, to fulfil those material needs. Those who are living in poverty and who are socially and economically marginalized are usually permanent residents in the category of 'strongly dependent'. However, families in other classes can also fall into this condition of 'strongly dependent', depending on the circumstances. For example, a family that is not necessarily poor but has a young member who is desperately looking for a job, or a family that is urgently seeking school admission for a child, or a family that needs some favour (often illegal or non-regular) or some kind of relief from legal authorities and police, or a family that has to depend on government rations, or person living under a government welfare dole (*pin padi*) are strongly dependent on external assistance and hence are easily vulnerable to promises of politicians or political mediators. Such families and individuals have almost no capacity to fulfil their need(s) and therefore are often motivated to approach mediators who can link them with state authorities. As pointed out, these mediators play a crucial role in our society where institutions and the bureaucracy are subservient to the political authority. Citizens who are in a stage of 'strong dependency' reach out to local power centres in village political networks, who act as mediators to address their pressing needs. Those citizens are aware of the 'rules of the game'—that they have to exchange their vote and often the votes of relatives and friends for assistance from those mediators. For those at the stage of 'strong dependency', their identity interests such as caste, class, religion and even ethnicity are hardly an obstacle in approaching mediators across party lines. In any electorate, the party and politicians from the ruling coalition enjoy clear support from areas where most socially and economically 'backward' social groups live. They are the recipients of most government welfare schemes and mediation of local politicians of the ruling party. Often the allegiance of these groups shifts from party to party depending on who is in power. They are often the foot soldiers of ruling politicians in the electorate. For example, in Weligama, according to Bandu Sarathchandra, the fishing community that lives along the coast and the Muslim community who are concentrated in the urban (town) area cannot extend support overtly to the opposition, as they are very much dependent on ruling party mediators.[38] The fishing community depends on politicians of the ruling party/coalition for economic assistance and other benefits, while the Muslim community has to depend on those mediators for their economic and physical security, being a minority in a Sinhalese-majority electorate.

The **weakly dependent** stage is when a family or individual, despite possessing the capacity to fulfil the most pressing needs at a given time, seeks external assistance to fulfil other 'non-pressing needs' that cannot be met entirely with their existing capabilities. Often those in this category have the capacity to fulfil their basic needs and are not as helpless as those in the previous group. Such people, if they so desire, can live without external assistance, but often they resort to fulfiling non-basic needs as they find them important for upward mobility. Hence, generally, people strive to achieve non-essential needs even when these are beyond their individual capacity. However, unlike in the case of 'strongly dependent', in this instance, people do not expose themselves to external assistance unconditionally and usually appreciate the external assistance, provided their identity interests remain intact. They can afford to pick and choose external assistance as they are less dependent and can even cope with their needs until they find the external assistance that comes with agreeable conditions. In this case, individuals exercise some agency when fulfiling needs, which is noticeably absent amongst individuals in the category of 'strongly dependent'.

Thushara Obeysekara of Weligama was from a strong SLFP family but decided to vote for the UNP Urban Council member and help his electoral campaign covertly, as he had been promised a job. He and his sister supported the UNP Local Council member, Ajith Sir, at that election as both were badly in need of jobs.[39] On the other hand, conditions were not unacceptable, as they were required only to support Ajith Sir and not to change their party. One of the most interesting accounts that emerged in this regard during field interviews was the story of Wijethilake's (coordinating secretary to UNP minister and Kelaniya organizer Cyril Mathew) immediate neighbour. According to Wijethilake, he had helped his neighbour, who had been struggling to find a school for a niece despite being from a family of strong SLFP supporters. On election day morning (2010 Parliamentary election), the neighbour had attempted to give him all (five) polling cards of that household in gratitude for his assistance, and had asked him to use them for the benefit of the party that Wijethilake supported. This was a suggestion to illegally cast five votes for the UNP. The interesting aspect of the story is that he told Wijethilake that since they had been supporters of the SLFP for generations, they could not cast votes for the rival UNP. They, however, would not mind sparing their votes for Wijethilake, as he had done a great favour to the family. These examples show that the voting decisions of communities who are in the category 'weakly dependent' can also be influenced by mediators due to their material interests.

The **independent stage** is when a family or individual possesses the necessary capabilities to meet their needs without seeking external assistance. Usually, those below the poverty line do not fall into this category. People in higher income categories and those in command of higher positions in the community or society usually come under this category. Sometimes even those in possession of comparatively less capital (economic and symbolic) can also fall into this category if they have fewer needs. Communities belonging to the 'independent' category are more concentrated in Kelaniya than in Weligama and Dedigama. In semi-industrial settings and in places where private enterprises play a crucial role in the economy, communities (except those that belong to extremely poor strata and who live in shanty housing settlements or encroached lands) are less dependent on political mediators to fulfil their needs. It should be noted that those who are in this stage may not be motivated to approach political mediators to fulfil their needs, basic or otherwise. Nevertheless, they may not be averse to accepting, and even appreciating, external assistance and benefits as long as these comply with their identity interests.

These three categories of dependence are neither completely independent nor dependent on a person's economic status. The categories are not only subject to a person's capability but are dependent on a person's needs. These categories of dependence reflect the capacity of the individual or his/her family to meet the needs of a given moment. Since, the needs and the capacity to meet them can vary from time to time, due to different life circumstances, the level of dependency can also change over time. The three stages are a product of individual capacity and what a person considers as needs. Hence, the category one resides in at any given moment is partly defined by attitudes and practices of a person including his/her family. However, it is also possible for external factors and actors to influence the level of dependency that one belongs to, by either influencing a person's needs or limiting or enabling the person's capabilities. For example, the higher status granted to government jobs in rural society may influence youth to strive for them, irrespective of the availability of jobs or their capacity to obtain them.

Let's look at another example. Even an economically secure person can seek the mediation of political elites under unexpected circumstances such as neighbourhood conflict or on issues such as political victimization. In such situations, irrespective of wealth or status, they can still be vulnerable enough to fall into the stage of 'strong dependency'. Therefore, the stage of dependency of a person is not exclusively dependent on the attitude and perceptions of the person but can also be affected or manipulated by external factors.

VOTER'S ATTITUDES TOWARDS POLITICIANS AND ELECTIONS

Thus far we have discussed different interests that influence the behaviour of the voter and the levels of dependency of the voter that determine the influence of each interest when forming the electoral choice. In addition to interests and the level of dependency, the attitudes of the voter towards politicians, political parties and elections in general also play a vital role in the electoral choice. Traditional political party literature has treated these categories of political parties, politicians and elections as objective categories as well as necessary players in any functioning democracy. However, the ground reality indicates that these categories are far from being objective, and voters are often apathetic towards them. Therefore, it is important to understand the attitudes of voters towards politicians, parties and elections to comprehend their rationale in making a voting decision.

If one examines voter attitudes towards politicians, parties and elections, it is evident that a majority of voters do not know much about politicians, parties and elections. They are often not interested in knowing them either. Although most voters do not trust parties and politicians, ironically, they do participate in elections. Examining this dilemma would help us to understand the various rationales that voters use to explain an electoral decision. In this case, the survey on "Democracy in Post-War Sri Lanka",[40] conducted in 2011, can be used to examine the macro picture.

When asked how often they read newspapers, listen to the radio and watch TV for political news, 66%, 45% and 20%, respectively, of the Sinhalese community said either, rarely or never. Of course, this shows that four out of every five individuals, quite an impressive proportion, watch TV for political news despite their considerably low attention to newspapers and radio. It is noteworthy that due to the uneven TV coverage in Sri Lanka, people have limited access to private channels as compared to government channels. It obviously follows that whatever knowledge a voter acquires through TV is highly biased towards state propaganda. Further, survey data state that almost half of the Sinhalese population is not at all interested in politics (*deshapalanaya pilibanda unanduwak*) other than at election times.

Those who claim to be knowledgeable about politicians and parties often think that they have made a sound electoral choice at the most recent election. However, these knowledge claims do not by any means suggest that persons who possess the information needed to compare the available options at an election actually do make a rational choice. For example, Suba of Kelaniya, despite being a graduate and the daughter of a strong SLFP family, did not have much knowledge about any politician.[41] Her mother is the political coordinator of the SLFP in Gonawala, Kelaniya, and she claims that they like the policies of the SLFP. Nevertheless, neither Suba nor her mother could describe these policies despite their strong support. Usually, a person's knowledge of politicians is limited to the family background, community services, patronage distribution and illegal or criminal record.

Often people do not know and perhaps are not interested in the policy programmes of the politician they voted for. On the other hand, it is unfair to expect people to have perfect information, as politicians hardly present serious policy programmes when contesting elections. Instead, they either present a list of patronage goods that will be offered if elected, or some highly ambiguous but 'sounds good' policies, such as fighting corruption, stopping the waste of public funds or development of the area. Almost all Local Council members and rank-and-file members at the village level interviewed in this study had not read the manifesto of their own party published during the general election in 2010. However, they claimed that they were aware of the policies of their party, as to them the rhetoric of party leaders at election campaigns meant, more or less, the policies of the party. Ironically, these very same individuals had distributed the party manifesto in their villages during the election campaign. Interestingly, a Local Council member confessed that he and his colleagues were well aware that nobody reads the party manifesto. Nevertheless, they distributed it as it was the standard document that needed to be distributed at election time, and failure to do so was bad for the party.

What transpired in the interviews with most of the ordinary citizens was that they picked the party and politicians based on some criteria (which will be discussed later) and then searched for information to justify their decision. Hence, people invariably look for positive information about their party and candidate(s). In this case, not only was the information about politics at the election biased and subjective, but what the reader attempted to access and comprehend was also selective and subjective. The results of the "Political Participation of Women in Sri Lanka" survey conducted by the Social Scientists' Association[42] confirms this phenomenon. According to the survey results, 55.9% of male and 46.9% of female voters claimed that they decided whom to vote for even before the campaign started (Social Scientists' Association 2012). A little more than one quarter of men and women made the decision during the campaign. Therefore, it is not incorrect to assume that most of the information (or misinformation) flowing during the campaign helps people to confirm rather than revise their decision.

Not only were people unaware of the parties, but parties were also the least trusted democratic institution amongst South Asians (CSDS 2008).

Across South Asia, political parties were listed as the least trustworthy institution amongst democratic institutions such the central government, local government, civil service, army, police, courts, election commission and Parliament. Another survey, "Democracy in Post-War Sri Lanka" (Social Indicator 2011: 46–49) reveals that two-thirds of the Sinhalese community believed that corruption was prevalent at least to some extent amongst members of Parliament. Commenting on corruption in other institutions, 65.6%, 63.4%, 57.1% and 42.6% believed it prevailed to some degree amongst the police, local government members, civil servants and non-government organizations, respectively. Therefore, politicians were perceived as being the most corrupt amongst a majority of the Sinhalese community.

National newspapers (not only partisan tabloid papers and blogs) report on numerous incidents, accusing politicians ranging from village council members to cabinet ministers, of involvement in various kinds of corruption and misbehaviour. The moral conduct of politicians has declined to such a low level that some even implicitly acknowledge allegations of corruption without worrying about potential electoral consequences. For example, the Chairman of the Kelaniya Local Council, Mr. Prasanna Ranaweera, one-time close associate of Mervyn Silva, held a press conference with other members of the Council and accused the minister of extortion and misappropriation of funds.[43] Responding to the allegations, Minister Silva made counter-allegations of corruption. Interestingly, and quite ironically, Minister Silva told the press that he was aware of the Chairman's corruption but decided to ignore it, as he thought the Chairman had as much right to prosper in Kelaniya as himself. This shows how behaviour and conduct contribute to the negative perception that people have of politicians.

The qualitative interviews provide a deeper insight into a voter's attitudes towards politicians and parties. Irrespective of whether they supported a particular political party or not, most agreed that parties were untrustworthy, and politicians were opportunists. A three-wheeler driver from Kelaniya, Asiri, expressed this understanding of politicians as "they are reminded of our existence only on the eve of an election" (*Egollolanta apiwa mathak wenne chande lang unama vithri*).[44] Expressing his cynicism he further said that: "We will eat if we earn. Nobody will care for us" (*Api hummberkaroth api kanawa, kauwuruth apiwa rakinna enne neha*). They assume that political parties and politicians are there for their own benefit, rather than to serve the community.

It is interesting and somewhat ironic that sometimes those who have received material benefits from politicians too articulate the same sentiments. For example, Mr. Silva, a retired electrical technician of the Weligama Urban Council and one-time staunch supporter of the current Chairman of the Urban Council, expressed his disappointment and anger when discussing party politics. He said that he is disgusted with his own party (SLFP) and party men as they were thugs and thieves. Of course, he was frustrated because he could not secure government employment for his graduate daughter. He believes that he is entitled to this favour from his party, which is in power at the moment, and he views the failure to achieve his ambition as a fault of the party and politicians. Similarly, everybody has something to complain about regarding political parties and politicians. Politicians are also well aware of how people perceive them. They admit and acknowledge their negative reputation. Simon Dias of Kananke, Weligama, a local political actor in the village and representative of the political network of the Weligama SLFP party organization, stated that they were aware that people thought that politicians were only intent on collecting votes and disappear afterwards. According to Simon, voters expect solutions from politicians for all their problems, and hence frustration and disappointment were unavoidable. Voicing similar sentiments, the Chairman of the Warakapola Local Council stated that it was not possible to satisfy the voter even though politicians receive their votes. Giving an example he said:

> Every day so many people come to see me and request me to find them jobs irrespective of my ability to provide jobs in any government institution being a Chairman of a Local Council. However, I never tell those people the truth and instead I ask them to give an application and say that I will try my best to find a job. If someone comes without an application I ask that person to bring an application. If that person is with an application, I will accept it and ask the person to come in two weeks. The strategy is to drag each case as long as possible instead of telling people that I cannot give them a job. Therefore each applicant visits my office several times and eventually they stop bothering me. It is much better to do that instead of telling the truth as it could antagonize the people who may have voted for me.

Therefore, this attitude of disdain towards political parties and politicians is not only common amongst communities but, ironically, is acknowledged by politicians too who are well aware of it. However, the dilemma

Table 4.2 Voter turnout in recent Parliamentary elections (%)

Year	1994	2000	2001	2004	2010*
Voter turn out	76.24	75.62	76.03	75.96	52

*Election was held three months after the massive Presidential election victory of Mahinda Rajapaksa, and turnout hit the lowest in recent times
Source Department of Election Commissioner, Sri Lanka

is that the electoral participation of Sri Lankans is impressively high at almost every election, despite such negative attitudes towards politicians and political parties. Table 4.2 shows the high voter turnout figures of the five most recent general elections. Except in 2010, in general, voter turnout for Parliamentary elections is high as compared to South Asian neighbours and mature democracies such as the US (International IDEA 2002: 80).

According to democratic theory, participation in an election itself is considered a good indication of the legitimacy of the electoral process and its political actors (Birch 1993: 80). Elections provide an opportunity for people to rule the country by electing their rulers. Hence, voting at an election is widely considered as an important right of any citizen in a democracy. However, the dynamics of electoral participation in our society hardly provides evidence of Sri Lankans considering voting to be a right. If one examines the semiotics of the way elections are held and voter participation in them, it is far from being an exercise of a 'right'. Generally, election centres are set up either in school buildings or at religious premises. Ordinary people, unless they are campaigners of a particular political party, usually wear sober attire to the polling booth in order to respect the election and symbolically assert their party neutrality. For many voters, participation in elections is very much a civic responsibility more than a right. For some, especially poor and socially marginalized communities, participation in elections is an important event that provides them the opportunity to enjoy equal status or some attention from others in the village. Many think that not participating in voting will make them look peculiar. Interestingly, Nishamalee, a poor housewife from Tholangamuwa, Dedigama, promptly answered the question as to whether she voted in the last election, even though she could not recall whether it was a local government election or a Parliamentary election and which politician she had voted for.[46] If one examines the voting intention in pre-election surveys or participation in voting in post-election surveys, it is quite common to find that more than 90% (far higher than the actual turnout) of respondents assert that they either will vote or had voted.[46]

Therefore, in a nutshell, the attitude of the majority of Sinhalese voters towards politicians and parties is that politicians and parties are worthless and opportunistic. Nevertheless, people should participate in elections and vote for somebody even if they do not expect anything good to result. This is not to disregard the feelings of staunch supporters of the UNP and SLFP for whom the party is almost a religion and politicians they support are akin to spiritual gurus. However, the attitudes of these people do not offer much help to comprehend the dynamics of electoral choices of voters in general.

CONCLUSION

This section has delved into the practice and logic of voting from the point of view of the voter, during and after an election, as an individual and as a member of the community. Drawing on phenomenology, this section sought to understand how electoral decisions are made by voters who vote for the UNP and SLFP. The data herein were drawn from fieldwork in the three electorates and was supplemented by data from a survey examining the practice of voting amongst men and women in Sri Lanka. Through this, I have sought to produce new knowledge on the rationalities at work in the practice of voting.

Although election results are often used to interrogate the choice of citizens, this study argued that electoral results are a reflection of the consciousness of voters at the height of the election. In this section, a significant argument is advanced that the rationalities at work during the time of elections differ significantly from periods when elections are not being held. Therefore, in other words, electoral choice is less a reflection of the rationality of citizens as of voters.

The electoral choice of a voter is influenced by two types of interest—identity interests and material interests. This section pointed out that both types of interest influence each other, and voters may often use one type of interest to represent the other. However, the extent to which the voter relies on either type of interest to influence electoral choice is determined by the level of dependency. I also noted that voters with higher levels of dependency are more likely to rely on material interests, while those with lower levels of dependency rely more on their identity interests when making the electoral choice. Furthermore, in this, I have also argued that the level of dependency is not only determined by the life history or personal choice of the individual voter, but can also be shaped, to a certain extent at least, by state policies and through the choices of political actors.

Finally and due to this, this section examined the rationalities of voters to argue that voting decisions are made by individuals within cognitive structures. Political and social associations in everyday life form and shape the structures within which voters narrate and justify their electoral choice. I noted that the voter does not function autonomously but rather that a choice is informed and influenced by patriarchal and cultural structures, economic networks, family status and the status of the neighbourhood. Therefore, the rationality of the voter is defined by the cultural, economic and political fields within which she/he operates. As a result, electoral choices that are often considered irrational from the point of view of normative frameworks may well appear completely rational and justifiable to the voter.

Therefore, this section contributes to the knowledge on the practice of politics in Sri Lanka by arguing that both the UNP and SLFP are recognized by voters as mediators that cross identity and material interests as well as dependency levels. As a result, the catch-all nature of both parties provides a framework for voters to articulate, justify and narrate their electoral choices from within their own cognitive frameworks.

NOTES

1. Albert Galloway Keller, ed. *Democracy and Responsible Government—The Challenge of Facts and Other Essays*, New Haven: Yale University Press, 1914.

   Parties are Irresponsible. Party responsibility is not, however, any guarantee of civil liberty nor any bond for the organization of governmental organs. It could not be very serviceable to good government unless parties were very free in their formation and dissolution and the public criticism of party politics very active. It is in this connection that the fast organization of parties, which seem, as we have seen, essential to democracy, is most mischievous, for it neutralizes the only form of responsibility which exists in a democracy. In our experience it has been proved that the Presidential election rallies and confirms party organizations every four years and that in the interval they decline and tend to freer combinations. The legislature, elected partly at these intervals and elected by detached constituencies in which the varieties and minor fluctuations of public opinion find expression as they do not in the great mass vote for President, constitutes a far more satisfactory exponent of national feeling and will than the executive. I do not hesitate to express the opinion that the government would to-day stand on a much higher plane of purity, energy and efficiency than it now does, if it had followed the lines indicated in Congressional elections, without the periodical shocks of the Presidential elections. We define the functions of our public offices and elect men to perform those functions for limited times. If we do not elect good ones, we have no one to blame but ourselves. This is the only conception of responsibility which the system seems to admit, and the consequence of the political education which it gives is that people scarcely seem to understand what the notion of responsibility in government is (https://oll.libertyfund.org/title/keller-the-challenge-of-facts-and-other-essays).

2. Interview with Ruwan Karunaratne, from Kananke, Weligama, 19 December 2010.

3. Kanchan Chandra, in her formulation, conceptualizes 'mediated democracies' as a state where only a small number of voters are autonomous and others depend on this small group of people (2004: 64). Therefore, she says, when only some of the votes are autonomous and control the votes of the rest, politicians can target a small and selected pool of beneficiaries. Chandra cites 'traditional' politics as an example and in which landed and other powerful classes are autonomous and control the votes of subordinate groups through ties of differences and coercion. Taking a similar but slightly different approach, Berenschot (2009) states that in mediated states, political actors control the distribution of state resources. Hence, state agents and citizens depend on the mediation of political actors to deal with each other. This system of political mediation reproduces dependency of bureaucrats and citizens on politicians.

Mick Moore's concept of 'guided democracy' also resembles very much the features of 'mediated democracy'. Drawing examples from Taiwan, Moore says that in guided democracies, the state apparatus is closely integrated to the organization of the ruling political party, and this ruling party-state apparatus appropriates a substantial volume of state economic capital. This leaves opposition parties in a permanent state of dependence and internal conflict. Moore argues that this entrenched state power ensures a permanent electoral majority for the ruling party.

4. The problem of structure and agency has rightly come to be seen as the basic issue in modern social theory (Margaret Archer, cited in Ritzer 1996: 526). Those who belong to the structuralist school view social practice as determined by social structures, while on the contrary, those who believe in agency argue that it is human agency that determines social practice. As Giddens says, "every research investigation in the social sciences or history is involved in relating action (agency) to structure ... there is no sense in which structure 'determines' action or vice versa" (Giddens 1984: 219).

Many social theorists—Anthony Giddens, Pierre Bourdieu, Margaret Archer and Jurgen Habermas—came forward to solve the problem of the structure-agency duality of social theory and introduced their conceptual framework to integrate structure and agency. In this study, I will use Bourdieu's concepts of 'habitus' and 'field' to transcend the structure-agency duality.

5. Phenomenology is concerned with the study of experience from the perspective of the individual, bracketing taken-for-granted assumptions and usual ways of perceiving. Pure phenomenological research seeks essentially to describe rather than explain, and to start from a perspective free from hypotheses or preconceptions (Husserl 1970). This is powerful for understanding subjective experience, gaining insights into people's motivations and actions, and cutting through the clutter of taken-for-granted assumptions and conventional wisdom.

A variety of methods can be used in phenomenology-based research, including interviews, conversations, participant observation, action research, focus meetings and analysis of personal texts. If there is a general principle involved it is that of minimum structure and maximum depth, in practice constrained by time and opportunities, to strike a balance between keeping a focus on the research issues and avoiding undue influence by the researcher. The establishment of a good level of rapport and empathy is critical to gaining depth of information, particularly when investigating issues where the participant has a strong personal stake.

6. Interview with Karunanyake, Mirissa, Weligama, 20 December 2010.

7. Interview with Dassanayake, Weligama town, Weligama, 20 December 2010.

8. Social Indicator (SI), the survey unit of the Centre for Policy Alternatives (CPA), conducted this survey with the financial assistance of *Friedrich Naumann Stiftung* (FNST) of Sri Lanka. The preliminary survey report, "Democracy in Post-War Sri Lanka", publicized some of the survey findings, and I am using the data set for some of the analysis appearing in this thesis. This survey was conducted in all 25 districts in order to ascertain the knowledge, attitude and practices of all ethnic communities using a structured questionnaire. The sample was chosen randomly using a multistage stratified random sampling technique. I am using the Sinhalese interview as this thesis limits its focus to the party-voter relationship of the Sinhalese community. The author was the principal researcher in this survey and was solely responsible for designing and conducting the survey as the head of Social Indicator (November 1999 to May 2011).

9. Interview with Weerasekara, Pelana, Weligama, 29 January 2011.

10. Interview with Victor, Kananke, Weligama, 19 December 2010.

11. Interview with Dhanushka Silva, Sinharamulla, Kelaniya, 12 May 2011.

12. A set of core values and discourses that a field articulates as its fundamental principles and that tend to be viewed as inherently true and necessary. For Bourdieu, the 'doxic attitude' means bodily and unconscious submission to conditions that are in fact quite arbitrary and contingent. Doxa is implicit and unformulated and reflects how people most of the time take themselves, their perceptions and the social world they relate to for granted (Jenkins 2002).

13. Interview with Nalika, Priyantha (husband) and Nalika's parents, 16 October 2011.

14. Habitus is a concept that expresses, on the one hand, the way in which individuals 'become themselves'—develop attitudes and

dispositions—and, on the other hand, the way in which they engage in practice. In other words, habitus is a cognitive property of social agency that regulates behaviour without being subject to rules (Maton 2008).

15. Interview with Edwin and his wife at their residence, Weligama town, 15 October 2011.

16. The economy is at the center of Marx's sociological theories; he considered society to be the result of an economic base and a social superstructure; it is the economic base that determines all other social structures including ideology, politics and religion. Marx's earliest development of his social and economic theories can be found in *The German Ideology* (1998).

   Marx also distinguishes between the economic base and the superstructure of capitalist society. In capitalist society the economic base is such that production is increasingly organized in large companies with the aim of securing profits, which in turn result in the exploitation of the proletariat in the interest of the bourgeoisie. By the superstructure Marx means the political, legal, religious and education systems, the mass media and the organization of family life. Marx then argues that the economic base of society heavily influences the organization and operation of its superstructure and that the institutions of the superstructure operate so as to maintain the dominance of the capitalist class within the economic base (http://www.earlhamsociologypages.co.uk/marxclasscap.htm).

17. The Sri Lanka Muslim Congress (SLMC) is a political party that is totally focused on giving voice to the Muslim minority who comprise 8% of the population, http://www.slmc.lk.

18. Interview with Appuhamy, Weniwellakaduwa, Dedigama, 26 February 2011.

19. Appuhamy was not explicit on caste oppression, probably due to the presence of my *goigama* field assistant. This is a good example of the methodological challenges faced when inquiring into phenomenon such as caste, which is considered to be a taboo topic in society.

20. Interview with Jayasinghe Banda, Waddeniya, Dedigama, 26 February 2011.

21. Information based on interview conducted by Minna Thaheer for her PhD thesis.

22. As defined in the free dictionary, http://www.thefreedictionary.com/ideology.
23. Interview with Suchithra Jayasinghe, Gonawila, Kelaniya, 12 December 2011.
24. Interview with Sarath Dewarathne, Hunupitiya Kelaniya. 12 December 2012.
25. Interview with Saman Gamage, Kananke, Weligama, 10 December 2010.
26. Many political leaders after completing their education in the West began to don *Ariya Sinhala* attire (traditional Sinhalese attire comprising a sarong and long-sleeved collarless shirt) in sharp contrast to their western orientation and upbringing. Often journalists made fun of politicians embarking on foreign tours. They left their native shores wearing Sinhalese national attire and landed on foreign soil in western attire. The sarcasm did contain a cruel reality. I met with a group of young provincial council members at a hotel pub in Colombo. While having drinks both men and women (including wives) discussed their plan to hold a *bodipuja viyaparaya* to evoke blessing for the defeated presidential candidate General Sarath Fonseka who was in prison at that time. Politicians had to hide their true selves to varying degrees to portray themselves as being attuned to the consciousness of their voters. Many politicians acknowledge that so-called Sri Lankan 'consciousness' or 'ideals' is far from the reality, but nobody dares to challenge them as it could be fatal for their political careers.
27. Interview with Simon Dias, Kananke, 15 October 2011.
28. Ranasinghe Sudatta, "The Challenge of Developing and Optimizing Human Resources in Sri Lanka: Current Issues and their Implications", HRM Perspectives, http://www.ipmlk.org/downloads/HRM%20Perspectives%202,012.pdf .
29. Ibid.
30. Saleem Rishar, "Sri Lanka's Underemployment Rate Has Come Down, *Ceylon Today*, http://www.ceylontoday.lk/22-2422-news-detail-sri-lankas-underemployment-rate-has-come-down-cbsl.html.
31. Interview with Ms. Shamila Perera, one of the coordinating secretaries of late Minister Lalith Athulathmudali, 14 June 2010.
32. Interview with Ruwan Ranathunga, one of the late Minister Reggie Ranathunga's sons, 14 June 2010.

33. Interview with Hendage Susantha, one of the coordinating secretaries of former Minister Mahinda Wijesekara, 16 October 2011.
34. Interview with Chaminda Perera Hewa, Mahaweediya, Weligama, 31 January 2011.
35. http://www.nhda.lk/.
36. Interview with Hendage Susantha, one of the coordinating secretaries of former Minister Mahinda Wijesekara, 16 October 2011.
37. Interview with Gunarathne of Algama, Dedigama, 9 August 2010. He is an old political actor who played an important role in the UNP's network in the electorate.
38. Interview with Bandu Sarathchandra, Midigama, Weligama, 27 February 2011.
39. Interview with Thushara Obeysekara, Weligama, 27 February 2011.
40. Interview with Suba Apsara, Ganawela, Kelaniya, 24 May 2012. This interview was held while her parents were present. Her mother is the SLFP's local contact in the area while her father is the driver of a prominent UNPer in Kelaniya.
41. Social Scientists' Association, Sri Lanka, conducted this survey in 2012 on women and political participation in six districts: Colombo, Gampaha, Galle, Kurunegala, Nuwara Eliya and Batticaloa. The survey was conducted using face-to-face interviews and administered using a semi-structured questionnaire amongst a sample chosen through a multi-stage random sampling technique. Since the women sample has been over sampled, the gender-segregated results should be used instead of totals. The author served as the coordinator of this survey and designed the project in consultation with his supervisor and other gender experts in the country.
42. *Daily Mirror*, 9 January 2012.
43. Asiri Devasiri, Hunupitiya, Kelaniya, 12 December 2012.
44. Interview with Nishamalee Perera, Tholangamuwa, Dedigama, 27 February 2011.
45. CSDS. *State of Democracy in South Asia*, Oxford University Press, 2008; Social Indicator, "Democracy in Post-War Sri Lanka", Colombo: Social Indicator-Centre for Policy Alternatives, 2011; Social Indicator, "The Sri Lankan Voter and the April 2004 Elections—Wave 1", Colombo: Social Indicator-Centre for Policy Alternatives, March 2004.

References

Bastian, Sunil. 2007. Politics and Power in the Market Economy. In *Power and Politics: In the Shadow of Sri Lanka's Armed Conflict*, ed. Camilla Orjuela, 101–125. Sida Studies No. 25. Sida.

Berenschot, W.J. 2009. *Riot Politics: Communal Violence and State-Society Mediation in Gujarat, India*. Unpublished PhD thesis, University of Amsterdam.

Birch, Anthony. 1993. *The Concepts and Theories of Modern Democracy*. London: Routledge.

Bourdieu, Pierre. 1977. *Outline of a Theory of Practice*. Cambridge: Cambridge University Press.

———. 1984. *Distinction: A Social Critique of the Judgment of Taste*. Cambridge, MA: Harvard University Press.

———. 1990. *The Logic of Practice*. Stanford, CA: Stanford University Press.

———. 1998. *Practical Reason*. On the Theory of Action, Cambridge: Polity Press.

Bourdieu, P., and L.J.D. Wacquant. 1992. *An Invitation to Reflexive Sociology*. Cambridge: Polity Press.

Central Bank of Sri Lanka. 2010. *Annual Report 2010*. Colombo: Central Bank.

Centre for the Study of Developing Societies. 2008. *State of Democracy in South Asia*. New Delhi: Oxford University Press.

Chandra, Kanchan. 2004. *Why Ethnic Parties Succeed: Patronage and Ethnic Head Count in India*. Cambridge: Cambridge University Press.

Chatterjee, P. 2004. *The Politics of the Governed: Reflections on Popular Politics in Most of the World*. New York: Colombia University Press.

Chibber, P., and M. Torcal. 1997. Elite Strategy, Social Cleavages and Party Systems in a New Democracy: Spain. *Comparative Political Studies* 30 (1): 27–54.

de Silva, K.M. 1998. *Reaping the Whirlwind*. New Delhi: Penguin Books India (P) Ltd.

DeVotta, Niel. 2006. Ethnolinguistic Nationalism and Ethnic Conflict in Sri Lanka. In *Politics of Conflict and Peace in Sri Lanka*, ed. P. Sahadevan and Neil DeVotta. New Delhi: Manak Publications Pvt. Ltd.

———. 2007. *Sinhala Buddhist Nationalist Ideology: Implications for Politics and Conflict Resolution*, Washington, DC: East-West Center.

Downs, Anthony. 1957. An Economic Theory of Political Action in a Democracy. *The Journal of Political Economy* 65 (2) (April): 135–150.

Duverger, Maurice. 1954. *Political Parties, Their Organisation and Activity in the Modern State*. London: Methen & Co. Ltd; New York: Wiley.

Fernando, T., and F. Farook. 2000. Echoes of Zimbabwe Roar in Negombo. *Sunday Times*, 11 June. http://www.sundaytimes.lk/000611/news2.html. Accessed 28 October 2009.

Giddens, Anthony. 1984. *The Constitution of Society: Outline of the Theory of Structuration*. Oxford: Polity Press.

Gunasekara, T. 1992. Democracy, Party Competition and Leadership: The Changing Power Structure in a Sinhalese Community. In *Agrarian Change in Sri Lanka*, ed. James Brow and Joe Weeramunda, 229–260. New Delhi, Newbury Park/London: Sage Publications.

———. 1994. *Hierarchy and Egalitarianism: Caste, Class and Power in Sinhalese Pleasant Society*. London: The Athlone Press.

Gunasinghe, N. 1990. *Changing Socio-Economic Relations in the Kandyan Cuntryside*. Colombo: Social Scientists' Association.

Hettige, S. 1984. *Wealth, Power and Prestige: Emerging Patterns of Social Inequality in a Peasant Context*. Colombo: Ministry of Higher Education.

Husserl, E. 1970. *Logical Investigations*, trans. D. Carr. New York: Humanities Press.

International IDEA. 2002. Voter Turnout Since 1945: A Global Report. http://www.idea.int/publications/vt/upload/VT_screenopt_2002.pdf. Accessed 28 May 2013.

Jayanntha, D. 1992. *Electoral Allegiance in Sri Lanka*. Cambridge: Cambridge University Press.

Jayasuriya, L. 2000. *Welfarism and Politics in Sri Lanka*. Perth: School of Social Work and Social Policy, University of Western Australia.

Jenkins, Richard. 2002. *Pierre Bourdieu*. Revised. London: Routledge.

Jiggins, J. 1979. *Caste and the Family in the Politics of the Sinhalese 1947 to 1976*. London: Cambridge University Press.

Jupp, J. 1978. *Sri Lanka: Third World Democracy*. London: Cass.

Kearny, R.N. 1973. *The Politics of Ceylon (Sri Lanka)*. Ithaca and London: Cornell University Press.

Kitschelt, Herbert, and I. Steven Wilkinson. 2007. Citizen-Politician Linkage: An Introduction. In *Patrons Clients and Policies, Patterns of Democratic Accountability and Political Competition*, ed. Herbert Kitschelt and I. Steven Wilkinson. Cambridge: Cambridge University Press.

Kirchheimer, O. 1966. The Transformation of Western European Party Systems. In *Political Parties and Political Development*, ed. J. La Palombara and M. Weiner, 177–199. Princeton, NJ: Princeton University Press.

Leiserson, A. 1958. *Parties and Politics: An Institutional and Behavioral Approach*. New York: Alfred A. Knopf Publishers.

Lipset, S.M., and S. Rokkan. 1967. *Party Systems and Voter Alignments: A Cross-National Perspective*. New York: The Free Press.

Macy, M.W. 1997. Identity, Interest and Emergent Rationality: An Evolutionary Synthesis. *Rationality and Society* 9 (November): 427–448.

Maton, Karl. 2008. Habitus. In *Pierre Bourdieu: Key Concepts*, ed. Michael Grenfell. Durham: Acumen.

Melis, M.M., Milanga Abeysuriya and Nilakshi De Silva. 2006. Putting Land First? Exploring the Links between Land and Poverty. In *Centre for Poverty*

Research, Symposium on Poverty Research in Sri Lanka. Colombo: Centre for Poverty Analysis.

Moore, M. 1985. *The State and Peasant Politics in Sri Lanka*. Cambridge: Cambridge University Press.

Oberschall, A. and H. Kim, 1996, "Identity and Action," *Mobilization: An International Quarterly*, vol. 1, March, 63–86.

Ranugge, S., ed. 2000. *State*. Bureaucracy and Development, Delhi: Macmillan.

Ritzer, George. 1996. *Sociological Theory*. New York: The McGraw-Hill Companies Inc.

Robinson, M.S. 1975. *Political Structure in a Changing Sinhalese Village*. Cambridge: Cambridge University Press.

Richardson, Jr., John M.. 2005. *Paradise Poisoned: Learning about Conflict, Terrorism and Development from Sri Lanka's Civil Wars*, Kandy: International Centre for Ethnic Studies.

Sen, Amartya. 1999. *Development as Freedom*. Oxford: Oxford University Press.

Social Indicator. 2011. *Democracy in Post-War Sri Lanka*. Colombo: Social Indicator-Centre for Policy Alternatives.

Spencer, Jonathan. 1990. *A Sinhala Village in a Time of Trouble, Politics and Change in Rural Sri Lanka*. Delhi: Oxford University Press.

Shastri, Amitha. 1983. The Political Economy of Intermediate Regimes: The Case of Sri Lanka. *South Asia Bulletin*, III (2): 1–14.

Uyangoda, Jayadeva. 1998. *Studies in Caste and Social Justice in Sri Lanka: Caste in Sinhalese Society, Culture and Politics*. Unpublished manuscript. Colombo: Social Scientists' Association.

———. 2010. Politics of Political Reform—A Key Theme in the Contemporary Conflict. In *Power and Politics: In the Shadow of Sri Lanka's Armed Conflict*, ed. Camilla Orjuela, 29–78. Sida Studies No. 25. Sida.

———. 2012. The State in Post-Colonial Sri Lanka: Trajectories of Change. In *The Political Economy of Environment and Development in a Globalized World: Exploring Frontiers*, ed. D.J. Kjosavik and Paul Vedeld, 345–373. Colombo: Social Scientists' Association.

Venugopal, R. 2011. The Politics of Market Reform at a Time of Ethnic Conflict: Sri Lanka in the Jayewardene Years. In *Liberal Peace in Question: Politics of State and Market Reform in Sri Lanka*, ed. Kristian Stokke and Jayadeva Uyangoda, 63–76. New York and London: Anthem Press.

Warnapala, W.A.W., and D.E. Woodsworth. 1987. *Welfare as Politics in Sri Lanka*. Quebec: Centre for Developing-Area Studies, McGill University.

Weerakoon, T.S. 1997. Management Turnaround of a Public Enterprise: A Sri Lankan Case Study. *Asian Journal of Public Administration* 19 (1): 102–122.

Wilson, A.J. 1975. *Electoral Politics in an Emergent State: The Ceylon General Election of May 1970*. London: Cambridge University Press.

Woodward, Calvin A. 1969. *The Growth of a Political System in Ceylon*. Cambridge: Cambridge University Press.

CHAPTER 5

Examining Party Allegiance

Introduction

The term 'party allegiance' is often used casually to cover a broad range of phenomena in reference to the relationship between a political party and the citizen. It varies from party functionary (rank and file), to party activist and party sympathizer, to the wavering voter. Hence, it is necessary to unravel a great many misconceptions with regard to the term party allegiance that will in turn allow us to understand the party-voter relationship. Accordingly, this section attempts to examine how party allegiance to the UNP and SLFP is formed and sustained over time in Sinhalese constituencies. In the case of these two political parties, Uyangoda (2012: 164) refers to them as 'catch-all' parties[1]; 'party allegiance' is given less attention and is often misinterpreted as voting behaviour. This section shows the nuanced difference between voting and party allegiance and discusses how party allegiance is formed and sustained by the two parties. I previously focused on the agency of the voter in arriving at his or her voting decision. This section will focus mainly on the agency of the political party in influencing the electoral decision of the voter. Thereby, I argue here that in the process of mobilizing electoral support, the two parties form 'party allegiance' amongst their constituencies. However, party allegiance is not an objective that the UNP and SLFP aim to achieve

© The Author(s), under exclusive license to Springer Nature Singapore Pte Ltd. 2022
P. Peiris, *Catch-All Parties and Party-Voter Nexus in Sri Lanka*, Politics of South Asia,
https://doi.org/10.1007/978-981-16-4153-4_5

in their functions; it is rather a by-product of the electoral organizing strategies and election propaganda strategies of the two parties that aim to influence the voting decision of voters at elections.

DEFINING PARTY ALLEGIANCE

Given the ambiguity of the term in popular usage of politics as well as amongst some scholars of political parties, it is important to define the term 'party allegiance' as a point of departure in this study. Allegiance to a particular party involves far more than merely voting for a party. Party allegiance can be construed as a citizen's desire to be bound (emotionally) to a particular course of action and subscribe to a policy or policies of a party. In this case, a citizen's allegiance can be a mixture of several dispositions such as faith, devotion, commitment, cooperation and even the willingness to resort to violence on behalf of the party. However, a survey of literature on political parties indicates that scholars have treated party allegiance and electoral allegiance as synonyms (e.g. Woodward 1969; Kearney 1973; Jupp 1978; Jiggins 1979; Weiner 2006). Of course, electoral allegiance of the voter influences the electoral performance of a party and is therefore more visible than the attribute of party allegiance. However, electoral affiliation should not be regarded as a measure of party allegiance for three principal reasons: (i) electoral allegiance captures only the preferences of those who have voted at a particular election and does not reflect the views of those who refrained from voting at a particular election, (ii) it is not completely correct to consider everyone who voted for a party at a particular election as loyalists of that party and (iii) electoral allegiance reflects transitory support of the voter for a particular political party at a particular moment, which is not quite the same as party allegiance, which is a phenomenon that could last a comparatively longer time. From society to society or from one party system to another, the distance between party allegiance and electoral allegiance can and indeed does vary. However, in a society such as that in Sri Lanka, it is important to recognize the difference between party allegiance and electoral allegiance when inquiring into the party-voter relationship. I use the term 'party loyalty' to refer to party allegiance.

VOTING FOR A PARTY VS. PARTY ALLEGIANCE

The act of 'voting' produces two distinct outcomes, namely, election of a politician and election of a political party. It is correct to say that electing a politician of a particular party also results in the election of the party to which the particular politician belongs. Nevertheless, under the proportional representation system, casting a ballot for a particular party does not necessarily imply voting for the politician of that electorate, unless the voter chooses him/her specifically. Technically, it is the political party that selects the candidate to contest the election. In this context, it has been the common practice for political parties to interpret election results as expressions of party allegiance in general. In studies of electoral behaviour scholars in general have interpreted the electoral support a particular political party receives at an election as party allegiance (e.g. Woodward 1969; Kearney 1973; Jupp 1978; Jiggins 1979; Weiner 2006). There is no doubt that many who cast their vote for a particular party in an election do extend their loyalty to the party as well. Especially, the existence of party allegiance can be assumed amongst a majority of voters who vote for political parties that are in the Opposition. However, it is not always correct to infer voting patterns as patterns of party allegiance. There are instances where the voter who extends allegiance to a particular party votes for a different party or candidate in other elections. Similarly, all voters who vote for a particular party cannot be considered as loyalists of that party. This may appear contradictory. Nevertheless, in practice, one can find individuals who make a strategic decision to vote for one party while being emotionally close to another party. There are many reasons to do so, especially in the case of voters who support 'catch-all' parties such as the UNP and SLFP. Political parties contest elections at different levels such as Presidential, Parliamentary and Provincial and Local Councils. At different levels, the prominence received by the political party as against its local candidate can vary for multiple reasons. First, parties adopt different organizing strategies and varying degrees of emphasis at different elections. For example, a Presidential election is usually organized by a centralized campaign committee of the Presidential candidate, which overrides the organization structure of the political party the candidate represents.[2] Hence, the Presidential candidate receives greater attention than the party at a Presidential election. Candidates form new alliances across party lines and present their own manifesto independently of their own party.[3] It is often the Parliamentary election that requires the specific and intense focus on the political party. In this instance, electorate organizers are in charge of mobilizing the entire party organization in the electorate. In Provincial and Local Council elections, the party organization structure of the electorate is not utilized fully. In fact parties often encourage their candidates to campaign in their individual capacity, as at the local-level candidates need to obtain a fairly small number of votes and they often contest individually with or without the effective support of the party organizational structure.[4] Therefore, the role of the voter and the perception of the voter drastically differ at different levels of election.

Hence, voters device varying voting strategies at different elections, even independently of their party allegiance. This explains the possibility for an individual to vote for different parties at different elections while remaining loyal to a particular political party. During the Weligama Local Council elections, I interviewed Hemal Gunasekara, a Parliamentarian and the Kamburupitiya SLFP organizer, whose house is located in the Weligama electorate.[5] I witnessed him advising his Local Council candidates who were in the middle of their electoral campaign. Offering specific advice to one candidate privately—his personal choice for the Kamburupitiya Pradeshiya Sabha Chairman—he said:

> You must work hard [referring to the election campaign] as the other fellow [another candidate who just left the place to campaign] has a big family network in the electorate. He will get more votes making it difficult to appoint you as the Chairperson. In Local Council elections what matters the most is the family and kinship.

Chamila Lorenzo, a UNP Local Council member in Weligama, also confirms that at Local Council elections, family and kinship matter a great deal.[6] According to him, parties are very conscious about this fact when appointing candidates for wards. The party appoints candidates in such a manner that allows the prominent kinship group or caste group to be represented in each ward. Therefore, often both the UNP and SLFP put forward candidates from the same family, caste group or community in the ward. I have presented evidence indicating that both parties use individuals of the same family (kinship group) and caste group as their local leaders. They often contest for local government elections eventually. It is clear that people sometimes (especially at Local and Provincial

Council elections) vote for politicians outside their party allegiance. In other words, electoral allegiance and party allegiance are not always the same, although it can be a similar phenomenon. Even though this difference has not been explicitly recognized or mentioned, Dilesh Jayanntha (1992) termed his scholarly intervention as 'electoral allegiance in Sri Lanka' instead of 'party allegiance'. There is no doubt about the importance and practical relevance of studying electoral allegiance. However, it is important to stress the difference between party allegiance and electoral allegiance when dissecting the party-voter relationship.

As illustrated previously, not all people who vote for the UNP or SLFP (or for a politician from one of the parties) can be considered as loyalists of the two parties. Clientelistic politics, life circumstance of the voter and several other issues such as campaign strategy of politicians can also influence the voting decision and distinguish it from the party loyalty of the voter. In addition, at every election, there is a substantial proportion of eligible voters who do not participate in voting due to other reasons. Often loyalists of a political party who are popularly seen to be a loser at an upcoming election shows less enthusiasm to participate at that election. Therefore, at an election where the result is highly predictable, the voter turnout tends to drop drastically. For example, despite the high voter turnout (74.49%), at the Presidential election held in January 2010, only 61.26% of eligible voters turned out at the Parliamentary election that was held a mere two months later. Therefore, it is possible for party loyalists (especially those with less chances of winning at the election) to not turn out for the polls. These voters are not reflected in the electoral result. This further emphasizes the difference between party allegiance and electoral support. In addition, party allegiance is a comparatively long-term process that can be explained through Bourdieu's concept of doxa.[7] People inherit allegiance to a particular political party from their families and often pass it on to the next generation. Those who extend allegiance to a particular party often remain consistent to that loyalty without questioning it. Even though party allegiance can shift from one party to another, the change does not happen as often as every election. Therefore, party allegiance should be understood to be independent of the electoral choice of voters. This distinction is crucial in understanding the party-voter relationship of parties such as the UNP and SLFP.

PARTY ALLEGIANCE AS A NON-HOMOGENEOUS CATEGORY

I have defined 'party allegiance' as a composition of several types of loyalty—faith, devotion, commitment, etc. Those who extend allegiance to a political party can exhibit either one or many such loyal dispositions. In this backdrop, varying degrees of loyalty are displayed by those who extend allegiance to a political party. Party allegiance in militant parties, cadre-based parties and extremist parties can often be considered far more homogeneous than that in catch-all parties such as the UNP and SLFP. Levels of party allegiance amongst supporters of a given political party can be summarized in three broadly defined categories: Active party loyalists, passive party loyalists and pragmatist voters.

Active Party Loyalists

They have deep loyalty to the party and actively participate in party affairs and are recognized for these attributes as 'active loyalists' of the political party. Often they are strongly linked to the village political actor network of the political party. They often sponsor the activities of the party either through personal resources or by contributing their time and labour. They consistently vote for their party irrespective of whether it is in the government or the Opposition. Even under severe pressure, at times, when the party is in the Opposition, these loyalists do not desert the party. Parties such as the UNP and SLFP rely on these loyalists as the main pillars of their village party organizing structure. A retired school principal, Dassanayake from Dedigama, who shared his experience with me said that there were only a few SLFP supporters in the area at the time.[8] He and his other SLFP stalwart friends in the electorate had to act on behalf of the party during 17 years of UNP regime. While he had to face numerous difficulties at the hands of local UNP leaders, his allegiance to his party remained strong and consistent. Kulasiri is a close associate of former Dedigama electoral organizers Nissanka Wijerathna and his son Manoda Wijerathna.[9] Despite serious economic difficulties, he still remains a supporter of the UNP in Wathdeniya, Dedigama. Even after Manoda Wijerathna crossed over to the ruling UPFA coalition, Kulasiri did not abandon his party. His deep commitment to it remained intact. He and a few likeminded active loyalists of the UNP provided leadership to the silent UNP supporters in the village. They continued to lead party activities with minimal resources. They often had to face intimidation and violence by the ruling SLFP supporters in the village. On the eve of the 2010 Parliamentary election, his small shop was attacked by supporters of the Chairman of the Warakapola Pradeshiya Sabha. The proportion of active loyalists of both the UNP and SLFP is considered very small. To retain their support, parties are not required to resort to party propaganda or offer patronage goods. However, even when the party cannot offer any special incentive to retain allegiance, it is careful to avoid hurting their interests. Both parties are concerned with keeping this core support well cared for in the party organization at ground level.

Passive Party Loyalists

Those who are loosely connected to the party's network of village political actors, but express allegiance to the party fall into this category. These loyalists differ from the first category as their allegiance is not as visible as that of the 'active loyalists'. However, they retain a deep sense of loyalty towards their party. This loyalty does not easily fade, irrespective of whether their party is in power or in the Opposition. Often their allegiance is not secret amongst the community. Yet, they hardly come forward on behalf of the party. Unlike active loyalists, they are either not ready or cannot afford to be victimized or intimidated by the violence of the party in power within the electorate. Lal Hettiarachchi, a poor labourer from Weligama town, continued to support the SLFP (in his terms 'the party of Blue') despite not having any support from the politicians of the electorate.[10] He was disheartened with SLFP politicians after being cheated by the most senior SLFP politician in the town. Nevertheless, he continues his allegiance to the SLFP. He does not take part in any campaign activities or openly work for any SLFP candidate. Senevirathne is a retired senior civil servant from Kelaniya.[11] He does not speak much about his party allegiance and does not participate in party activities in his area. Yet, the UNP party network in Gonawala, Kelaniya, recognizes him as one of its key supporters. Understandably, he finds it difficult to participate in local party work, which is in the hands of less privileged and less-educated party supporters, while he is a retired senior civil servant. Those who are in this category of 'passive loyalty' can approach politicians of rival parties if they need their support/mediation to receive state patronage. Unlike 'active loyalist', changing allegiance is much easier for the passive loyalist. It does not cost much for them to switch sides, and hence, the village party network of the rival political party formulates its clientelistic programmes aimed at weaning away these passive loyalists of the rival party. Those in a state of 'strong dependency'—as discussed before—can fall prey to the electoral strategies of the ruling party and surrender their votes to receive material benefits. However, very often, they return to their old party once they feel that the new party cannot offer them any further benefits. Sriyalatha is a poor single mother of three. Explaining her disappointment with the ruling coalition, she said that she was from a UNP-oriented family but supported the SLFP at the recent elections as her young son was promised a job by SLFP politicians.[12] She says that she felt cheated as her son failed to secure a job and her family did not get any assistance in return for their support to the ruling party at several elections. Since, her son had joined the security forces as a soldier she does not think she needs any further assistance. She said that she will return to the UNP despite it being in the Opposition. The field research of this study suggests, despite the absence of systematically collected empirical data, that a majority of UNP and SLFP voters fall in to this 'passive loyalist' category.

Pragmatist Voters

They do not offer allegiance to a particular political party. They vote strictly on the basis of party policies or for the material benefits that the party has promised or already provided. Pragmatist voters do not maintain long-term links with the village political actor network of any political party. They prefer to evaluate the parties at each election and decide on their electoral support. Some pragmatists look for the policy programmes that parties put forward. Some look for personal benefits that each party promises and the credibility of those promises. Either way, pragmatist voters are those who seek utility maximization as described in Downs's Rational Choice Theory. However, the proportion of prag-matists who evaluate the policy programmes of the party—UNP and SLFP—is extremely small as compared to those who evaluate the potential material benefits. A young security guard, Kamal, explaining his frustra-tion with these parties, stated that "politicians from both the parties are the same and whoever comes to power will look after their well-being (*"Unuth ekai munuth ekai. Kavuru awath un balanne un hadenna"*).[13] He said that he would vote for any party if he got something in return. He believes that election time presents the only opportunity to get something from politicians. Making a similar point, Wilfred Karunarathne said he came to meet Hemal Gunasekara to get a job for his son-in-law.[14] He said he received his job (now retired) from the UNP during Minister Jayewickrema's time, and he managed to get jobs for his two daughters from Minister Mahinda Wijesekara under the SLFP government. Karunarathne believes that the only way to get a job is to get it through politicians, and he was blunt in saying that his association with politics is only to get something done. In response to pragmatist voters, both parties offer clientelist programmes on the eve of elections.

These three categories capture almost all existing practices that determine party-voter relationships. There are people who claim that they make their electoral decision based on the manifesto or the past performance of parties and politicians. However, despite many such 'politically correct' claims, the actual practice of such laudable convictions is limited to a numerically negligible proportion. It should be noted that a citizen who falls into any one of the three categories would not remain static. In response to his/her life conditions at a given moment, they would adopt certain kinds of social practices. These would determine whether the person remains an active party loyalist, a passive party loyalist or a pragmatist voter. On the other hand, these three categories do not have fixed and well-defined boundaries.

FORMING PARTY ALLEGIANCE

As shown above, political parties in Sri Lanka, especially the UNP and SLFP, do not secure the allegiance of a person purely because it managed to secure his/her vote at an election. As has been argued, party allegiance is a deeper commitment. It is necessary to inquire into how allegiance to a party is formed and maintained. As discussed previously, the UNP and SLFP have not maintained starkly different policies, and the initial differences faded in the 1990s. In addition, the policy positions of the two parties have sometimes converged and sometimes diverged depending on the party leadership. Especially at the electorate level, the differences of the bases of the village political leadership that existed in the 1950s have disappeared to a great extent. Therefore, in the absence of such distinct and diverse identities, how do the parties attract the allegiance of the Sinhalese community? In other words, why does one choose to extend his/her allegiance to one and not the other? I have made it clear that the two political parties focus on maximizing their votes rather than on building a strong base of party loyalists. The base of party loyalists of the two parties is mainly a by-product of the campaign that aims to maximize votes and not the result of a calculated party strategy. Building a loyalist base was never a priority of either party. The process of forming party allegiance of both the UNP and SLFP will be discussed in detail in the following section.

The conceptualization depicted in Fig. 5.1 can be used to summarize the formation of party allegiance of the two political parties—the UNP and SLFP. This conceptualization summarizes the fieldwork of this study on how party allegiance to the two political parties is formed. Assume that a particular society consists of 'loyalists' (active or passive) of party A and 'others' (who support any other party or no party at all). Loyalists of party A and the 'others' are subject to the party organizing strategy and the electoral propaganda strategy of party A, as well as of the other parties. For simplicity, assume that loyalists of party A and the other parties are exclusively subject to the influence/pressure of party A. In this scenario, the allegiance of the loyalists of party A will not necessarily be tested

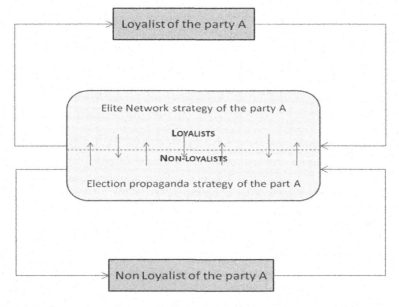

Fig. 5.1 Formation of party allegiance

by the influence of its own party's electoral and party organizing strategies. However, the party allegiance of loyalists of other parties is tested by the electoral strategies of this party A. In this process, party A emerges successful in wooing some loyalists from other parties and shifting their electoral allegiance towards itself. Those who switch to party A during this process can switch back to their old party at the next election. However, some of them who switch sides to party A can continue to remain loyal to the party and increase their allegiance to the new party.

Sumanadasa Silva, a poor labourer from Kelaniya, has been a strong UNP supporter since 1977 despite his father, siblings and entire village remaining staunch SLFPers.[15] He says that he decided to vote for the UNP at the 1977 election, and since then he has never voted for any other party. According to him, he used the 1977 election to take revenge against the SLFP-led coalition, as he was subjected to humiliation and harassment at the hands of SLFPers despite being a member of an SLFP family. Now he is retired and most of his relatives in the village actively support the SLFP, but he continues his allegiance unchanged. Unlike Sumanadasa Silva, Jeyraj Chandrasekara is a highly educated elite from Gonawela, Kelaniya.[16] According to him, his grandfather was the main SLFP point person in the village during the 1950s and 1960s. Chandrasekara was exposed to politics through his grandfather; however, he decided to extend his allegiance to the UNP in the 1977 election as he was heartbroken by the fact that the United Front (UF) government's economic policies had prevented him from going abroad after leaving school, as had many of his other friends. Since 1977, he considered the UNP as his party and never felt that he should shift allegiance. Tikiribanda Gunapala is a graduate and retired government servant from Warakapola, Dedigama.[17] He decided to vote for the SLFP coalition in 1965 despite his family being known supporters of the UNP in the village. He said he was attracted to Leftist ideas during that time and decided to vote for the SLFP in his first election. Since then he has continued to vote for the SLFP.

Priyantha Amarasekara received his hospital labourer job from a UNP minister in the electorate during the 1980s in appreciation for his work in the election campaign of the minister.[18] Despite being from an SLFP family in the village, he and his sister joined the election campaign of the UNP minster as it was their only way to secure jobs. Since then, Amarasekara continued to support the UNP at every election until 2010. He said it was difficult to vote for the UNP this time (2010 general election) as it was the SLFP, under the leadership of President Mahinda Rajapaksa, that managed to end the 30-year-war with the LTTE (Liberation Tigers of Tamil Eelam). However, two years after the 2010 election, he was utterly disappointed with the SLFP-led UPFA government and said he would not vote for this government again. Bandula Liyanage, a middle-aged school teacher from Midigama, asked how one could vote for the UNP, as there were huge cut-outs of Mahinda Rajapaksa with soldiers, and various pictures depicting the war victory around the polling booth and on the way to the polling station.[19] Hence, Liyanage says that many UNPers who did not want to vote for the UPFA decided to stay at home.[20]

The research in all three locations shows that the influence of the village political actor network is not usually confined to the time of elections. It continues even beyond them. However, the village political actor network of the party intensifies the pressure on voters during the election campaign. Parties are primarily focused on increasing their share of votes by drawing the votes of loyalist as well as non-loyalist blocs. They are not focused on developing a loyalist base for the party. Although voters are constantly subject to the influence of rival parties during times of elections, the switching of loyalty is not a regular occurrence. Often, as the above interviews demonstrate, the traffic is towards the ruling party or parties in a ruling coalition. Those currently in power have the resources to execute a strong party organizing and propaganda campaign as compared to the party or parties in the Opposition.[21]

INHERITING PARTY ALLEGIANCE OF THE FAMILY

Like religion, everyone inherits a political party from parents. If someone says he/she does not have a party it's a lie. (Wijethunge, Chairman of the Warakapola Pradeshiya Sabha)

While this statement could be an exaggeration, I assume it is not totally devoid of relevance and truth. As was shown before, many inherit party allegiance from their parents and often pass it on to the next generation. Due to the family centric nature of party allegiance that has developed over time, the loyalty of a household is hardly a secret in the closely knit village society. This public knowledge usually reinforces the individual's allegiance further. Such a voter finds it difficult to renegotiate his/her party allegiance. To some, party allegiance is an honour. Others find it as hard as the dogma of a religion inherited from his/her ancestors and consider it betrayal to change it. For yet others, it helps assert their position in the neighbourhood or work place and is therefore to be defended at any cost. If the party they owe allegiance to is not in power, these families come under harassment by the ruling party and are subjected to various forms of discrimination. Political victimization in the village or work place due to perceived allegiance to a political party is a common grievance when the party finds itself in the Opposition. Intimidation and harassment by ruling party supporters often serve to galvanize party loyalty instead of undermining it. The common feeling amongst almost all those interviewed for this research was that the high visibility of family based party support has faded to a great extent in the past decades. One of the leading political economists sharing his field experience made the point that a few decades ago, he went to villages with an informant on the eve of elections to get a sense of the election results.[22] Today, he finds it very difficult to gauge the party allegiance of villagers as it was no longer patently visible.

I used survey data to explore the family connection in party allegiance. It will help us to expand the microscopic view already presented in a macro picture. The results of the "Post-War Democracy in Sri Lanka" survey by Social Indicator provide valuable insights into voter behaviour amongst citizens (Sinhalese in this analysis) in relation to voting practices within families. Of course, voting habit is not exactly party allegiance. The long-term electoral allegiance of a person should provide valuable insights into party allegiance. This survey provides data on the voting habits of individuals and their recollection of the voting habits of their fathers. It was earlier argued that a father or husband enjoys considerable weight as an agency in determining the electoral decision of the household in the rural Sinhalese society (this could be so with other socio-cultural groups as well). Therefore, if the father in a family has voted for one party in almost all elections, we can assume that the family supports that particular party. Exceptions are possible but rare. The survey findings provide data on: (i) whether the respondent's father voted almost always for the same political party or not, (ii) whether the respondent and the father voted for the same party and (iii) whether the respondent almost always voted for the same party. Answers to these questions can provide valuable insight into the history of the family's voting behaviour. The following diagram illustrates the findings of the survey and demonstrates how the influence of party allegiance of the family has impacted on the electoral behaviour of the individual.

The above table attempts to summarize the survey data on voting patterns linking respondents and their fathers. The first column of the table shows (as recalled by the respondent) whether the father often voted for the same political party or not. The second column indicates whether the respondent and the father voted for the same party. However, percentages are derived only from those respondents whose fathers always or often claimed to have voted for the same party. The third column shows whether respondents have always or often voted for the same party.

The results show that 78.6% of voters claim that their father almost always voted for the same party, while 21.4% stated that the father casts his vote for different parties at different elections, or that she/he does not remember the father's electoral choice. Children also tend to vote for the father's choice of a party in families where the father has supported a specific party in almost all elections. For example, according to the survey findings (Fig. 5.2), 69.9% of children whose fathers have often or always voted for the same party, also vote for the same party that their father voted for. In addition, survey findings show that like their fathers, children too continued to vote for the same party in almost all elections. As shown in table, 93.8% of children who vote for the same party as their father claim that they too always or often voted for the same party (which is the party that their father always or often voted for). Only a negligible percentage (6.2%) of children who vote for the same party as their fathers state that they did not always or often vote for the same party. Even when those children switched their support to another party, the survey reveals that a majority of them would vote for the new party in almost all elections. Further, 67.5% say that despite not having followed their father's footsteps, children of those who have always or often voted for the same party state that they maintain strong allegiance (vote always or often) to their party.

Tikiribanda is a *Goigama* peasant from Waddeniya. His family had been strong supporters of the UNP and connected to the UNP's village elite network in which Balin was also a member. Tikiribanda was a close aid of Manoda Wijerathna who crossed over to the SLFP in 2006. Yet, Tikiribanda did not switch allegiance to the SLFP, despite his old master, a minister in the SLFP government, giving a job to his wife at the Kegalle National Hospital. In the verandah of Tikiribanda's humble home, a

Father's voting behaviour	Did your father and you vote for the same party?	Your voting behaviour
Almost always voted for the same party (78.6%)	Yes (69.9%)	Almost always voted for the same party (93.8%)
		Didn't always vote for the same party (6.2%)
	No (27.5%)	Almost always voted for the same party (67.5%)
		Didn't always vote for the same party (32.5%)
Didn't always vote for the same party or I do not know (21.4%)		Almost always voted for the same party (54.2%)
		Didn't always vote for the same party (45.8%)

Fig. 5.2 Influence of family's voting behaviour history on individual electoral choice

portrait of Manoda Wijerathna hangs alongside wedding photographs of family members and deceased relatives.

The children of weak-party loyalists tend to remain comparatively less committed to one political party. For example, only 54.2% of those from families that had weak-party allegiance stated that they voted for one particular party in almost all elections. This shows that families that associated with a political party as a faith or with a strong allegiance passed such behaviour onto their children. Weerasekara of Kelaniya provided an interesting explanation of this phenomenon.[23]

.... we all have a religion and we practice various religious rituals. Not only do we practice those rituals by ourselves but we also train our children to observe them. For example, we have been going to Katharagama as an annual pilgrimage for years. We have been taking our son also, as any parent would do, on these annual pilgrimages. Now he is in his twenties and one day when he has a family, he will also continue these rituals.

Attitudes towards political parties are also formed in a similar manner. Sometimes we take our children to election rallies. We discuss politics and about our party at home. We decorate the neighbourhood with green flags and posters and invite politicians home. In all these activities we involve children who participate in various activities. Therefore, it is not surprising to see children too following in the footsteps of their parents.

Party Allegiance and the Influence of Electoral Strategies

Party allegiance formation cannot be solely attributed to family influence. If party allegiance is a family phenomenon, then no party would be able to draw new supporters or increase their support base. As shown in Fig. 5.2, not everyone, even in families that maintain long-term loyalty, would support the same party. While acknowledging the role of family influence in 'party allegiance formation', we also need to recognize other factors that contribute to it. Some voters extend allegiance to a political party contrary to the party affiliation of their family. When listening to the life experiences of people who switched their party allegiance or those who extended allegiance to a party for the first time, there emerges a general pattern in rationale behind that decision.

People decide to extend their electoral allegiance to a new party at a particular juncture in their life. This then gradually grows into party allegiance due to continuous association with that party. In the case of the UNP and SLFP, as the discussion in the previous sections suggests, it is the aspect of 'material interest' that triggers the decision to switch parties more than a person's 'identity interest'. Often, switching of party allegiance takes place when the person is engaged in the search of recognition and economic stability. For example, Balin and Siriwardane both moved in opposite directions when they were young and striving for recognition as new village leaders. Both the UNP and SLFP gave them the space and a platform to emerge as new village leaders. While people switch their electoral allegiance, they also begin to affirm deep loyalty for the party that addressed their most pressing needs such as jobs, houses and land. The following stories I collected during fieldwork provide valuable insights in support of these assertions.

The Story of Somalatha

Somalatha's story is an ideal illustration of what we have seen up to this point. Somalatha is the eldest sister in a SLFP family, and she switched allegiance to the UNP along with her sister. She was educated and was employed as an English stenographer at the electricity board. Her husband was a government executive who obtained employment through a left-leaning minister during the SLFP government. Following the electoral defeat of the SLFP in 1977, Somalatha's family, as with so many other SLFP-leaning families, had to struggle for access to government jobs and services with the UNP now in power. Due to her relatively high social standing in the neighbourhood as an English-educated woman, she managed to establish the first link to the UNP's elite network within the village. Gradually, she managed to get close to the Member of Parliament in the area who was also a cabinet minister in the UNP government of the time. She actively participated in the election campaigns of the politician and hosted several meetings at her home. She says that she did those things as one of her UNP neighbours advised her to do so in order to secure government jobs for her daughters who had completed their education. Following the electoral victory, many in the village who had worked for that politician were given jobs. Somalatha's eldest daughter and her niece also obtained government jobs. A few years later, she managed to find two other government jobs for her second daughter and her brother-in-law. In her eyes, these were critical achievements. According to her, government jobs are the best occupations for her children. They ensure job security and other social benefits such as loans and old-age pensions. In addition, government jobs bestow a higher status on her children, an important factor in marriage.

Somalatha and her family continued their allegiance to the UNP over the past 20 years in gratitude to the patronage her family enjoyed. Now her life conditions are far different from what they were in the mid-1980s when she sought the help of the UNP to resolve those pressing needs of her family. The three daughters are now married. They are economically settled. She now lives with one of her daughters in a new neighbourhood. She no longer associates with the UNP, except for the ritual telephone call she makes on *Sinhala Auvrudu* day (Sinhala New Year) to the politician of her old electorate.

The story of Somalatha is one amongst many that demonstrates how an average voter switches allegiance to a new party in order to address individual 'material interest'. Solving her pressing problems was what motivated her to change her allegiance to the party. Nevertheless, if not for the presence of an effective patronage network in the village, such a shift of allegiance would be less possible or even not probable at all. This story has many similarities with the stories of Balin Wickramasinghe and Siriwardane of Ragalakande. In the case of Balin Wickramasinghe, his father was a strong SLFP supporter from the *Wahumpura* caste. He was also a *chandiya* (thug) in the village who openly challenged the oppression of the *Goigama* caste that dominated UNP politics at the time. However, since Balin fell out with his father due to his choice of a bride, he was drawn to the UNP network that was led by *Goigama* elites. The District Revenue Officer (DRO) of Kegalle suggested to Balin that he assists Dudley Senanayake in his election campaign. The DRO had helped Balin to conduct social work in the village (giving Balin recognition in the village), and Balin responded positively to the request by the DRO. Since then, he became not only a supporter of the UNP but an active member of the UNP's elite network under three electorate organizers. This also illustrates that the desire to switch party allegiance is sparked at a particular point in a person's life, and an effective party organizing structure helps the individual take this otherwise difficult decision. The experience of Siriwardane of Ragalakanda also serves to further reinforce this point. Siriwardane is a member of a *Goigama* family of government bureaucrats with feudal ancestry. Given this background, the family network represented the UNP leadership in the village. However, the dazzling oratory and charismatic appeal of S.W.R.D. Bandaranaike excited Siriwardane while he was still a student. His attraction to Bandaranaike further deepened when he witnessed how the then UNP local leadership humiliated and harassed his hero during the 1952 election campaign in Dedigama. Despite the objections of his parents, he supported the SLFP, which was in its early stage and was also critical of the class that his family represented in the village. He, together with oppressed villagers, joined the SLFP and worked against the dominance of the UNP in the village. He successfully replaced the old feudal-minded leadership in the village. This marked the beginning of the switch of party allegiance of his family members and relatives to the SLFP.

Even though the critical point that triggers change of party allegiance is somewhat unpredictable, those moments occur under certain conditions that are determined by the electoral strategies of political parties, which can be conceptualized as 'electoral organizing strategies' of political parties. As in the case of conceiving a child where a womb is needed to provide the right conditions for conception and growth of the embryo, a random conceiving process occurs when political parties generate the right atmosphere through their electoral strategies. They trigger new conceptions in the form of crossovers to their party within the constituency. The concept of 'electoral strategies' needs to be discussed in some detail. It will enable us to understand the concepts of party allegiance and electoral allegiance while arriving at two distinct definitions of the two concepts.

ELECTORAL STRATEGIES

> Victory of an election depends 60% on party organizing and 40% on the campaign propaganda of the party and the politician (Saman Gamage, a former Local Council Chairman).[24]

This quote by a grassroots political activist serves to summarize the electoral strategies of the two main political parties. This comprises two principal components:

   i The party organizing strategy and
   ii Election campaign propaganda.

The first is a long-term strategy. Parties and politicians need to engage voters throughout the year irrespective of whether there is an election or not. This greatly depends on how well the party and the politician manage to establish and maintain an elite network in the electorate. In the case of the latter, party election campaign propaganda is usually aimed at a particular election. It lasts only for the duration of the election. As a former Chairman of the Weligama Pradeshiya Sabha, Saman Gamage, says, a successful election campaign requires the party to have a powerful party organizing structure and a strategy that couples it with effective election campaign propaganda. I previously examined the psyche of the voter, to understand the agency of the voter in the electoral decision. Here, I attempt to explain what parties and politicians do in order to garner votes and retain electoral allegiance by responding to the voter psyche.

Party Organizing as Electoral Strategy

A brief recapitulation of the core points on party organization strategy is helpful to describe the electoral strategies of the two parties and how they respond to the interests and attitudes of voters.

I previously argued that the party organization structure in the electorate is an informal one that is largely based on the village elite networks that spread across the electorate. Party branches and other ancillary organizations become visible and active when there is an election, and at other times, they are reduced to a mere network of socio-political actors in the electorate. Sociological stratifications such as ethnicity, religion, caste, class within the electorate define the boundaries of these village political actors. They are connected to powerful national elites through intermediates. I also showed that these networks are usually lubricated by the distribution of clientelist goods by electorate organizers. Electorate organizers form their party organization structure by giving leadership to the networks of these elites. Two concepts, 'oscillation' and 'transformation', introduced therein describe the changing dynamics of these village political actor networks. The concept of oscillation—that an object moves from one place to another and returns to the original place by travelling in the opposite direction—describes how the dynamics of party organization shift from an active and enlarged network to a weak and less visible organization depending on whether the party is in power or out of power. When a party is in power (even as part of a coalition), the party organization in the electorate becomes active with a large amount of supporters. It becomes very powerful as it often makes use of state authorities (police and local agents) and state resources for its party activities. However, when the party becomes an Opposition party, its supporters become hesitant to identify their party identity. Once it returns to the Opposition, the party loses access (authority over) to state authority and resources. However, the party organizations of both parties, the UNP and SLFP, oscillate in such a way that while one party enjoys strong and enlarged party organization, the other party experiences a weak-party organization with a shrinking network of village political actors.

The other concept introduced earlier was the 'transformation' of the party organization structure. Organizational structures of the two parties in the electorate transformed due to the introduction of the proportional electoral system and the position of the Executive President. As a result, the coherence of the party organization network in the electorate is diluted, and intraparty rivalry is intensified. Under the PR system, the structure of elite networks in electorates has become extremely complex. This has paved the way for a new breed of village elites to emerge over the traditional leaders who enjoyed their elite status due to their economic and cultural capital. With that recapitulation, I now proceed to discuss how parties and politicians use their party organization strategies as electoral strategies.

The party organization strategies at the electorate level of both the UNP and SLFP aim at maximizing votes instead of aggregating the interests of the constituency, as classical political party literature assumes (e.g. Duverger 1954; Leiserson 1958; Lipset and Rokkan 1967). Under the PR system, the architecture of the organizing network is mainly focused on collecting the maximum number of votes with a minimum outlay of resources. In this context, the question of the ability of a party organizer to make a meaningful representation to the constituency is often irrelevant. As mentioned, the party organization in the electorate does not maintain active party branches when there is no election to prepare for. Instead, a party organizer maintains a loosely connected network of village political actors to sustain the relationship with his/her electoral base. It is extremely important to have a vibrant and effective network of village political actors for a successful party organizer to maintain the supporters of the party and his/her personal followers. Through these networks, the party organizer addresses the needs of voters as well as potential voters. As pointed out earlier, by addressing the material interests of the voter, the party and the politician manage to address both material and identity interests of the voter. Clever politicians distribute material goods—such as houses, jobs, promotions, new roads—amongst their supporters in keeping with the social cleavages in the constituency, in such a manner that each social group feels that its interests have been served by the party organizer.

Augustine Daluwatta of Weligama, expressing his frustration with his party (UNP), said that there was no one available any longer for people to approach when they are harassed by the police.[25] He said that during Mahinda Wijesekara's time, UNPers in Weligama (referring to the fisher folk community living along the coastal belt) felt secure and empowered as their party organizer (Mahinda Wijesekara) was able to get his supporters released from police custody within a few hours of arrest. What Daluwatta emphasized was that party supporters expect their party organizer to be strong and active enough to mediate on behalf of them irrespective of their guilt or innocence. In this manner, the party organization through its local political actor network has sustained relations with its supporters. Of course, when parties are in power, they have ample resources to empower their village political actors to serve their party supporters and potential supporters. Therefore, as discussed before, when in power, the two parties distribute various forms of patronage. Many forms of techniques are used in the constituencies to sustain village political actor networks and to preserve the allegiance of supporters. Rathnayake of Dedigama is an opposition UNP member of the Warakapola Local Council.[26] He points to the *Gama Naguma* and *Maga Naguma* programmes of the SLFP-led UPFA coalition government as the best contemporary examples of patronage programmes. On the surface, they appear to be necessary programmes for development. In reality, they play a very important role in sustaining the village political actor network and helping supporters of the ruling party. The works of James Brow (1992) on *Agrarian Change and the Struggle for Community in Kukulewa* and Laksiri Jayasuriya's (2000) *Welfarism and Politics in Sri Lanka* explain the role played by those welfare programmes in strengthening the support bases of the two ruling parties—the UNP and SLFP.

Lalinda Edward is a popular teacher of private classes (a tuition master) from Gonawela, Kelaniya.[27] According to him, a road in his neighbourhood was recently carpeted by the Pradeshiya Sabha to benefit SLFP supporters and members of the ruling party in his neighbourhood. He said they made the request through individuals who liaise with the politicians at the Pradeshiya Sabha. Despite the preference indicated by the people in his neighbourhood to tar the road, the Pradeshiya Sabha laid concrete, according to Lalinda, as it was profitable for the contractors who sponsored politicians of the Local Council. Therefore, through these social programmes, the government was able to kill two birds with one stone; its development programmes provided opportunities for its local leadership to strengthen their own networks with state resources—in this case contracts.

However, being in power also has its disadvantages. Wielding power creates an endless string of issues that the party network has to solve. The practice of patronage politics results in disappointments amongst many while pleasing some. Therefore, the very strength of being the ruling party can be counterproductive when preparing for elections. Voters generally do not expect many material benefits from the party in the Opposition because it cannot deliver. It can only promise to deliver, in contrast to the party in power which already has the means to deliver at least in the eyes of its supporters. However, when these parties (UNP and SLFP) are in the Opposition, they use their village political actor networks, which consist of elites with substantial economic and social capital, to address the needs of their supporters as much as possible. Dassanayake, an old SLFP elite from Dedigama, described the 1977–1994 period[28] saying that they could not do much for the supporters of the SLFP because the UNP was very powerful. Many SLFPers joined the UNP or at least befriended UNP elites to avoid political victimization and gain some benefits.[29] The supporters of the SLFP understood that the SLFP elite network could not do much while being in the Opposition. Nevertheless, when an SLFP loyalist approached them for assistance, Dassanayake says that they endeavoured strongly to help the family or the person using their own connections. Sometimes they would introduce the person to the party hierarchy. Another example from Dedigama is Champika Premadasa, who is a businessman and the UNP Member of Parliament. He has provided many job opportunities for the youth of UNP families in his private capacity and using his personal contacts.[30] This demonstrates that even when in the Opposition, parties attempt to address the needs of their supporters. They are well aware of the fact that maintaining the patron-client relationship through the village political actor network of the party is crucial for future electoral campaigns. However, as argued earlier, patronage politics is largely effective amongst communities at the stage of *strong dependency* and not for those that are *independent* or in a stage of *weak dependency* where the material benefits provided have little impact.

Party organizers and village elites of the parties use innovative methods to sustain and expand their support base. An alternative mechanism is attending funerals in the constituency. Amongst Sinhalese (as perhaps with other communities in Sri Lanka), it is important to visit a funeral home to pay homage to the dead. Irrespective of whether the dead person or his family members are personally known, it is an accepted custom to visit the house of the bereaved. Often the bier is kept for a few days for people to visit and pay their last respects—or join in the rituals observed. On the other hand, who visits the funeral home, the frequency of visits and the number of visitors who pay their last respects are matters of great concern to the family of the bereaved as well as the village elites on both sides of the political divide. It is a measure of the status of the family in the village. It is also a measure of the concern and care shown by the party and politicians for the dead as well as for the family. Visiting funeral houses is almost an unwritten rule for politicians and is observed by every politician.[31] Hilary is a Tamil Christian from Kelaniya who maintains a close friendship with a number of UNP parliamentarians in the district.[32] He explained how the UNP maintained its support base in his middle-class urban neighbourhood. He said that he routinely informs his parliamentarian friends of every funeral in the village. According to Hilary, these politicians always visit those houses. These are gestures with great potential to earn future votes and support. A young boy from an extremely poor family in Weligama interrupted my interview with his mother to make the point that Minister Gajadeera will not get the votes of his family next time.[33] They had voted for the SLFP-led coalition of which Gajadeera was now a minister. The boy said that he did not have the courtesy to visit his grandmother's funeral. He praised Minister Mahinda Yapa Abeywardana for not only visiting his grandmother's funeral but also for sending his brother to visit as soon as he learned about the funeral.

Patronage politics favours the supporters of the ruling political party while discriminating against those who support the party in the Opposition. Loyalists of parties in the Opposition are not only deprived of equal access to state recourses and services but are also subject to intimidation and violence by supporters and leaders of the party in power. This point regarding political victimization has been observed and commented on by many scholars (Hettige 1984; Spencer 1990; Gunasekara 1992; Brow 1992). These discriminatory practices of the ruling party and the forms of harassment meted out to supporters of the rival party serve to further strengthen bonds amongst the loyalists of the Opposition political parties. In fact, it helps the Opposition political parties to sustain the allegiance of their supporters. The expansion of the Kelaniya temple area during the SLFP regime resulted in Wijethilake's parents losing their land.[34] This further strengthened their party allegiance to the UNP. Madanayake said that he was interdicted from his job at the weaving mill in the neighbourhood by the management affiliated to the then-ruling SLFP. He says that anger and the desire to avenge the injustice he and his family suffered at the hands of the village SLFP leadership prompted him to volunteer to campaign for the UNP in 1977. Expressing similar sentiments, the Chairman of the Warakapola Pradeshiya Sabha shared the following experience.[35]

My father was a very strong SLFP loyalist. We were the people in this village who did not change our loyalty during the time of the UNP. Our house was completely burnt down as we resisted the pressure of the UNP leaders in the electorate at that time. Amidst growing UNP pressure, we stood fearlessly loyal to our party.

Before 1977, under the FPTP system, regime changes were frequent, and every election from 1956 to 1977 resulted in a new government. Between the UNP and SLFP, one formed the government and the other became the main Opposition in Parliament. Therefore, supporters of the Opposition party (be it UNP or SLFP) were deprived of access to state patronage distribution only for a limited time period. As Tamara Gunasekara observes, supporters of the Opposition have to bide their time until the next election, when they hope their party will return to power and it will be their turn to obtain perks and other patronage goods (1992: 240).

As regime change has become less frequent under the PR system, waiting for the next election does not solve the problem of Opposition supporters. Therefore, in this context, supporters of Opposition parties have changed their allegiance dynamics to ensure that they are not completely shunned from state patronage distribution channels. In addition, as discussed previously, politicians too have had to alter their strategies under intensified intraparty competition in the PR system. Therefore, even ruling party politicians do not close their doors to Opposition supporters when they are approached for assistance. These new electoral realities have paved the way for loyalists of Opposition political parties to remain loyal to the old party without being completely cut off from state patronage. Unlike in the FPTP system, loyalists of both parties have adjusted to these new political realities. They have distanced themselves from old party-based rivalries in the village. After Manoda Wijerathna crossed over to the SLFP in Dedigama, some UNP loyalists enjoyed government patronage on the basis of their personal connection with their former electorate organizer who crossed over to the government. Kithsiri, a UNP youth leader in Waddeniya, says he helped Minister Ranjith Siyabalapitiya (SLFP Kegalle organizer) by pasting posters in the area where the minister did not enjoy the allegiance of his own party supporters. In return, Keerthi managed to obtain six jobs for fellow UNP loyalists in his area. In addition, intraparty competition under the PR system has prompted politicians of both parties in the electorate to share resources and opportunities with local political leaders in the rival party.

Propaganda as Electoral Strategy

The propaganda campaign of a political party intends to propagate what the party believes in the form of ideas, promises and policies to the community to obtain as many votes as possible. Propaganda is much more than dissemination of information. Parties intentionally craft news in order to influence beliefs and shape opinions. For this purpose, they use words as well as symbols, such as pictures, items, processions, songs. As in the case of party organizing strategy, political parties maintain their propaganda strategies well beyond the election period. However, outside of the election period, propaganda activities of the party are mainly confined to the national level. When parties prepare for an election, propaganda campaigns are intensified.[36] During the election period, propaganda campaigns are activated at both national and electorate levels. While a continuing propaganda campaign is important for party politics, it is not sufficient to ensure success. This results in propaganda blitz campaigns launched on the eve of elections at both the local and national levels.

There is a qualitative and quantitative difference in the propaganda strategies of parties during election and normal times. During the election period, parties are open about their propaganda campaigns. At other times, political parties do not call their efforts of mass mobilization as propaganda. The propaganda strategies of a party in power or parties in power as a coalition differ from the propaganda of parties in the Opposition. In Sri Lanka, the ruling party is capable of executing a sophisticated propaganda campaign by emphasizing all 'good' activities in which the government is engaged. Often the routine work of the government is depicted as some hitherto unheard of innovative initiatives made solely for the benefit of the people. The government's decision to introduce a fertilizer subsidiary to farmers aiming at elections is a good example.[37] It is a practice that has been in existence for several decades and has been adopted as policy by successive governments. The occasion is often used to hold mega ceremonies with government politicians in attendance and is thus used as a platform for propaganda. When the UNP was in government from 1977 to 1994, it used events such as *gamudawa* and *mahapola* as exhibitions and carnivals.[38] Immediately after the 1977 victory, J.R. Jayewardene revived the ancient tradition of the *vap magula* ceremony in order to draw a parallel between his rule and that of Sinhalese kings.[39] The inauguration of major development projects, such as the *Uda Gam* housing project and Mahaweli project, were used to increase the popularity of the UNP during the 1980s and early 1990s.[40] Similarly, SLFP-led UPFA governments held public events such as the *Dayata Kirula* exhibition and war victory commemoration ceremonies, which were made into extravagant events.[41] The final objective was to use them as propaganda to create and boost the party's image in the public psyche (especially Sinhalese-Buddhist communities).

When in the Opposition, parties do not have the resources and opportunities to carry out mega propaganda campaigns to match those of the ruling party. They respond with alternative propaganda techniques to sustain their image-building campaigns. However, the Opposition can also carry out effective propaganda campaigns with protest marches, *satyagraha*, strikes and religious ceremonies to show its strength while countering government propaganda. The *Jana Gosha* civil disobedience campaign and *Pada Yathra* organized by Mahinda Rajapaksa as an Opposition MP during the 17-year-UNP regime are good examples of effective campaigns of Opposition parties.[42] Political parties construct their ideology and policy positions through their propaganda programmes. They also use them to exhibit their perceived electoral strength, which is very important in maintaining the support base in electorates.

However, the propaganda of political parties becomes explicit, intensive and at times violent and aggressive during election campaign periods. During this period, depending on the type of election—Presidential, Parliamentary, Provincial or Local Council—the features and intensity of the campaigns differ. During election campaigns, candidates also launch their personal propaganda campaigns in addition to that of the party. As Saman Gamage, a former Chairman of the Weligama Pradeshiya Sabha, says, the party at the national level should create a winning aura with its propaganda machine to allow local politicians to mobilize grassroots supporters.[43] Therefore, election propaganda takes place at two levels i.e. the national and electorate levels. A party's leadership and sponsors execute national-level propaganda using various propaganda instruments, such as advertisements on popular media, TV and radio discussions/debates, newspapers and new media articles, rallies, mega meetings and sometimes even the systematic spreading of rumours. All these activities are planned by the national leadership and executed by the centre at the national level.

According to my field research observations, the election propaganda campaigns of the UNP and SLFP at the national level are designed to:

i Create confidence amongst the voters that a particular party has the opportunity (chance) of coming to power
ii Construct a party ideology and values that are in conformity with the popular imagination
iii Make voters believe that they would gain material benefits if that party wins
iv Galvanize voters by emphasizing social cleavages (sociological, cultural and political) to mobilize support for the party

These objectives together form the main focus of national-level propaganda campaigns. For example, election propaganda at the national level does not expect to generate hope for the victory of a particular candidate unless that candidate has a national appeal that will directly bear on the national-level performance of the party. Similarly, electorate-level propaganda confined to a particular area is insufficient to stimulate hope for the victory of the party at the national level. The national-level election propaganda, during a Parliamentary election, focuses mainly on the party, while the electorate-specific propaganda focuses on candidates.

National-level propaganda, through mass media, attempts to build the confidence of voters by creating a palpable sense of winning the election. The parties that are in government are usually in an advantageous position in executing the most effective and successful electoral propaganda campaigns. They have the means of manipulating state agencies (public office) and deploying state resources for campaign purposes (Welikala 2008). The Centre for Monitoring Election Violence (CMEV), referring to the 2010 Presidential election campaign, described the election as marred by blatant partisanship by state-controlled media and the failure of the police to obey the Election Commissioner's orders to cease illegal campaigning.[44] On the eve of the 2010 Presidential election, the Central Bank of Sri Lanka printed 1,000-rupee currency notes with the picture of the incumbent President Mahinda Rajapaksa who was also a candidate at that election. Many government agencies ran expensive and expansive advertisements on television and in newspapers offering good wishes to ministers on birthdays or in commemoration of some event or another. The advertisement or announcement invariably carried a large picture of the minister who was also a candidate. Ruling parties often misuse government media institutions for propaganda. Commenting on the 2010 Presidential election, Reporters without Borders said that "state media has turned into a presidential propaganda outlet".[45] They also coerce

private channels to provide free propaganda for them, offer more exposure for news favourable and less to no exposure for news unfavourable,
and more and more exposure for reports unfavourable to the Opposition.[46] Despite all such limitations, Opposition parties also execute their
national-level campaigns to renew hope amongst voters and sympathizers
who provide funds that they indeed could bring about a regime change.
Successful propaganda helps electorate organizers mobilize supporters
and potential supporters. Every politician interviewed from the UNP, the
main Opposition party, emphasized the importance of effective national-
level propaganda to create a positive image by arousing hope.[47] Such a
national-level propaganda campaign maximizes the election turnout of
supporters.

The other function of national-level propaganda is to convince people
that they will be provided various material benefits following an election
victory. In this case, ruling parties enjoy unparalleled advantage compared
to the Opposition, as they have many options in propagating this message.
For example, on the eve of elections, the government could announce
its recruitment plans and call for applications for government jobs.[48]
Sometimes government politicians distribute letters of appointment or
application forms to unemployed graduates. At times, Opposition parties
also include such programmes in their national election propaganda
campaigns but with little effect as compared to the parties that are already
in power. Through national-level electoral propaganda, parties spell out
their ideological and policy positions. These positions have little meaning,
as often they are extremely ambiguous and at times contradictory.[49] They
are nevertheless important for voters who have already decided on their
electoral allegiance. This is to say that parties can communicate a specific
ideological and policy position to voters irrespective of whether they practice it or not. For example, a party can successfully convince a majority
that it stands for a socialist-welfare economy, while privatization and
private enterprise is the real agenda. However, as already discussed, this
type of propaganda material is important for those who have decided to
support a party or who need to justify such a decision. Both the UNP and
SLFP, as shown in their manifestos for the 2010 general election, did not
display stark differences in political ideology or policy. What both parties
strived to do instead was argue about who is more efficient in delivering
these programmes. The propaganda line is to claim better, accurate and
honest delivery, which has consistently superseded any ideological debate
between the two parties. Election propaganda campaigns play a major role

in transforming citizens into voters, as described earlier. As the electoral campaign heats up, dormant social cleavages within the village community come into the open. In this context, parties highlight divisions within the village in 'us' verses 'them' terms. Therefore, as illustrated earlier, generally silent citizens begin to be inquisitive of party politics. Some come forward to actively participate in the election campaign. The leadership and an aggressive party organization at the national level are seminal for a successful propaganda campaign. Electorate-level propaganda is largely dependent on the success of the national-level campaign.

Election propaganda of the two main parties in Parliamentary elections is focused on mobilizing votes for candidates at the electorate level. Election propaganda in the electorate is mainly designed and executed by the electorate organizer. However, in the PR system, parties appoint a leader for each district. Therefore, district-level overall propaganda is designed by the candidates under the leadership and supervision of the district leader. However, heavy intraparty competition prevalent under the PR system, where each candidate has to maximize his/her preference vote, makes the propaganda campaign a complex operation (Chang 2004: 4). Therefore, each candidate usually has his/her own propaganda campaign that is not only designed to counter candidates of other political parties, but also to counter candidates from their own party. Hence, the instruments used for electorate-level propaganda are diverse, complex and innovative. Electorate-level election propaganda campaigns, as observed during the field research, attempt to construct a popular opinion that:

i The particular candidate or group of candidates is/are certainly going to get elected to Parliament

ii The candidate is powerful and has the capacity to deliver either using her/his own wealth or, more importantly, using state capital

iii The candidate will deliver and she/he has a record of delivering material benefits in the past

iv The candidate is someone who not only subscribes to popular cultural and religious (*aagama*, *sanskruthiya* and *sadacharaya*) values but will also safeguard them for the future generation

v The candidate is one of their own (*ape kenek*)

vi Discredit the image of rival political parties and politicians (including ones in their own party)

Most importantly, election propaganda at the electorate level attempts to communicate all these messages. Hence, a variety of communication tools and instruments of mind manipulation can be identified. Politicians pick what they consider the best messages for each community in the constituency, because at the micro level of contact communities are not homogeneous in terms of their state of dependency, culture and taste.[50] Therefore, election propaganda uses not only different messages for different communities but also relies on different communication instruments and strategies targeting different groups in the electorate.

Propaganda has become somewhat easier to design but far more expensive as compared to the period before the PR system was introduced. Under the FPTP system, competition was confined to a few candidates in a relatively small geographical territory. This required fewer resources to communicate messages to voters. The people in a constituency usually possessed fair knowledge about the candidates and their political histories.[51] In addition, competition was between candidates of rival political parties (often between the UNP and SLFP). This made the electoral decision fairly simple. In contrast, under the PR system, competition within an electoral district is not only interparty but also turns into an intraparty contest. This system allows many options of multiple propaganda strategies for candidates, provided they can afford to mobilize the required resources.

An extravagant campaign is considered to be very important in shaping public opinion that a particular politician is a winning candidate. Expensive cut-outs, posters and decorations, hundreds of supporters wearing T-shirts or caps depicting the identity of the candidate, and thousands marching in processions and attending rallies serve to convey the message of the candidate's popularity and winning streak. The success of the communication of this message attracts more crowds and develops a snowball effect, at least to the extent of intensifying the message. If a candidate fails to communicate winning potential, she/he will fail to attract the needed percentage of supporters for his/her election campaign. Along with the message of 'winning capacity', candidates attempt to convince people that they have the capacity to deliver various 'material goods' after the election. They use various strategies and symbols in their election propaganda campaign to convey this idea effectively. One of the most popular as well as effective strategies used by candidates during the 2010 election campaign was to portray themselves within

the constituency as the 'first amongst equals', as closely related or intimately associated with the Head of State or at least with a member
of his family. Candidates used words as well as symbols to communicate this message. The electorate organizer for Kamburupitiya (but very
much based in Weligama), Hemal Gunasekara, successfully spread the
word that President Rajapaksa was known to his family, and that he
would be given a ministerial position after election. It was true that President Rajapaksa was known to Hemal Gunasekara's father. The President
had visited Hemal Gunasekara's house after assuming office. The claim
boosted Hemal Gunasekara's symbolic capital. It allowed him to conveniently propagate the message that, once elected, he had the capacity to
serve and care for his supporters. Many candidates put up billboards with
photographs that featured them with the President, his brothers or at least
with his son. These symbolic displays were aimed to communicate their
proximity to the real seat of power. It was an effective way of convincing
voters of their capacity to deliver material goods and serve material interests. As Coomaraswamy (1989) observes, over time, state capital has
replaced private capital of politicians when sourcing for patronage distribution, and hence, the best indication of the politician's capacity to deliver
patronage goods was his/her capacity to tap into state resources and not
how much wealth the candidate had. In addition, politicians use various
other symbolic tools to exhibit their capabilities and capacity. The use of
expensive vehicles, even security convoys, and distribution of pre-election
goods such as food, drink, etc., are also widely used as propaganda strategies by politicians, especially in PR systems. It is important to make people
believe that he/she has the command of resources not only as compared
to candidates from rival political parties, but also those within his/her
own party. To cite another example from Weligama, Mrs. De Mel, wife
of one of the most powerful senior politicians in the country Ronnie De
Mel, distributed sewing machines amongst a few selected women in a
women's organizations set up in the Matara District several months before
the election. Chandima, a Local Council member from Weligama, says
that people believed that she would distribute sewing machines amongst
all members of that particular women's association, and she managed to
convince people that she was capable of delivering such assistance, being
the wife of the country's most experienced finance minister.[52] According
to Chandima, that strategy worked well and people voted for her in
the hope of receiving the promised assistances. According to many local
politicians, she did not visit those villages once elected to Parliament. As

this discussion suggests, 'manufacturing hope' is one of the most powerful electoral tactics used by politicians of the UNP and SLFP when they are in power as well as out of power.

The other important aspect of propaganda strategy at the electorate level is the construction of the cultural and religious persona of the candidate. Members of the village political actor network of the candidate in his/her constituency organize programmes and events that help in building a culturally conformist and religiously recognizable image for the candidate. *Bodipuja viyapara*, *shramadana viyapara*, cultural and sports events are organized to reinforce his/her religious and cultural credentials. Village elites, such as priests or other religious dignitaries, educationists or other respected leaders in villages are mobilized to organize these events. Hence, they succeed in ensuring wide participation and lend credibility to those events. Those candidates who are not capable of organizing such popular events strive to ensure that there are no negative perceptions of their religious and cultural affinity with the constituency. There are many examples to illustrate this point. The best is the symbolic religious practice of Marxist politicians in Sri Lanka. It is not easy to convince numerous social groups that a candidate is from their community. However, clever politicians successfully operate their propaganda machinery to make a majority believe that she/he is associated with the community that the voters belong to (implicit in this is the assumption that as a member of the community s/he is the most reliable representative of the community.) It is interesting to see how candidates connect themselves to other caste groups through their propaganda machines. It has been seen how Montague Jayewickrema, a *Karawa* elite of Weligama, relates himself to the majority *Goigama* community in the electorate. His rubber estates and the *Goigama* wife of his brother, Eral Jayewickrema, were used to construct his *Govi-Karawa* hybrid caste identity in his election campaigns. This was a strong enough reason for the majority *Goigama* caste community to accept him as one of their own. The *Wahumpura* community extended their support to the *Goigama* leader Dudley Senanayake in Dedigama for decades. They felt that he was connected to them in their life experience of living under the oppressive social norms of the *Goigama* elites in the Kandyan districts. The *Wahumpura* community believes that they were brought to Sri Lanka when a princess from India brought the sacred Bo tree sapling which stands today as the *Sri Maha Bodhiya*. Legend claims that they were brought to preserve the sacred tree. They also believe that King Parakram-abahu brought one of the off-shoots of the *Sri Maha Bodiya* to Beligala in the Dedigama electorate while attempting to hide the sacred tooth relic of the Buddha.[53] Folklore claims that an ancestor of Dudley Senanayake was in charge of both the tree and relic. Hence, the Senanayake family is considered to have close kinship ties with them traced through the centuries in a misty past. There is no evidence to prove this claim but the legend persists. It helped Dudley Senanayake to hold the *Wahumpura* community in thrall for several decades starting from his election to the State Council in the 1930s. Election campaign propaganda is executed not only on matters people discuss but also on what people do not discuss openly. One example was discovered during the field interviews. A poor labourer from Weligama, who belonged to the marginalized caste group *Berawa*, said that *Goigama* feudal elite member Panini Illangakoon was a distant relative, and hence, he used to vote for him.[54] In reality, the poor man was referring to one of the many mistresses that Panni Illangakoon had. She was a domestic servant in the Illangakoon household. He later married the woman and she bore him a daughter.

It should be noted that election organizing strategies and propaganda strategies primarily aim at maximizing votes. Therefore, both strategies seek to reach beyond the traditional support bases. At every election, the party loyalty of the citizen is tested by these electoral organizing and propaganda strategies of political parties. Some manage to remain loyal to their old party while others switch electoral allegiance to a new polit-ical party. Those with deep-rooted loyalty to a particular party stick with the party despite the pressure they are subjected to by the organizing and propaganda strategies of rival parties. Others either temporarily or permanently decide to switch allegiance to a new party. Political parties such as the UNP and SLFP do not attempt to nurture party allegiance amongst new groups while holding on to old party allegiances. Once a family embraces a political party as their party, that allegiance is sometimes transferred from generation to generation. Hence, party identity has also begun to produce a form of 'social cleavage' in the electorate.

CONCLUSION

In this section, I sought to shed light on the formation and sustenance of party allegiance of the UNP and SLFP. The findings of this section are based on my ethnographic fieldwork and supplemented through survey data. Through this, I have sought to produce new knowledge on the processes and role of the political party in the formation of allegiances.

Although scholars often conflate party allegiance and voter allegiance, this chapter argues for the differentiation between both forms of allegiance. In the course of this section, I demonstrated that whereas voter allegiance is temporary and contingent on the voter's circumstance at the time of the election, party allegiance is a more enduring relationship between the voter and the party that is not limited to the act of voting for the party alone.

The formation of party allegiance is the result of a complex, recurring and long-term process of party competition at the level of the electorate. Party competition involves both the carrying out of electoral propaganda at the time of the election as well as the organizational strategies between elections. The first result of this process is the formation of voter allegiance to a party, which is extended solely during the course of the election. However, elections are the testing grounds for the affirmation of allegiance to a party. Over time and as a result of this process, the extension of voter allegiance is transformed to a deeper attachment and commitment to the party, which is the hallmark of party allegiance. However, it should be noted that the main focus of parties is on maximizing votes at an election rather than on the formation and sustenance of a strong voter base. Therefore, this section argued that the formation of party allegiance is a by-product of the election campaigns carried out by the parties.

The sustenance of party allegiance, however, takes place as a result of two processes. On the one hand, the function of the organizational strategy of the party embeds these loyalists into the party's political actor network. On the other hand, party allegiance is also sustained through the handing down of party identification from one generation to the next. However, this section also argued that these processes are not mutually exclusive. On the contrary, they are interconnected, interdependent social practices that are ritualized within Sri Lankan society.

In this context, I made an argument for the importance of differentiating between voter allegiance and party allegiance when attempting to understand the practice of politics in Sri Lanka. This differentiation is crucial in order to understand the continued ability of both the SLFP and UNP to maintain their support bases irrespective of whether they are in power or not.

NOTES

1. Larry Diamond and Richard Gunther (2001) provide a detailed scheme to categorize political parties. In it, a catch-all party is one that seeks to attract people with diverse viewpoints. The party does not require adherence to a particular ideology as a criterion for membership.

2. Interview with Mangala Samaraweera, former cabinet minister of Ports and Aviation and chief campaign organizer of the 2005 presidential election, 5 December 2008.

3. At the 2006 and 2010 presidential elections, the SLFP (UPFA coalition) presidential candidate, Mahinda Rajapaksa, introduced his own manifesto called *Mahinda Chinthanaya*.

4. Interviews with parliamentarians and electorate organizers, such as Champika Premadasa of Dedigama and Hemal Gunasekara of Kamburupitiya, indicate that electorate organizers let their village political candidate contests independently within the electorate. It is important for an organizer to be independent from the election campaign of the local councillor in order to maintain that he/she does not favour any of the candidates. However, there are enough strategies available to them to ensure that their loyalists eventually get elected to the local bodies.

5. Interview with Hemal Gunasekara, parliamentarian from Kamburupitiya, 31 January 2011.

6. Interviews with Chamila Lorenzo Hewa, Mahaweediya, Weligama, 20 May 2010, 12 October 2010 and 31 January 2011. The point that he made on kinship and local council election were made by many interviewees, including Saman Gamage, Wijethilake, and Susantha and Kulasiri, who are also local-level political actors of the UNP and SLFP, respectively.

7. A set of core values and discourses that a field articulates as its fundamental principles and that tend to be viewed as inherently true and necessary. For Bourdieu, the 'doxic attitude' means bodily and unconscious submission to conditions that are in fact quite arbitrary and contingent. Doxa is implicit and unformulated and reflects how people frequently take themselves, their perceptions and the social world they relate to for granted (Jenkins 2002).

8. Interview with Dassanayake, Kahabiliyawa, Dedigama, 8 October 2010.

9. Interviews with Kamal Gamanayake, 12 November 2009 and 9 October 2010.
10. Interview with Thushari Hettiarachchi, daughter of Lal, Galborella, Weligama, 30 August 2012.
11. Interview with Senavirathne Gonawela, Kelaniya, 16 February 2011.
12. Interview with Sriyalatha Udupila, Mirissa, Weligama, 29 January 2011.
13. Interview with Kamal Chaminda, Tholangamuwa, Dedigama, 6 January 2011.
14. Interview with Wilfred Karunanrathne at Hemal Gunasekara's political office (house), 31 January 2011
15. Interview with Sumanadasa Silva, Enderamulla, Kelaniya, 16 February 2011.
16. Interview with Jayraj Chandrasekara, the Basnayake Nilame of Kelaniya temple and former chairman of Hatton National Bank, 29 June 2013.
17. Interview with Tikiribanda Gunapala, 12 October 2010.
18. Priyantha Amarasekara, Algama, Dedigama, 14 October 2012.
19. Interview with Bandula Liyanage, Midigama, 30 January 2011.
20. As described in this chapter 5 (Table 5.2), voter turnout at the 2010 Parliamentary election was the lowest since 1947 (see Jayasuriya 2000: 111).
21. My observation of electorate campaigns of the UNP and SLFP in the field locations and beyond indicates that, in general, election rallies, meetings, pocket meetings and even posters of the SLFP were extravagant and more vibrant than those of opposition parties.
22. From many discussions I had with Sunil Bastian on electoral politics in Sri Lanka, he is one of the country's leading scholars in political economy and has published extensively on rural economy, democracy and market economy, and peacebuilding in Sri Lanka.
23. Interview with Weerasekara, Kelaniya, 19 February 2011.
24. Interview with Saman Gamage, 20 December 2010.
25. Interview with Augustine Daluwatta, Weligama, 18 December 2010.
26. Interview with Rathnayaka Wickramasinghe, Waddeniya, 11 October 2010.

27. Interview with Lalinda Edward, Gonawela, Kelaniya, 17 February 2011.
28. Interview with Dassanayake, Kahabiliyawa, Dedigama, 8 October 2010.
29. Brow, in his study in Kukulewa, succinctly illustrates how village opposition party members and supporters suffered at the hands of members and supporters of the ruling party (Brow 1992).
30. Many village political actors of the UNP confirmed that MP Champika Premadasa has provided many job opportunities to poor villagers of Dedigama. Most of these jobs are in his businesses around the country. However, some criticize that these jobs are mainly given to members of his caste group.
31. I was invited to a workshop with a senior and a junior parliamentarian from the UNP and SLFP, respectively. Over tea, the two compared the number of funerals each had attended in a day. One said that he had attended 12 funerals in one day.
32. Interview with Joseph Hilary, Wanawasala, Kelaniya, 16 February 2011.
33. Interview with Siriyalatha, Udupila, Weligama, 29 January 2011.
34. Interview with Wijethilake, Kelaniya. I had a series of interviews with Wijethilake over three years, and he was instrumental in my meeting many old political notables in Kelaniya.
35. Interview with Wijethunge, chairman of Warakapola Pradeshiya Sabha, 11 October 2010.
36. Parties and candidates spend huge amounts of money for the campaigns on the eve of elections, especially for national-level election. In Sri Lanka, there is no law that demands parties disclose their campaign financing; therefore, it is extremely difficult to calculate how much they spend on election campaigns. However, the report released by Transparency International (TI) on the 2010 presidential election campaign provides some indication of the level of spending by the two main parties for recent presidential campaigns. According to the calculation, the cost of advertising at the presidential election was estimated to be Rs. 823,809,000 by the two main candidates ("Special Report on Election Expenditure", http://www.tisrilanka.org/).
37. Numerous examples can be given on successive governments' attempts to use its welfare for electoral gain. On the eve of provincial council elections in the Northern, North Western,

Sabaragamuwa and Central provinces, the government decided to increase the fertilizer subsidy given to farmers for the 2013/2014 Maha season by 15% over the last season's amount. The government increased the fertilizer subsidy for the coming Maha season, expecting that about 700,000 hectares will be cultivated (http://www.colombopage.com, 4 September 2013).

38. Gam Udawa refers to the total process of the reawakening of villages, concentrating on both economic and cultural aspects of life. The basic idea of Gam Udawa is to take development to rural areas outside of the core region centred around Colombo. It is designed to provide housing for the poor and enhance basic infrastructure facilities, such as roads, electricity and other services, in less-developed areas. From its start in 1978 until 1992, Gam Udawa exhibitions were held every year. As Hennayake observed, Gam Udawa became a routinely held festival that many awaited (Hennayake 2006:147–49).

39. *Vap magula* (ploughing festival) is an ancient ceremony in which Sinhalese kings traditionally entered the paddy field behind a bullock to plow the first furrow in preparation for the main rice crop.

40. Uda Gam was a housing project with the aim of building ten million houses by the year 2000. Initially, the government built the houses and allocated them to selected families. At opening ceremonies of the Uda Gam, songs written by villagers were sung to greet the chief guest. As Hennayake says, these songs thanked the leader (R. Premadasa) for the benevolence he extended to poor people (Hennayake 2006: 138).

41. Dayata Kirula Chairman, Minister Ranjith Siyambalapitiya, states that the objective of the exhibition is to identify and combine all development work within the selected district and to educate the public on development activities throughout the country. However, critics accuse Dayata Kirula of being a white elephant and unnecessary extravaganza only meant to boost the image and ego of President Mahinda Rajapaksa.

42. Addressing the 59th anniversary of the Sri Lanka Freedom Party at Temple Trees (2 September), President Rajapaksa said, "When the party office was abandoned, when 60,000 innocent youth were killed, we were able to organize the longest *Pada Yatra* in Sri Lanka – *Janagosha* and human chains to reorganize the party. We

withstood all pressures for 17 years and stayed firm without leaving the Party".

43. Interview with Saman Gamage, 20 December 2010.
44. Centre for Monitoring Election Violence, *Final Report on Election Related Violence and Malpractices: Presidential Election 2010* (Colombo: CMEV, 2010).
45. Reporters Without Borders, monitoring on 18 and 19 January, found that out of a total of 472 minutes and 5 seconds of news and current affairs on Rupavahini and ITN, Gen. Fonseka and other opposition candidates were granted only 7 minutes and 50 seconds, or 1.6%, while the president, his government and party were granted 465 minutes and 25 seconds—in other words, nearly 8 hours of air-time in just 2 days.

    On ITN, one had to wait until the 7 p.m. Sinhala-language news programme for coverage of opposition activity (Gen. Fonseka for 30 seconds, the UNP for 40 seconds, and the JVP for 45 seconds), while President Rajapaksa received 3 minutes on the 9 a.m. programme, 2 minutes on the 10 a.m. programme, 4 minutes 45 seconds on the noon programme and 4 minutes 20 seconds on the Tamil-language programme at 6 p.m.

    Rupavahini gives the government an overwhelming air-time advantage. On the 8 p.m., Sinhala-language news programme on 18 January, for example, the government received 8 minutes and 30 seconds, and the president 7 minutes and 10 seconds, while Gen. Fonseka, the UNP and JVP received a combined total of just 1 minute; it is deplorable that the 20 or so other candidates were totally ignored by the state media (http://en.rsf.org/sri-lanka-state-media-turned-into-21-01-2010,36164).
46. Election coverage by private media is more diverse, but they have become more consolidated in recent years with many private media outlets now owned by government officials or their close associates (Global Advanced Network Integrity Solutions, http://www.business-anti-corruption.cn/country-profiles/south-asia/sri-lanka/initiatives/private-anti-corruption-initiatives.aspx).
47. This is the common point that almost all the UNP national, provincial and local politicians that I interviewed emphasized. MP Champika Premadasa, MP Buddhika Pathirana, provincial councilors such as Srilal Lakthilaka, George Perera, R. Pallepopla and numerous local councillors expressed their frustration with

the UNP's inability to create a favourable political environment through its national propaganda in order for them to launch their local campaigns effectively. Even some opposition MPs acknowledged that UNP village politicians are helpless without effective national-level propaganda.

48. For example, two months prior to the presidential election in 2010, the government announced that it had decided to provide employment to over 17,000 unemployed graduates. Finance and State Revenue Minister Ranjith Siyambalapitiya made this announcement in a statement of 12 November 2009.

49. Wijewardene, analyzing the two manifestos, says that fundamentally the UNP's manifesto (three pages) is an overview of the party's stand, with the most pressing challenges confronting the country including education, employment, rural development and raising living standards. Each section contains a handful of bullet points, and pledges include a laptop for every university student, lower interest rates on loans and the immediate removal of taxes on essential goods including canned fish, onions and milk powder. Given its brevity, the document is hardly exhaustive and focuses on providing the public with an outline of the UNP's solutions for some very complex, multifaceted problems.

On the other hand, *Mahinda Chinthanaya Idiri Dakma* provides details in 100 pages. As one *Sunday Leader* columnist stated, there are specific plans for cities and regions with step-by-step plans for everything from public transport to the establishment of a space agency. He further stated that this vision is of course incredibly saccharine and often fails to accept a number of practical constraints. However, it succeeds in creating a saleable vision—a vision of the country as a beacon in Asia that members of the public would like to subscribe to.

While the manifestos differ in style and size their fundamental purpose is the same—to convince the public to vote in support of the parties' respective visions.

50. Interview with Ajith Kumarasinghe, Weligama, 10 December 2010. Describing his leader, Mahinda Wijesekara, and his campaign strategies, Kumarasinghe said that he was always careful when addressing a crowd in the electorate about their caste. When addressing non-*karawa* groups, he never mentions caste and addresses the group as his people in Weligama. However, amongst

his own *karawa* groups, he is always explicit about his caste group
and stresses his commitment to the people of it. Similarly, close
associates of Cyril Mathew of Kelaniya and Champika Premadasa
of Dedigama also describe how their leaders change their topics
and caste identity from village to village.
51. "Proportional Representation System that killed Democracy in Sri
Lanka", Dr. Sudath Gunasekara, president, Mahanuwara Senior
Citizens Movement (http://www.lankaweb.com/news/items/
2010/04/04/proportional-representation-system-that-killed-dem
ocracy-in-sri-lanka/).
52. Interview with Chandima Ranweera, 10 December 2010.
53. Interview with the chief monk of the Manikkadawara Rajamaha
Viharaya, 9 August 2010.
54. Interview with Victor from Kananke, Weligama, 29 January 2011.

REFERENCES

Brow, James. 1992. Agrarian Change and the Struggle for Community in
Kukulewa, Anuradhapura District. In *Agrarian Change in Sri Lanka*, ed.
James Brow and Joe Weeramunda, 261–291. Newbury Park/London and
New Delhi: Sage.
Chang, Eric. 2004. Electoral Incentives for Political Corruption Under Open-
List Proportional Representation. *The Journal of Politics* (forthcoming), www.
msu.edu/~echang/Research/JOP_final_draft%20_proofread.pdf. Accessed 18
May 2013.
Coomaraswamy, Tara. 1989. *Parliamentarian Representation in Sri Lanka 1931–
1986*. Unpublished PhD thesis, University of Sussex.
Diamond, Larry, and Richard Gunther, eds. 2001. *Political Parties and Democ-
racy*. Maryland: The Johns Hopkins University Press.
Duverger, Maurice. 19540. *Political Parties, Their Organisation and Activity in
the Modern State*. London: Methen & Co. Ltd; New York: Wiley.
Gunasekara, T. 1992. Democracy, Party Competition and Leadership: The
Changing Power Structure in a Sinhalese Community. In *Agrarian Change
in Sri Lanka*, ed. James Brow and Joe Weeramunda, 229–260. New Delhi
and Newbury Park/London: Sage.
Hennayake, Nalani. 2006. *Culture, Politics and Development in Post-colonial Sri
Lanka*. Lanham: Lexington Books.
Hettige, S., 1984, "Wealth, Power and Prestige: Emerging Patterns of Social
Inequality in a Peasant Context," Colombo: Ministry of Higher Education.

Jayanntha, D. 1992. *Electoral Allegiance in Sri Lanka*. Cambridge: Cambridge University Press.

Jayasuriya, L. 2000. *Welfarism and Politics in Sri Lanka*. Perth: School of Social Work and Social Policy, University of Western Australia.

Jenkins, Richard. 2002. *Pierre Bourdieu*. Rev. London: Routledge.

Jiggins, J. 1979. *Caste and the Family in the Politics of the Sinhalese 1947 to 1976*. London: Cambridge University Press.

Jupp, J. 1978. *Sri Lanka: Third World Democracy*. London: Cass.

Kearny, R.N. 1973. *The Politics of Ceylon (Sri Lanka)*. Ithaca and London: Cornell University Press.

Leiserson, A. 1958. *Parties and Politics: An Institutional and Behavioral Approach*. New York: Alfred A. Knopf.

Lipset, S.M., and S. Rokkan. 1967. *Party Systems and Voter Alignments: A Cross National Perspective*. New York: The Free Press.

Spencer, Jonathan. 1990. *A Sinhala Village in a Time of Trouble, Politics and Change in Rural Sri Lanka*. Delhi: Oxford University Press.

Uyangoda, Jayadeva. 2012. The Dynamics of Coalition Politics and Democracy in Sri Lanka. In *Coalition Politics and Democratic Consolidation in Asia*, ed. E. Sridharan, 161–240. New Delhi: Oxford University Press.

Weiner, M. 2006. Party Politics and Electoral Behaviour: From Independence to 1980s. In *India's Political Parties*, ed. P. DeSouza and E. Sridaran, 116–154. New Delhi: Sage Publications India Pvt. Ltd.

Welikala, Asanga, 2008, "Independent Elections Administration in Respect of Public Resources and State Media: The Constitutional Framework in Sri Lanka," in *Report of the Regional Workshop of Experts on Inclusive Electoral Process*, Colombo: South Asians for Human Rights, 104–12.

Woodward, Calvin A. 1969. *The Growth of a Political System in Ceylon*. Cambridge: Cambridge University Press.

CHAPTER 6

Desertion of the Party

INTRODUCTION

This book has thus far discussed how the two main parties of Sri Lanka—the UNP and the SLFP—have organized themselves, the rationale on which voters make their electoral choice and how party allegiance is formed and sustained. This chapter brings the analysis of the party-voter nexus to a completion by focusing on the way in which—and the rationale on which—voters desert these catch-all parties. The previous chapters were written at a time when the country's electoral politics were divided between the UNP and the SLFP. However, this power constellation started undergoing significant changes since the defeat of Mahinda Rajapaksa (MR) at the January 2015 Presidential election. Following the 2015 Presidential election, under the leadership of Maithripala Sirisena (MS), the SLFP joined its arch rival the UNP to form a national government. This then led to the formation of a joint opposition by the faction of the SLFP led by Mahinda Rajapaksa. This new political force later culminated into a new political party, the Sri Lanka Podujana Peramuna (SLPP). In the wake of 2019 Presidential election, the UNP too has faced the same plight as the SLFP. The leadership crisis of the UNP that has been hurting the party for decades finally pushed the rebels to desert the party and contest the 2020 Parliamentary election as the Samagi Jana Balawegaya (SJB). The results of the 2018 local government election and

© The Author(s), under exclusive license to Springer Nature
Singapore Pte Ltd. 2022
P. Peiris, *Catch-All Parties and Party-Voter Nexus in Sri Lanka*,
Politics of South Asia,
https://doi.org/10.1007/978-981-16-4153-4_6

222P. PEIRIS

the 2020 Parliamentary confirmed that an overwhelming majority of the supporters of both the SLFP and the UNP had deserted their respective parties to support these new parties. In this context, this chapter investigates how these two new parties emerged or rather those two main parties that dominated the country's politics for more than half a century lost their bases to two new political forces that emerged from within them. The chapter thereby inquires into the process, logic and conditions within which the party-voter nexus of the main catch-all parties has transformed. Inquiring into how voters desert their party will bring this examination of the party-vote nexus to a logical end.

To this end, this chapter first discusses the context in which the two old parties' support bases started eroding, paving way for the emergence of new parties from within them. It then explains how national-level developments were mirrored on the local level as well, by explaining the defection of local level organizers following the actions of national politicians. The chapter then describes the realignment of the old networks in the service of the new parties, and using this discussion as an entry point, moves on to analysing the mobilization strategies of the new party. Drawing from field observations as well as national-level developments, the chapter makes certain concluding observations about the disappearance of the party-voter nexus in the old parties equation.

THE CONTEXT

Since the emergence of the two-party electoral system in Sri Lanka, Sinhalese electorates have been mainly divided between the two main parties—the UNP and the SLFP. The history of electoral results demonstrates that over 90% of the electorate in most of the Sinhalese electorate is divided between these two parties. For decades, due to the domination of the UNP and the SLFP, there has not been space for another political force to thrive within the Sinhalese electorates. Since the SLPP and the SJB were carved out of the SLFP and the UNP, respectively, instead of emerging as alternative forces, they may be considered as simply having replaced the two old parties. The results (see Table 6.1) of the 2018 Local Government election, where the SLFP and the SLPP contested against each other, confirmed that the SLPP has consolidated its position amongst the majority Sinhala Buddhist electoral base essentially by appropriating the SLFP. At the 2018 Local Government election, the SLPP, despite being a newcomer, secured 40% of the total votes while

Table 6.1 Summary of the 2015 Parliamentary election results

Party	Votes received	Percentage (%)	Seats allocated
United Nations Front for god governance (led by UNP)	5,098,927	45.66	106
United people'sFreedom Alliance (led by SLFP)	4,732,669	42.38	95
Janatha Vimukthi Peramuna	543,944	4.87	6
Tamil National Alliance	515,963	4.62	16
Sri Lanka Muslim congress	44,193	0.40	1
Ealam people's democratic party	33,481	0.30	1
Democratic party	28,587	0.26	0
Other	169,227	1.52	0

the SLFP could only achieve 12%. Although most of the councils turned out to be hung councils, the SLPP managed to capture the power of 231 out of the 340 of Local Authorities where the election was held. The SLFP's power was limited to only 9 authorities. It was such irony that the SLFP suffered this humiliating defeat while its leader functioned as the Executive President of the ruling coalition. Therefore, the 2018 Local Government election results clearly indicated that a majority of the SLFP's support base had deserted the party at least temporarily. However, it did not take that long for the UNP also to experience the same fate. The UNP's long-standing crisis finally exploded on the eve of the 2020 Parliamentary election. Many young energic UNP parliamentarians and many partners of the 2015 United National Front for Good Governance (UNFGG) coalition joined Sajith Premadasa to form the SJB to contest this election. Although this coalition was formed about three months before the Parliamentary election and contested under a new symbol (telephone), it managed to emerge as the second largest force in Parliament by securing 54 seats. For the first time in its 74 year history, the UNP's Parliament strength was reduced to one seat—a seat allotted from the national list. The results of the Parliamentary election indicated that the support base of the UNP had clearly deserted the party and rallied around a new political coalition, the SJB.

Therefore, the result of the elections that were held during the past three years—from 2018 to 2020—clearly demonstrates that support bases can desert catch-all parties despite them being mainstream and even ruling parties for decades. The UNP and SLFP have been considered as the 'party of the family' for generations of voters in many families, though such family-based party allegiance has been on the decline for some time now. The humiliating defeat that both the UNP and the SLFP experienced post-2018 demonstrates that family-based party allegiance is no longer significant enough to count at elections.

No Sri Lankan political party analysis has ever predicted the possibility of the desertion of supporters of the two main parties on such a scale. Kirchheimer, who coined the term "catch-all party" viewed that they are "highly successful electoral machines, sufficiently adept at winning votes that it would force its competitors to adopt similar ploys" (as cited in Wolinetz 2002: 160). However, comparative scholars of European political parties have identified not only the strengths of catch-all parties as efficient vote generating machines, but also their vulnerability to desertion and defections (Panebianco 1988; Wolinetz 2002; Katz and Mair 2009). The mass desertions from the UNP and SLFP may, however, not have followed the same trajectory of Western European democratic parties. Following detailed discussions on these desertions and the forming into new parties, it came to light that the previous 'electorates of belonging' were in fact what triggered such mass scale desertion, and not the lack of it. In the case of SLFP, it was the electorate's sense that it belonged to the Rajapaksas which subsequently led to the desertion of the SLFP in favour of the SLPP. Although it is too early to comment on the desertion of the UNP by its supporters at the 2020 Parliamentary election, it is clear that they too did not defect to their rival SLFP or its new incantation, the SLPP (Table 6.2 and Table 6.3).

Table 6.2 Summary of the 2018 local government election results

Party	Votes received	Percentage (%)	Members	LG bodies
Sri Lanka Podujana Peramuna	4,941,952	44.65	3369	231
United Natins front	3,612,259	32.63	2385	34
United Nations people's Freedom Alliance	989,821	8.94	674	2
Janatha Vimukthi Peramuna	693,875	6.27	431	0
Sri Lanka Freedom party	491,835	4.44	358	7
Tamil National Alliance	339,675	3.07	407	41

Table 6.3 Summary of the 2020 Parliamentary election results

Party	Votes received	Percentage (%)	Seats allocated
Sri Lanka pepople's freedom alliance (led by SLPP)	6,853,693	59.09	145
Smagi jana Balawegaya	2,771,984	23.90	54
Tamil National Alliance	327,168	2.82	10
Jathiga Jana Balawegaya	445,958	3.84	3
Others	804,995	6.92	13

LOCAL NETWORKS DESERTING NATIONAL LEADERS

In Sri Lankan politics, national is local too (Peiris 2018: 34; Uyangoda 2015: 207). The strategies and actions of the local political notables are very sensitive to the developments in the national political theatre. In the backdrop of national leaders deserting the SLFP and the UNP, substantial sections of their local leadership also followed in the same footsteps. However, this local level desertion of the two old parties cannot be reduced to a phenomenon that was solely triggered by the actions and decisions of national politicians. Local level political actors of both the UNP and the SLFP also played a key role and exercised agency in shifting the allegiance of their party loyalists to these two new political forces. In both cases—shifting electoral allegiance from the SLFP to the SLPP, and from the UNP to the SJB—the local level leadership had made a calculative decision and a concerted effort to that end. Not only did they shift their own allegiance, but also mobilized their supporters in support of these new parties. This is understandable as their political survival depends on the success of these new political forces that they now represent.

Meanwhile, one cannot ignore the seminal role played by the national leadership of the SLPP—and to a lesser extent that of the SJB—in mobilizing the local political leadership and triggering mass exodus from their old party. Therefore, the pattern and dynamics of desertion of the two main parties are far from being uniform across electorates. The transition of these allegiances is defined by both inter- and intraparty contexts in each constituency, as well as the strategies executed by the national leaders of both the SLPP and SJB.

Deserting SLFP for SLPP

As already demonstrated in Chapter 2, both the UNP and SLFP used loosely knitted networks of local elites or political actors to organize their party institutions at the electorate level. These party networks earn their strength by representing the many social cleavages in the electorate. Their ability to distribute various patronage goods determines how effective they are. Therefore, as demonstrated in Chapter 3, the party or the coalition that forms the government enjoys the most efficient and effective party network at the electorate level, while those in the opposition possess a comparatively weaker and more ineffective network at that level.

Having been in power for more than two decades continuously—except for a brief interruption from 2001 to 2004, the strength of the SLFP's party network at the local level, by 2015, was unparalleled to its rival UNP. Especially under Mahinda Rajapaksa's leadership, the country underwent massive infrastructure development changes which, in addition to their contribution towards the national economy, contributed to the strengthening of the financial capacities of various local level Rajapaksa loyalists. During the decade of his Presidency, Mahinda Rajapaksa managed to groom and sustain a sophisticated web of support networks at the electoral level comprising various local level organizations as well as businessmen who are well connected to national-level politics and especially to the Rajapaksa family. Many such individuals also got the opportunity to serve as members of the relevant Provincial or local council (also known as *Pradeshiya Sabha*). Such extensive patronage programmes were what was chiefly responsible for the electoral success of the Rajapaksas: "The bloc vote and the loyalty factor are part of a cascading patronage pyramid, flowing from the top by political leaders to the lowest rung of the political ladder in villages" (Kulatunga 2020, as cited in Macan-Marcar 2020)[1]. As a result, especially after 2010, local constituencies started identifying themselves more with Mahinda Rajapaksa than the SLFP.

As such, many supporters of the SLFP and its electoral allies rallied around MR at the 2015 election to defeat MS—a Minister of the Rajapaksa government and then secretary of the SLFP—who contested under the UNFGG coalition. Although MS had been the General Secretary of the SLFP, he did not receive considerable support from the SLFPers for his Presidential bid. Although the former President and the daughter of the SLFP's founder Chandrika Bandaranaike Kumaratunga

(CBK) was instrumental in introducing MS to the UNFGG, not many traditional SLFPers voted for MS during the 2015 Presidential election. He was seen as an agent of minorities, with the "two biggest minorities – Tamils and Muslims – [having] voted for [him which] probably swung the vote his way" (Haviland 2015)[2]. This popular opinion, in fact, worked in favour of MR's campaign to further consolidate the support of Sinhalese voters. Although MR managed to obtain "a narrow majority of Sinhalese votes" (Dibbert 2015)[3], he lost the election since an overwhelming majority of the minority communities—as well as a sizeable portion of Sinhalese largely from the urban upper middle and educated classes—came forward to vote for his main contender.

The defeat of the all-powerful MR at the January 2015 election left his supporters utterly nonplussed about their future[4]. This is because supporters at the electorate level were in shock as they did not anticipate such an astounding defeat as early as 2015, and it appeared as though minorities held the swing vote (Kelegama 2015)[5]. Therefore, many village level MR supporters voluntarily organized themselves to visit MR's ancestral house in Beliatta where he shifted to after leaving his official residence at Temple Trees[6]. The SLFPers found themselves further disillusioned when MS took up the leadership of the SLFP while heading the UNP dominated unity government. In this backdrop, MR loyalist political actors in the SLFP started distancing themselves from MS's SLFP and began to organize themselves informally as a separate bloc. For example, Ajith Gurusinghe[7], a local councilor from Dedigama said "since we felt defeated by rival forces and betrayed and abandoned by our own party leadership, friends in the neighbourhood started discussing what to do". At the same time, some such disgruntled groups received backing from their leaders in the electorate and district, who also wished to be organized under the leadership of MR again. It was these various factions of disgruntled supporters that rallied around the SLPP when MR's support base in Parliament reorganized itself as the Joint Opposition and later formed the SLPP. It is therefore clear that there should be certain psychological and material conditions present for local political actors to desert a catch-all party.

However, a few who considered themselves to be '*paaramparika*' (ancestral) SLFPers refused to leave the old party. This group was mainly composed of families with 'weak patronage dependency'—as described in Chapter 5—and a certain amount of continued ideological affinity with the 'Bandaranaike politics' of the olden days. There was also another group that defied mass desertion, viz. the SLFP supporters who had experienced discrimination under the local political leadership of MR loyalists. Their animosity with their former local leadership now aligning with MR, and/ or their hope that mass desertion had opened up space for better career prospects within the ranks of the party chiefly accounted for this decision[8]. However, such groups constituted a very small minority.

Deserting UNP for SJB

The SJB was formed only three months prior to the 2020 Parliamentary election. The loyalists of the UNP had shifted their electoral allegiance to the SJB because the local level political actors who previously organized the UNP's votes in the electorate had shifted their support to the new political entity. In any case, over the past decades UNP supporters have voted for various coalitions sometimes under different symbols and even under different leaders (for example, UNPers campaigned for Sarath Fonseka in 2010 under the symbol of the swan). As already discussed in the previous chapters, the efficiency and the strength of the political actor network in the electorate is more effective than the election manifesto of the party. Therefore, for an average UNP voter, voting for SJB did not constitute a drastically different experience. While the deputy leader of their party contested the election, the local level campaign was led by the same old party supporters. Therefore, for a majority of supporters, the SJB is simply the UNP minus Ranil Wickramasinghe. The result was that in the run-up to the 2020 Parliamentary election, there was no serious competition between the UNP and the SJB at the local level. In many villages, the entire UNP organizing structure had been transformed to become the support structure of the SJB, and hence voting for the SJB was not seen as desertion of the UNP, but rather supporting their old party with a new leader at the helm.

Some UNP loyalists, especially the ones who had been political inactive for years, stayed on with their old party as they felt it is not right to leave their ancestral party. Yet another group made a similar decision as their local party organizers had decided to do so. However, since there is data on only one election, it is too early to make any substantial claims about the relationship between voters and local political actors with regard to the newly formed SJB.

The above discussion on the desertion of supporters of the UNP and the SLFP is clearly different from the dynamics that previous literature highlights as important in explaining defection of party members. As **de Vet, Poletti** *and* **Wauters** *(2019) point out:*

> [...] party members defect because they have negative attitudes towards the party leadership, are displeased with the ideological direction the party is heading, or are attracted to ideologically close competitors. When party members are, in other words, dissatisfied with the current state of affairs within parties, they might not only deny them their own vote, but might also convince other party supporters to do the same.

It is true that supporters of both the UNP and SLFP were dissatisfied with their respective party leadership, but they did not defect to a rival party. Rather, the entire party organization in both parties have been appropriated by a new leadership. One can use a house as a metaphor to explain the emergence of these two new parties. This scenario is akin to an entire house being moved to a new location with all its furniture and inhabitants, leaving only the owner behind. In the case of the SLPP, it is the same old SLFP in a new address with most of its old furniture, inhabitants and even legitimate owners. The SJB's situation is somewhat different. It has most of the old furniture and inhabitants in it, but is yet to establish who the legitimate owner is. Future elections would determine who that would be, if SJB manages to sustain its current political identity. In the following section, an attempt is made to understand how the old networks were used to carve out the new parties.

FORMING INTO A NEW PARTY

Deserting an existing party and the formation of a new party constitute simultaneous processes. On the one hand, the elites who formed the local political actor networks of the older catch-all parties that relied on them for their party organization reconfigured their networks to suit the new political realities that emerged following MR's 2015 defeat. These newly reconfigured political actor networks formed the architecture of the new party for the deserters to come and join. On the other, the 2018 Local Council, 2019 Presidential and 2020 Parliamentary election campaigns, at the national as well as local levels, ushered those who are willing to desert their old party to the new party. In the next section, I look into the process in detail.

Realignment of the Old Political Actor Network

Following his defeat at the Presidential race of 2015, MR had to give up leadership of the SLFP—due to a policy that he himself had introduced a few years before, dealing a double blow to the leaders of the Rajapaksa camp of the SLFP-led United People's Freedom Alliance. The political future of these leaders who belong to different minor parties heavily relied on the electoral performance of MR. Therefore, leaders of the coalition parties that backed MR including Wimal Weerawansa, Vasudewa Nanyakkara, Denesh Gunawardana and Udaya Gammanpilla as well as their senior loyalists devised plans to ensure MR's return, as it was crucial for the survival of their political careers also. A countrywide campaign called 'Mahinda Sulaga' (Mahinda Wind) was launched at a rally held in Nugegoda on 18 February 2015. The campaign was aimed at getting rid of the defeatist psyche of their supporters and uniting them against the Yahapalana government. Further, it established the point that MR is still a formidable political force and though he lost the election he has not left politics. This narrative boosted the morale of local level MR loyalists and political actors, who then started organizing their wards and electorates in support of their national leader.

Although MS managed to force MR to handover the party leadership of the SLFP to him, he did not have a comprehensive strategy to unify the rank and file members of the party. Despite this internal division, the SLFP contested for the Parliamentary election of 2016 as one party under the leadership of MS. However, after the election, the faction loyal to MR decided to act as a separate group in Parliament. Therefore, out of 95 Parliamentarians who got elected under the SLFP led coalition (the United People's Freedom Alliance), 52 members decided to function as the Joint Opposition (JO). Not only did MS fail to win back the support of the MR faction of the party, but he simply did not make any meaningful attempt to attract the local level political actors who were loyal to MR. MS's decision to dissolve the local councils and postpone electing new councils cost him the valuable opportunity of winning over the party's local level leadership[9]. In this backdrop, Basil Rajapaksa approached the local leadership to organize their supporters for the upcoming election of Cooperative Societies. All the local level Rajapaksa loyalists interviewed in this research recognized the mobilizing for this fairly insignificant election as the beginning of the organizing of Rajapaksa's party—which later came to be known as SLPP.

Ending speculations about a new party, in late 2016, MR loyalists officially established the SLPP. The local level political actors loyal to MR were instructed to organize their electorates in order to recruit one million members to the newly formed party[10]. Within each ward, a party branch was formed and 10 families were assigned to each party supporter to monitor and report information on, in order to win their votes. Each party branch was organized under the supervision of a national-level politician and the district coordinator of the SLPP. After establishing ward level branch offices, SLPP supporters conducted regular meetings that witnessed increasing numbers of participants.

The 2018 Local Government election was a turning point of the SLPP's local party organizing drive. New electoral rules introduced by the mixed electoral system additionally complicated the election landscape for SLPP by requiring that 25% of all local councils be made up of women. Finding strong female candidates with relatively little experience in politics to contest for the new party running for the election for the first time was, needless to say, particularly challenging. Despite the many odds, the SLPP claimed a resounding electoral victory and managed to secure power in 231 of 340 local councils across the country[11], with a total of 3436 members getting elected. This unexpected victory boosted confidence amongst MR loyalists that the new party had the potential to grab power. Hence those who deserted the SLFP started rallying around the SLPP in numbers and the new party managed to efficiently organize them under local party branches. While these organizational structures were hardly different from the ones traditionally maintained by the SLFP and UNP, the SLPP also relied more on loosely knit collectives of political actors who used their private residence or a business place as the party branch office, instead of formal institutionalized mechanisms. Additionally, core office bearers often happen to also be family members of close friends of the local political actor of the party. Pulasthi Gunasekera, a secretary of the SLPP from Weligama, narrated how his party branch functions thus:

> As part of a one million membership drive, we were asked to recruit people to the party. One person from one family can get the membership by purchasing a Rs. 20 ticket. However, we do not maintain a membership registry or host regular meetings as we were instructed by Basil Rajapaksa, the national organizer. Technically we should have Youth and women organization meetings in addition to branch meetings, but it is only during

times of elections do we hold these meetings. In fact, we have not yet had a single meeting since the Parliamentary election.

The failures of governance of '*Yahapalana* regime', rivalry between the President and the Prime Minister, Easter Attack and anti-Muslim tensions further boosted the popularity that SLPP earned following the 2018 local government victory. The strong national-level campaign of the party, supplemented by the support of Buddhist monks, private media enterprises that were favourably disposed towards it, and various nationalist civil society organizations (technocratic groups such as *Viyath maga* and Sinhala Buddhist extremist organizations such as *Ravana Balaya, Bodu Bala Sena*) that provided added legitimacy, further strengthened local level voter mobilization for the Presidential election.

The fieldwork of this study only captures the four months of SJB's life as a political party. Since unlike the SLPP, it did not have time to form or mature, it is difficult to make serious claims about the nature of the network dynamics of the SJB.

Mobilizing the New Party for Presidential and Parliamentary Elections

The electoral mobilization strategies of the SLPP and SJB are not significantly different from their former institutions, namely the SLFP and UNP, except for the highly charged enthusiasm exhibited by their local political actors. As already argued in Chapter 3, electoral mobilization is twofold; on the one hand, catch-all parties carry out their national propaganda campaigns to attract voter allegiance (the 'pull' factor), while one the other, voter choice is informed by local electorate mobilization strategies (the 'push' factor). In order to discuss these push and pull factors, a brief understanding of the political climate in which the 2019–20 developments took place may be in order.

Political Climate

The SLPP contested for the 2019 Presidential election in an exceptionally favourable political climate. It was held at a time when the unpopularity of the *Yahapalanaya* regime has hit its peak. The corruption allegations against its ministers, inefficiencies in governance and internal conflicts between the President and the Prime Minister had eroded the credibility of the *Yahapalana* government, a situation aggravated by the October

2018 constitutional coup, where the President attempted to illegally sack the Prime Minister and appoint Mahinda Rajapaksa in his stead. However, the inability to prevent the Easter Attack despite warnings by various foreign intelligence agencies shifted the public opinion decisively against the government (Hewage 2020)[13].

In this backdrop, many started advocating, implicitly and explicitly, the importance of the return of Rajapaksa rule since the country's security was perceived to be at serious risk, a mentality he duly capitalized on in his manifesto as well (Hashim 2019)[14]. Soon after the Easter attack, the former Defence Secretary Gotabaya Rajapaksa (GR) announced his desire to run for Presidential office. This further boosted the enthusiasm of the Rajapaksa supporters who were somewhat confused about who their next Presidential candidate would be. GR was better placed for the job than SJB's candidate Sajith Premadasa, it was believed, because of the former's military and bureaucratic training that a career politician like Premadasa lacks.

On the other side of the political divide, the UNP leader Ranil Wickramasinghe was in a long drawn struggle to secure his leadership in the party, even at the cost of the election. This further contributed to an ever widening chasm in the UNP between Wickramasinghe loyalists and opponents who believed Sajith Premadasa to constitute a better candidate for the 2019 Presidential election. The candidate that the UNP produced for the 2019 Presidential election therefore suffered dual disadvantages, viz. an unfavourable national political climate as well as a party severely weakened due to internal divisions.

National-Level Campaign
Both candidates made an effort to entice their support bases by making popular patronage promises during their national-level propaganda campaigns. The 'Vistas of Prosperity and Splendor', (Gotabaya Rajapaksa's manifesto) promised priority to security and to build an efficient, disciplined and modern society[15]. In addition, he promised 50,000 jobs to unemployed graduates and 100,000 jobs for low-income earners[16]. Further, speaking his inaugural campaign rally in Anuradapura, he promised free fertilizers for farmers, a good fixed price for rice in the market and storage facilities for the farmers. He further stated that "[farmers] can sell their product without selling them for a lesser value or without a middle man (sic)"[17], and promised to cut off all the micro credit loans and any other loans of farmers for good[18]. Sajith Premadasa

also promised numerous patronage goods including housing for the poor, which was intended to be perceived as an extension of his father R. Premadasa's main patronage programme. However, in the light of the failure of the *Yahapalanaya* regime to honour their patronage promises during their 4 years in power, Premadasa's manifesto carried little weight. A strong former UNP supporter from Dedigama who was interviewed for this study said that they "cannot even ask our own party supporters to come for a meeting as our government did not do anything during the past four years"[19]. He further stated that supporters of the *Pohot-tuwa* party (the SLPP) know that they will be looked after if Mahinda (Rajapaksa) comes into power. In addition, the tug of war between the leader of the party and the UNP's Presidential candidate made the UNP's electoral promises even less credible.

The other major factor that added to the strength of the national-level campaign of the SLPP, the New Democratic Front and the JVP was the support they received from various political and civil society organizations. The SLPP was backed by 11 political organizations of a spectrum of ideologies ranging from socialist to capitalist, nationalist to pluralist and parties representing ethnic minorities to parties representing the ethnic majority. In addition, many civil society organizations including the technocratic and nationalist *Viyath Maga* and extremist Buddhist organizations such as *Sinhala Raavaya* and *Bodubala Sena* backed Gotabaya Rajapaksa's candidacy. The Centre for Monitoring Election Violence (CMEV) reported how a prominent Buddhist temple supported the Presidential bid of Gotabaya Rajapaksa right before the election, when campaign activity is legally prohibited:

> Some other events, such as a dhathu (relic) exhibition organised at the historic Kelaniya Raja Maha Viharaya during the last week of the election campaign, while not specifically held to promote any political party or candidate nevertheless featured Buddhist monks and laypersons expressing opinions about the SLPP candidate Mr. Rajapaksa. These events were also extensively covered by certain privately owned media channels, with television programming dedicated to them. Other incidents amounted to clear election law violations. For instance, a group of persons stationed in the vicinity of Kelaniya Raja Maha Viharaya during the cooling-off period of 48 hours after the end of election campaign promotion activities distributed lotus flower buds to temple attendees and asked them to vote for Mr. Rajapaksa.[20]

Cardinal Malcom Ranjith, the head of Sri Lanka's Catholic church whose criticism of the *Yahapalana* government was well known since the Easter Attack, issued the following statement on the eve of the election that was accused of being politically biased towards Gotabaya Rajapaksa: "This decision you make will be important for the future of this country and to take the country towards progress. I urge all of you to come forward to fulfill your duties as you are also a partner in the event of any harm to our country due to that omission" (UCA News Reporter, Colombo, 5th August 2020).

The fact that GR was new to politics and was supported by numerous organizations outside of traditional parties made his election campaign something radically new and refreshing to many frustrated Sri Lankan voters. Hence his platform promised a potential break away from the traditional corruption ridden way of doing politics that Sri Lanka has known since independence.

In contrast, Sajith Premadasa's campaign that was supported by the traditional electoral bases of the UNP did not offer anything novel to the national political landscape. Even the liberal civil society that supported Premadasa's campaign failed to constitute anything new and exciting by way of a political voice, as they stood for the same political agenda that they backed in 2015, which had proven to be an utter failure by 2019. Though Premadasa's campaign attempted to discredit its main opponent by highlighting the large-scale corruptions of the Rajapaksa family and their friends, and portraying GR as a leader with authoritarian tendencies, the corruption allegations circling its four-year term that the UNP failed to debunk meant that these attempts failed to create much of an impression.

Local Level Campaign
The local organizers of the SLPP and its constituent parties capitalized on the national campaign to mobilize their electorates. At the local level, SLPP local political actors organized meetings under the guidance of district leaders. Although the SLFP signed a national-level electoral alliance with the SLPP, most local political actors of the SLPP maintained a distance from the local level SLFP leadership. Although most of the current local SLPP political actors were SLFPers before 2015, they treated their old party as the main political rival in the village. This is understandable as the SLPP also primarily targeted the same social and ideological bases that the SLFP has been representing since its inception.

The following two narratives of two local political actors of the SLPP succinctly illustrate the electoral mobilizing strategy of their party.

Thakshala Damayanthi[21] from Kapparathota North, Weligama:

Damayanthi organizes the SLPP voters in her ward Kapparathota North in Weligama. She is originally from a UNP family but switched her allegiance when her local parliamentarian, Mahinda Wijesekara, crossed over to support Mahinda Rajapaksa in 2006. Since then, up until 2015, she had been actively engaged in SLFP politics. During her tenure at SLFP, she had met and developed a connection with Dallas Alahaperuma, a senior Mahinda-camp politician. Since then she has been working with Alahaperuma who is now an influential SLPP minister. She derives her political power by being connected to this national-level politician. Therefore, what is important for her political career is not the membership of the party or her position in the party, but the connectivity she maintains with the national-level politician. Under the guidance of Alahaperuma and the material support extended by Mahinda Yapa Abeywardena, another national politician, Damayanthi mobilized her ward in support of GR for the 2019 Presidential election. According to Damayanthi, at the local level, the SLPP worked independently of the other constituent partners, including the SLFP, to promote their candidate. This distance that the SLPP maintained with the SLFP turned in to clear rivalry at the Parliamentary election of 2020. The SLPP local political actors only promoted in their districts only those who stood by Mahinda Rajapaksa from 2015. According to Damayanthi, during the Parliamentary election campaign, the SLPP local political actors worked strategically to undermine the politicians who joined the *Yahapalana* government with Maithripala Sirisena.

Nirosha Preiyadarshani from Weniwelkaduwa, Dedigama:

Priyadarshani is also from a traditional UNP family. As a member of her family received a job from a SLFP government, she and her family switched their party allegiance to the SLFP, voting for Mahinda Rajapaksa at the 2015 Presidential election as well. Despite the electoral defeat, like many who supported MR then, a decision was made to stay with him and bring him back to power. This decision was not only an emotional one but a pragmatic one as well because, on the one hand, the new leader of the party, Maithripala Sirisena, had not made any attempt to look into their political career, while on the other, they witnessed that Mahinda Rajapaksa still attracts a huge support base. Against this backdrop, the Parliamentary and Provincial Council level politicians who stood with MR had approached Priyadarshani and other local political actors in her area to organize the electorate under the new party. She was given the task of overseeing 20 houses in her ward and reporting to the district and national-level leadership about the electoral choices of those households. During the process, many of the old SLFPers had joined them. Since the SLPP campaigned independently of their other electoral partners—National Freedom Front, LSSP, CP, etc., during the Presidential election campaign, Priyadarshani reported that for the Parliamentary election she mobilized her ward only in support of the politicians who were with the SLPP from its outset.

The campaigns for the Presidential and Parliamentary elections allowed the SLPP to further consolidate their electoral grip at the local level by eating into the bases of the SLFP. Due to the desertion of most of its supporters, the SLFP branches at the local level had been inactive at the time of Presidential election. A local political actor of the SLFP from Weligma, Nalika Galahitiyawa[22], states that she and her friends had to canvass individually using their own funds during the 2018 local council election since the local party organization was in no position to do so. Even though the SLFP supported the candidate of the SLPP at the Presidential election campaign, both parties carried out their campaigns independently and separately. According to Nimal Ranjith, from Watthegedara, Dedigama[23], though the SLFP worked to elect Gotabaya Rajapaksa at the Presidential election, the local organizers of the SLPP excluded the SLFPers from their election campaign activities in the area. This attitude towards SLFP members is not surprising given the rivalry between the two groups. According to Karunanyaka, at the local council of the area where the SLPP holds power, SLFP council members regularly experience discrimination. He further said during the Parliamentary election campaign, the SLPP local political actors in his ward openly campaigned against the SLFP candidates, despite both parties have signed an electoral alliance. Therefore, the 2019 Presidential and the 2020 Parliamentary elections helped the SLPP not only to establish itself as the ruling party, but also to undermine the remaining power bases of the SLFP at the electorate level.

The weak electoral campaign of the UNP at the local level was mainly a result of the infighting at the national level. The last minute acceptance of Sajith Premadasa as the party's Presidential candidate did not really allow enough time for the party to formulate a unified and powerful campaign at either the national level or the local level. Not all the Parliamentarians and district leaders of the UNP made a genuine effort to campaign for Sajith Premadasa. For example, Champika Premadasa, the Dedigama Parliamentarian, as he had already decided to quit politics, did not contribute to the UNP's campaign at the Presidential election[24]. Kabir Hasim, a senior UNP district leader had to bear that responsibility instead.[25] However, for the Parliamentary election, almost all the local political actors started supporting the SJB, the alliance led by Sajith Premadasa. Jayampathy Ekanayake, a long-standing UNP local political actor from Dedigama said that they did not feel they were supporting a different party because at the 2020 Parliamentary campaign, they were working for the very same politicians they have been supporting through the past few decades, and working with the same groups in the electorate that they have been organizing election campaigns with, also for decades. According to the opposition leader of the Warakapola Pradeshiya Saba, Ishtiaq Ahmed, the UNPers were deeply disappointed with the internal conflict within the party. Therefore, many did not even cast their ballot at the 2019 Presidential election.[27] He said his family has been with the UNP since the time of D.S. Senanayake, and cannot therefore just leave the party. According to Ishtiaq, traditional UNPers in his electorate are waiting for their party to resolve its internal issues and come forward as a single force once again.

Through these two election campaigns, the SLPP has clearly consolidated its position as the most dominant party amongst Sinhalese voters. Although the SLPP emerged as a new party, the nature of the local level party organization and its electoral campaign process indicate that it is the same as the old SLFP, only under the leadership of the Rajapaksas. The electoral success of the SLPP was chiefly dependent on the popularity of Mahinda Rajapaksa and electoral-engineering skills of the Rajapaksa family. Similarly, local level party organization and electoral mobilization strategies confirm that the SJB is nothing but the same old UNP minus Ranil Wickramasinghe. However, unlike between the SLFP and the SLPP, to an average supporter, the difference between the UNP and the SJB is less clear.

CONCLUSION

This chapter inquired into the phenomenon of the party-voter nexus disappearing in long-standing catch-all parties. Despite having enjoyed oligarchical dominance in the Sri Lankan electoral landscape for many decades, the UNP and SLFP both suddenly turned into parties of almost no electoral worth. It is striking that the shift happened over one election cycle (2015 to 2020) whereby both parties suffered a steep decline from being the two main coalition centres in the country to the status of two minor parties.

This chapter has illustrated the vulnerabilities that these two parties inherited through their choice to employ catch-all strategies to maximize votes. The weakening of the party institution and party discipline as a result of relying heavily on patronage-based politics while distancing from programmatic politics made both parties vulnerable to the politics of new entrants. In addition, the inability to defuse internal disputes stemming from family-based control made space for second-tier leadership and their rank-and-file to be disillusioned. Interestingly, those who defected have not joined their political rivals, but rather gone on to build replicas of their respective old parties that are in no way distinct from their old parties in terms of their policy programmes, ideological positions, electoral and party organization strategies or bases of representation, except in terms of efficiency and effectiveness.

The chapter demonstrated that regional and local level political actors and local party supporters of these parties exercise significant agency when they work for as well as against the old party. As much as they do when signing up for and continuing, they make equally strong utilitarian calculations when signing out of the party-voter nexus. In the absence of a large electorate that is emotionally attached (like the kind afforded by the FPTP system), catch-all parties find it difficult to retain the interest/loyalty of their local level support bases. Further, it could be stated that the emergence of the SLPP and SJB can be considered an instance of re-politicizing the party-voter nexus which was completely de-politicized within the patronage logic of the older catch-all parties such as the SLFP and UNP. However, given the electoral strategies underpinning the two new parties, it is safe to assume that the new party-voter nexus too will soon be equally de-politicized and vulnerable to desertion as the party model they follow is not different to their predecessors.

With its analysis, this chapter has demonstrated that the emergence of these two new parties does not constitute an abrogation of the two-party system that Sri Lanka has known over the past seven decades, but rather is a continuation of the system with new fronts playing the same old roles. Therefore, by deserting the UNP and the SLFP, their supporters did not breach the party-voter nexus but rather renewed it.

NOTES

1. Macan-Marcar, M. 2019. *Divide and Conquer: Sri Lankan Strongman Plots AN Election Return,* viewed 15 November 2020, https://asia.nikkei.com/Spotlight/The-Big-Story/Div ide-and-conquer-Sri-Lankan-strongman-plots-an-election-return.
2. Haviland, C. 2015. *Sri Lanka's Rajapaksa suffers shock election defeat,* viewed 15 November 2020.
3. Dibbert, T. 2015. *Sri Lanka's Surprising Election Victor,* viewed 22 November 2020, https://foreignpolicy.com/2015/01/21/sri-lankas-surprising-election-victor/ .
4. Field interviews conducted in Weligama, Dedigama and Keleniya electorate during the period of January 2020 to September 2020.
5. Kelegama, S 2015, *Sri Lankan presidential Election at a Glance,* viewed 15 November 2020.
6. Interview with Eranga Epa, young SLPP supporter from Galle. 10th February 2020.
7. Pseudonym. Interview at Weniwelkaduwa. 20th July 2020.
8. Interview with the SLFP supporters; Wijesekara in Mirissa, Weligama; Rathnayaka in Watthegedata, Dedigama.
9. Interview with SLPP local councilor of Warakapola Pradesha Sabha. 16th September 2020.
10. Interview with the SLPP local political actors in all three electorates.
11. https://elections.gov.lk/en/elections/results_lae_E.html.
12. Pseudonym. Interview at Weligama. 15th September 2020.
13. Hewage, K 2020, *Year in review: Sri Lanka's road to recovery in 2019,* viewed 15 November 2020.
14. Hashim, A 2019, *Gotabaya Rajapaksa wins Sri Lanka electiob,* viewed 15 November 2020.
15. Manifesto of Sri Lanka Podu Jana Peramuna (SLPP), https://gota.lk/sri-lanka-podujana-peramuna-manifesto-english.pdf.
16. Manifesto of Sri Lanka Podu Jana Peramuna (SLPP), https://gota.lk/sri-lanka-podujana-peramuna-manifesto-english.pdf.
17. https://economynext.com/gota-sajith-election-promises-freebies-to-boost-sri-lanka-state-spending-28258/.
18. https://economynext.com/gota-sajith-election-promises-freebies-to-boost-sri-lanka-state-spending-28258/.

19. Interview with Kulasiri Meepaga, in Dedegama. 10th October 2020.
20. https://anfrel.org/wp-content/uploads/2020/06/cmev-presid ential-election-2019-final-report-english-3.pdf.
21. Pseudonym.
22. Pseudonym. Interview at Kuhunugamuwa, Weligama. 8th October 2020.
23. Pseudonym. Interview at Watthegedara, Dedigama. 15 September 2020.
24. Pseudonym. Interview at Wathdeniya, Dedigama, 15th September 2020.
25. Pseudonym. Interview at Wathdeniya, Dedigama, 15th September 2020.
26. Pseudonym. Interview at Wathdeniya, Dedigama, 15th September 2020.
27. Pseudonym. Interview at Warakapola Town, Dedigama. 15th September 2020.

REFERENCES

Katz, R., and P. Mair. 2009. 2009. "The Cartel Party Thesis: A Restatement", of "Perspectives on Politics." *American Political Science Association* 7 (4): 753–766.

Panebianco, A. 1988. *Political Parties: Organization and Power*. Cambridge: Cambridge University Press.

Peiris, H.A. 2018. Politics of Citizens (Non-)Participation in Governance. *LST Review* 29 (345).

Uyangoda, Jayadeva. 2015. Local Government as Local Democracy: Challenges in Sri Lanka's Rural Society. In *Local Government and Local Democracy in Sri Lanka: Institutional and Social Dimensions*, ed. J. Uyangoda, 196–243 Colombo: Social Scientists' Association.

Wolinetz, Steven. 2002. Beyond the Catch-All Party: Approaches to the Study of Parties and Party Organizations in Contemporary Democracies. In *Political Parties: Old Concepts and New Challenges*, ed. Richard Günther, José Ramón Montero, and Juan Linz, 136–165. Oxford: Oxford University Press.

CHAPTER 7

Conclusion

This book examined the party-voter nexus of the UNP and the SLFP in order to inquire into an interesting paradox in Sri Lankan democracy. Since its independence, the country has been under the rule of two main parties with more similarities than differences. Although Sri Lanka is a multiparty electoral democracy, the UNP and the SLFP have been the main coalition centres for more than seven decades. Rural Sinhalese electorates are largely divided between these two parties. In urban and semi-urban Sinhalese electorates, most of the smaller parties contest elections as coalition partners of these two parties. Interestingly, not only have these two parties failed to represent a set of contrasting policy and ideological positions consistently, but they also have a sizable number of members in Parliament who have crossed over from the opposing camp. The hegemony of the UNP and the SLFP in Sri Lanka's electoral politics, however, seemingly ended with the 2020 Parliamentary election. The emergence of the Samagi Jana Balawegaya (SJB) and Sri Lanka Podujana Peramuna (SLPP) dwarfed both the UNP and the SLFP. Interestingly, these two new parties are offshoots of the UNP and the SLFP, respectively, and show no significant rupture from their old parties in terms of their ideology, policies and the way they function. Theoretically, the emergence of two new parties to replace ones that hegemonized post-colonial politics should have changed the political system, yet interestingly these

© The Author(s), under exclusive license to Springer Nature Singapore Pte Ltd. 2022
P. Peiris, *Catch-All Parties and Party-Voter Nexus in Sri Lanka*, Politics of South Asia, https://doi.org/10.1007/978-981-16-4153-4_7

two new parties continued to maintain the bipolar multiparty system in Sri Lanka.

This raises important questions about the nature of Sri Lankan democracy and representation, role of political parties, efficacy of voting and in general the nature of state-society relations in Sri Lanka. Sri Lankans can rightfully be proud of their post-colonial democratic credentials as they were able to seat and unseat many leaders through mostly free and fair elections. Nevertheless, the increasing erosion of the legitimacy of political parties and continued challenges to transform the country's political system on the revered principles of good governance and pluralism begs a critical reflection on the nature of the party-voter nexus in post-independence Sri Lanka. It is therefore important to inquire as to what citizens expect from their politicians, from parties and more fundamentally, from democracy.

THE STUDY

To comprehend how the state-society relationship is negotiated in everyday practice, this study interrogates the nature of the party-voter nexus in the two dominant catch-all parties in Sri Lanka through the lens of political sociology. Since the 1950s, in spite of the availability of multiple political party options and the introduction of the PR system that favours a multiparty system, the UNP and SLFP consistently attracted the majority of Sinhalese votes for more than half a century. This highlights an interesting puzzle about the Sri Lankan party-voter nexus; despite the fact that the two parties show more similarities than differences in terms of policy and ideological positions on some key spheres or not being able maintain clear differences consistently for over seven decades, they continued to be the main source of division within Sinhalese-majority electorates and amongst Sinhalese voters.

Field research conducted in Dedigama, Weligama and Kelaniya from 2010 to 2014 sheds light on how these two parties organize themselves at the electorate level and what strategies they use to mobilize the electorate around the time of election and in between elections. A fresh round of field research was conducted in the same electorates during 2020 to capture the emergence of the SJB and SLPP and thereby to understand how voters have deserted these two parties. As such, this study has captured all phases of the dynamics of party-voter nexus, i.e. formation, sustenance and decline.

Within the framework of political sociology, this study illustrates how formal and informal social relations and cultural practices in Sinhalese electorates influence the function of political parties. The traditional approaches to the study of political parties have not only masked the rationales and relationships shaping the party-voter nexus, but have also left us with an inadequate understanding of the function of democracy in a society like Sri Lanka. On the contrary, this study treats the party-voter nexus as a dialectical relationship in which the party as well as the voter exercise a degree of agency in shaping the nature of the relationship. In order to do so, it draws extensively on Pierrer Bourdieu's seminal work on the 'theory of practice' (particularly his ideas on habitus, field, capital and doxa) and proposes some key concepts that are useful to analyse the party-voter relationship beyond the structure-agency dichotomy. Therefore, the knowledge produced in this study provides fresh insights into the role of catch-all parties and how they operate at the electoral level. The study thereby contributes to a better understanding of the role of catch-all parties in (re)defining the party-voter contract in society and reconstituting the state-society relationship in Sri Lanka.

ROLE OF PARTY ORGANIZATION TO MAXIMIZE VOTES

Contrary to the traditional institutionalist understanding, the party institutional structures of the UNP and SLFP at the electorate level are extremely feeble and, at best, rather loosely organized. In addition, these organizational structures remain largely dormant and are generally activated only as an election nears. The study also observes that the guiding motivation for the party organization of both the SLFP and UNP at the local level appears to revolve more around attracting votes than on building a strong party membership base. Therefore, the feeble nature of the party organization continues to be reproduced at the level of the electorate.

In the absence of a strong organizational structure, these parties heavily rely on elites/notables—rarely groomed and often picked—for party organizational activities at the level of the electorate. When making this appointment, it does not matter whether that person is originally from the same electorate or in fact whether he/she share the party ideology. What matters is the unwavering loyalty to the party leader and his/her capacity to mobilize local-level political actors to collect votes for the party. The nature of the party institutional structure in the electorate is contingent upon the electoral organizer and his choice of strategy to mobilize voters in the electorate. Therefore, the party organizational structure draws on a variety of relationships, networks and forms of capital to keep the party machinery well oiled at the level of the electorate.

In this context, the local political actors who play key roles in the cultural and economic life of the village also come to constitute the rank-and-file membership as well as village-level leadership of these two parties. In the past, these local political actors were the local elites who drew on their cultural and economic capital to organize the party in the electorate. However, today—in the backdrop of an increasingly neoliberalized lifestyle and a proportional representative electoral system—the legitimacy of the local political actor rests more on his/her social capital than on the cultural and economic capital that the traditional elites relied on in the past.

PARTY MOBILIZATION: MOBILIZING LOCAL POLITICAL ACTORS INSTEAD OF MEMBERS

When mobilizing the electorates, political parties have to respond to numerous cleavages such as ethnicity, religion, caste, kinship and class. The UNP and SLFP, in the quest to expand their voter bases, instead of using ideological or policy programs, learned the art of accommodating the interests of various cleavage groups through political patronage. The electoral organizers of these two parties have reached out to actors within various social groups and connected them to the party's network at the electorate level by facilitating access to state patronage. This strategy not only enables the party to reach out to rival groups within an electorate, but also strengthens their local political capacity to be efficient vote collectors given that the legitimacy of the local political actor is dependent to a large extent on the symbolic capital that is and can be earned through facilitating voters within their groups to access these individual benefits. Therefore, it is unsurprising to note that the party organizers pay more attention to organizing local political actors rather than party members in the electorate. The key role played by local political actors in the everyday life and political activities of voters within these electorates is also important. Through patronage, brokerage and particularization, these actors have emerged as important nodal points in the everyday life and political decisions of the local community.

Additionally, the party mobilization strategy changes depending on whether a party is in power or not. When a party is in power, the political actor network tends to expand and become complex, and the expectations of individual benefits from this network also increase amongst the community. However, when the party is out of power, though this network of political actors tends to shrink and the expectations of actors from amongst the community decline proportionately, it continues to accommodate those who have no access to the networks of patronage in the current system. Therefore, the local political actor networks of the SLFP and UNP continue to survive (albeit on different scales) irrespective of whether the party enjoys the benefits of incumbency or not.

Furthermore, the introduction of the PR electoral system has increased the complexity and fragility of the party mobilizing strategies of the UNP and SLFP. The relationship between the party organizer and the local political actor networks that existed under FPTP and have been characterized as being 'one-to-many' has changed to a 'many-to-many' relationship after the introduction of the PR and the preferential voting system. This has increased the options available to electorate organizers, local political actors and most importantly voters. Therefore, the introduction of PR has in fact intensified intraparty competition and conflict. The introduction of PR and the attendant importance of the electoral district have also bene-fitted these two parties, since it has opened up opportunities for them to mobilize numerically small social groups within the district. The intended benefits of the PR system, then, have largely been appropriated by the UNP and SLFP, rather than smaller parties.

Rationalities at Work in the Practice of Voting

The standard practice is to interpret electoral results as a verdict on the policies of parties and qualities of the candidate—either incoming or outgoing. However, this study argues that the logic of voting for many is far more complex and constitutes a reflection of the conscious-ness of voters at the height of the election. In contrast to what Western democratic theory assumes, Sri Lankan voters are not autonomous indi-vidual rational beings in the modernist sense. Rather, the socio-cultural setting within which everyday life is embedded and collective understand-ings of how democracy works provide an epistemic frame for the voter's electoral rationale. Therefore, electoral choices that are often considered irrational from the point of view of normative frameworks may well appear completely rational and justifiable to the voter.

Irrespective of whether the electoral choice is collective or individual, it represents two types of interests—identity interests and material interests. Since these interests are subjective categories, it is not difficult for material interests to be recognized as identity interest and vice versa. However, the extent to which the voter relies on either type of interest when making their electoral choice is determined by the extent to which voter depends on state patronage. Voters with higher levels of dependency are more likely to rely on material interests, while those with lower levels of dependency rely more on their identity interests when making their electoral choices. Interestingly, the level of dependency is not necessarily a structural circumstance that the voter and his/her family happen to be in, but is also shaped, to a certain extent at least, by state policies and through the choices of political actors.

In this context, a majority of Sinhalese voters finds parties such as the UNP and SLFP or their potential coalition partners as a natural choice, because it enables them not only to meet their identity and material interests but also, justify the decision with the episteme of the democratic culture prevalent in Sri Lanka.

WEAKENED PARTY ALLEGIANCE

As already discussed, managing party membership has never been the main focus of the institutional design of the UNP and the SLFP despite their ritualistic recruitment drives in the run up to every election. However, it is common knowledge that most of the rural Sinhalese households label themselves with a party identity almost in the same way as their caste identity. Therefore, more than now, in the past, it was believed that these two parties enjoyed table party allegiance from a sizable proportion of each Sinhalese village. While acknowledging the existence of party allegiance, this study emphasizes the need to differentiate between party allegiance and voter allegiance—voting for a party either individually or as a whole family. Voter allegiance is a temporary phenomenon and contingent on the voter's circumstances around the time of an election.

However, the formation of party allegiance is the result of a complex, recurring and long-term process of party competition at the level of the electorate. It denotes a more enduring relationship between the voter and the party that is not limited to the act of voting for the party alone. Party competition involves both the carrying out of electoral propaganda at the time of the election and the organizational strategies between elections. The first result of this process is the formation of voter allegiance to a party, which is extended solely during the course of the election. Elections, therefore, are the test of allegiance to a party. Over time and as a result of this process, the extension of voter allegiance is transformed to a deeper attachment and commitment to the party, which is the hallmark of party allegiance.

However, as already discussed, the main focus of parties is on maximizing votes at an election rather than on the formation and sustenance of a strong voter base. Therefore, this study demonstrate that the formation of party allegiance is a by-product of the election campaigns carried out by the parties. The current strategy of the UNP and the SLFP to sustain party allegiance embeds these loyalists in the party's political actor network rather than incorporating them into institutionalized party organizational structures. As these political actor networks are highly fragile and dependent on individuals, especially under the PR system, the level of party allegiance these two parties traditionally enjoyed has steadily declined. As a result, these two parties have lost the assured party bases that they once enjoyed. In its stead, the efficiency of electoral engineering has become the stronger determinant of the election outcome.

VULNERABILITIES OF CATCH-ALL PARTIES

The UNP and SLFP party organization strategies had their own inherent weaknesses as well. Though these two parties managed to maximize votes, it came at the cost of weakening the party institution and party discipline. The decision to heavily rely on patronage-based politics while deliberately distancing from programmatic politics has exposed both parties to be vulnerable to new entrants. The party organization design that relies on a loosely knit network of political actors instead of a well-defined institutional structure has sapped these parties of their ability to resolve internal disputes not only at the local level but also at the national level. As a result, both the UNP and SLFP suffered defections especially when out of power.

The fact that for decades the party organization and management of these two parties have been all about managing local political actors— local businessmen, monks and local cultural elites—who are capable of amassing votes at elections further strengthened the national politicians against the party institution. As a result, whoever commands the loyalty and support of a majority of such local political actors determined the future of the party. As already discussed, winning efficient local political actors over means wining their vote banks as well. This explains the emergence of the SJB and SLPP to replace their old parties within a very short period of time since formation. It is interesting that those who defected the UNP and SLFP have not joined their political rivals, but rather gone on to build replicas of their respective old parties that are in no way distinct from their old parties in terms of their policy programs, ideological positions, electoral and party organization strategies or bases of representation.

DYNAMICS OF THE PARTY-VOTER NEXUS CONTINUE

Investigating the political life of three electorates, this book has discussed the nature of the party organizational structure and mobilization dynamics of the UNP and SLFP, logic of voting practices of voters and the formation, sustenance and retrieval of their allegiance to political parties, and the vulnerabilities of the model these two parties followed to maximize their electoral performance. It is now clear that not only the UNP and SLFP, but also the majority Sinhalese voters played a role in forming a kind of party-voter nexus that they found logical to meet their own interest within the framework of Sri Lanka's patronage democracy. The majority of the Sinhalese voters extended their support for party with the capacity to accommodate their identity as well as material interests. However, a major part of this party-voter nexus is mediated through local political actors who play an important role in the everyday life of the voters in between elections. Ideologies and policies are important for voting decisions and party allegiance as long as they are connected to the material interests of the people who depend on state patronage schemes at different levels. Sinhalese votes are willing to desert their party but they are not yet ready to take a risk to desert the system within which the party-voter nexus is formed and maintained.

Bibliography

Adrian, Wolfgang. 1987. Some Reflections on the Role of Political Parties in a Democracy. In *Political Party System of Sri Lanka*. Colombo: Sri Lanka Foundation Institute.

Allan, James P. 1997. The British Labour Party in Opposition, 1979–1997: Structure, Agency, and Party Change. Unpublished MA thesis, Virginia Polytechnic Institute and State University.

Andersen, Robert, and Anthony Heath. 2000. Social Class and Voting: A Multi-Level Analysis of Individual and Constituency Differences. Working Paper 107, Centre for Research into Elections and Social Trends.

Athukorala, Premachandra, and Sisira Jayasuriya. 1994. *Macroeconomic Policies, Crisis and Growth of Sri Lanka, 1969–1990*. Washington, DC: World Bank.

Babbie, Earl R. 1998. *The Practice of Social Research*, 8th ed. Belmont, CA: Wadsworth Publishing Company.

Bastian, Sunil. 2007. *Politics of Foreign Aid in Sri Lanka, Promoting Markets and Supporting Peace*. Colombo: International Centre for Ethnic Studies.

———. 2010. Politics and Power in the Market Economy. In *Power and Politics: In the Shadow of Sri Lanka's Armed Conflict*, ed. Camilla Orjuela, 101–125. Sida Studies No. 25. Sida.

———. 2012. The Politics of Land Reform and Land Settlement in Sri Lanka. http://www.panossouthasia.org/PDF/Politics%20of%20Land%20Reform%20in%20Sri%20Lanka.pdf. Accessed 12 November 2012.

Berenschot, W.J. 2009. Riot Politics: Communal Violence and State-Society Mediation in Gujarat, India. Unpublished PhD thesis, University of Amsterdam.

© The Editor(s) (if applicable) and The Author(s), under exclusive license to Springer Nature Singapore Pte Ltd. 2022
P. Peiris, *Catch-All Parties and Party-Voter Nexus in Sri Lanka*, Politics of South Asia,
https://doi.org/10.1007/978-981-16-4153-4

251

Bevir, Mark, and Rhodes Raw. 2002. Interpretive Theory. In *Theory and Methods in Political Science*, ed. David Marsh and Gerry Stoker, 131–152. New York: Palgrave Macmillan.

Birch, Anthony. 1993. *The Concepts and Theories of Modern Democracy*. London: Routledge.

Bourdieu, Pierre. 1977. *Outline of a Theory of Practice*. Cambridge: Cambridge University Press.

———. 1984. *Distinction: A Social Critique of the Judgment of Taste*. Cambridge, MA: Harvard University Press.

———. 1986. The Forms of Capital. In *Handbook of Theory and Research for the Sociology of Education*, ed. J.G. Richardson. New York: Greenwood Press.

———. 1989. Social Space and Symbolic Power. *Sociological Theory* 7: 14–25.

———. 1990a. *In Other Words, Essays Towards a Reflexive Sociology*. Cambridge: Polity Press.

———. 1990b. *The Logic of Practice*. Stanford, CA: Stanford University Press.

———. 1991. *Language and Symbolic Power*. Cambridge: Polity Press.

———. 1993. *Sociology in Question*. London: Sage.

———. 1998. *Practical Reason, On the Theory of Action*. Cambridge: Polity Press.

Bourdieu, Pierre, and L.J.D. Wacquant. 1992a. *An Invitation to Reflexive Sociology*. Cambridge: Polity Press.

———. 1992b. The Purpose of Reflexive Sociology (The Chicago Workshop). In *An Invitation to Reflexive Sociology*, ed. P. Bourdieu and L.D.J. Wacquant, 61–225. Chicago: University of Chicago Press.

———. 1994. *Practical Reason: On the Theory of Action*. Stanford and Cambridge: Stanford University Press.

Brass, P., ed. 1985. *Ethnic Groups and the State*. Totowa, NJ: Barnes and Noble.

Brow, James. 1992. Agrarian Change and the Struggle for Community in Kukulewa, Anuradhapura District. In *Agrarian Change in Sri Lanka*, ed. James Brow and Joe Weeramunda, 261–291. Newbury Park/London and New Delhi: Sage.

Budge, Ian. 1994. A New Spatial Theory of Party Competition: Uncertainty, Ideology and Policy Equilibria Viewed Comparatively and Temporally. *British Journal of Political Science*, 443–467.

Central Bank of Sri Lanka. 2010. *Annual Report 2010*. Colombo: Central Bank.

Centre for the Study of Developing Societies. 2008. *State of Democracy in South Asia*. New Delhi: Oxford University Press.

Chandra, Kanchan. 2007. *Why Ethnic Parties Succeed: Patronage and Ethnic Head Count in India*. Cambridge: Cambridge University Press.

Chandraratna, D., and L. Smith. 1997. *A Background Reader in Philosophy, Psychology and Social Science*. Perth: Curtin University of Technology.

Chang, Eric. 2004. Electoral Incentives for Political Corruption Under Open-List Proportional Representation. *The Journal of Politics* (forthcoming), www.msu.edu/~echang/Research/JOP_final_draft%20_proofread.pdf. Accessed 18 May 2013.

Chatterjee, P. 2004. *The Politics of the Governed: Reflections on Popular Politics in Most of the World*. New York: Colombia University Press.

Chibber, P. 1999. *Democracy without Associations: Transformation of the Party System and Social Cleavages in India*. New Delhi: Vistaar.

Chibber, P., and M. Torcal. 1997. Elite Strategy, Social Cleavages and Party Systems in a New Democracy: Spain. *Comparative Political Studies* 30 (1): 27–54.

Coomaraswamy, Radika. 2003. The Politics of Institutional Design: An Overview of the Case of Sri Lanka. In *Democracy Be Designed? The Politics of Institutional Choice in Conflict-torn Societies*, S. Bastian and R. Luckham. London: Zed Books.

Coomaraswamy, Tara. 1989. *Parliamentarian Representation in Sri Lanka 1931–1986*. Unpublished PhD thesis, University of Sussex.

Crotty, Michael. 1998. *The Foundation of Social Research: Meanings and Perspectives in the Research Process*. Crows Nest, Australia: Allen & Unwin.

Dahl, R.A. 1966. *Political Oppositions in Western Democracies*. New Haven: Yale University Press.

Dalton, R.J. 1996. The History of Party Systems. In *Citizen Politics: Public Opinion and Political Parties in Advanced Western Democracies*, ed. R.J. Dalton, 2nd ed., 149–164. Chatham, NJ: Chatham House.

de Grazia, Alfred. 1962. *The Element of Political Science: Political Behaviour*. New York: The Free Press.

de Silva, K.M. 1998. *Reaping the Whirlwind*. New Delhi: Penguin Books India (P) Ltd.

de Silva, K.M., and Howard Wriggins. 1988. *J.R. Jayewardene of Sri Lanka: A Political Biography, Volume One: 1906 to 1956*. Anthony Blond/Quartet.

de Souza, Peter, and E. Sridharan, eds. 2006. *India's Political Parties*. New Delhi: Sage.

de Zoysa, K.P. 2013. *Caste Matters: Democracy, Caste and Politics in Sri Lanka After the Promulgation of the 1978 Constitution: A Case Study of Sinhala Society*. Unpublished MA thesis, University of Colombo.

Deer, Cecile. 2008a. Doxa. In *Pierre Bourdieu: Key Concepts*, ed. Michael Grenfell. Durham: Acumen.

———. 2008b. Reflexivity. In *Pierre Bourdieu: Key Concepts*, ed. Michael Grenfell. Durham: Acumen.

Devine, Fiona. 2002. Qualitative Methods. In *Theory and Methods in Political Science*, ed. David Marsh and Gerry Stoker, 17–24. New York: Palgrave Macmillan.

DeVotta, Niel. 2006. Ethnolinguistic Nationalism and Ethnic Conflict in Sri Lanka. In *Politics of Conflict and Peace in Sri Lanka*, ed. P. Sahadevan and Neil DeVotta. New Delhi: Manak Publications Pvt. Ltd.

———. 2007. *Sinhala Buddhist Nationalist Ideology: Implications for Politics and Conflict Resolution*. Washington, DC: East-West Center.

Dewasiri, Nirmal Ranjth. 2008. *The Adaptable Peasant: Agrarian Society in Western Sri Lanka Under Dutch Rule, 1740–1800*. Leiden and Boston: IDC Publishers.

Diamond, Larry, and Richard Gunther, eds. 2001. *Political Parties and Democracy*. Maryland: The Johns Hopkins University Press.

Downs, Anthony. 1957. An Economic Theory of Political Action in a Democracy. *The Journal of Political Economy* 65 (2) (April): 135–150.

Dumont, L. 1999. *Homo Hierarchicus*. New Delhi: Oxford University Press.

Duverger, Maurice. 19540. *Political Parties, Their Organisation and Activity in the Modern State*. London: Methen & Co. Ltd; New York: Wiley.

Fernando, Laksiri. 1999. Three Phases of Political Development after Independence. In *Facets of Development of Sri Lanka Since Independence: Socio-Political, Economic, Scientific and Cultural*, ed. W.D. Lakshman and C.A. Tisdell. Queensland: Department of Economics, University of Queensland.

Fernando, T., and F. Farook. 2000. Echoes of Zimbabwe Roar in Negombo. *Sunday Times*, 11 June. http://www.sundaytimes.lk/000611/news2.html. Accessed 28 October 2009.

Fuller, C.J., and J. Harris. 2001. For an Anthropology of the Modern Indian State. In *The Everyday State & Society in Modern India*, ed. C.J. Fuller and V. Benei. London: Hurst & Co.

Geys, B. 2006. 'Rational' Theories of Voter Turnout: A Review. *Political Studies Review* 4: 16–35.

Giddens, Anthony. 1984. *The Constitution of Society: Outline of the Theory of Structuration*. Oxford: Polity Press.

Goodhand, J., J. Spencer, and B. Koef, eds. 2010. *Conflict and Peace Building Sri Lanka: Caught in Peace Trap?* London: Routledge.

Gosselin, Tania. 2008. The Impact of Cleavages on Political Participation and Electoral Volatility. Paper prepared for the Canadian Political Science Association Annual Conference, 4–6 June 2008, Vancouver, British Columbia. http://www.personal.ceu.hu/staff/Gabor_Toka/Papers/GosselinToka08Vancouver.pdf.

Grenfell, Michael, ed. 2008. *Pierre Bourdieu: Key Concepts*. Durham: Acumen.

Gunasekara, T. 1992. Democracy, Party Competition and Leadership: The Changing Power Structure in a Sinhalese Community. In *Agrarian Change in Sri Lanka*, ed. James Brow and Joe Weeramunda, 229–260. New Delhi and Newbury Park/London: Sage.

————. 1994. *Hierarchy and Egalitarianism: Caste, Class and Power in Sinhalese Pleasant Society*. London: The Athlone Press.

Gunasinghe, N. 1990. *Changing Socio-Economic Relations in the Kandyan Cuntryside*. Colombo: Social Scientists' Association.

Heath, Anthony. 1999. Were Traditional Voters Disillusioned with Labour? Working Paper 68, Centre for Research into Elections and Social Trends, March.

Heath, Anthony, Ian McLean, and Bridget Taylor. 1997. How Much Is at Stake? Electoral Behaviour in Second-Order Elections. Working Paper 59, Centre for Research into Elections and Social Trends.

Heath, Anthony, and Yogendra Yadev. 2002. The United Colours of Congress: Social Profile of Congress Voters, 1996 and 1998. In *Parties and Party Politics in India*, ed. Hasan Zoya. New Delhi: Oxford University Press.

Heath, Oliver. 2002. Anatomy of BJP's Rise to Power: Social, Regional and Political Expansion in the 1990s. In *Parties and Party Politics in India*, ed. Hasan Zoya. New Delhi: Oxford University Press.

Hammersley, Martyn, and Paul Atkinson. 2007. *Ethnography: Principles in Practice*, 3rd ed. New York: Routledge.

Hennayake, Nalani. 2006. *Culture, Politics and Development in Post-colonial Sri Lanka*. Lanham: Lexington Books.

Hettige, S. 1984. *Wealth, Power and Prestige: Emerging Patterns of Social Inequality in a Peasant Context*. Colombo: Ministry of Higher Education.

Horowitz, D. 1989. Incentives and Behaviour in the Ethnic Politics of Sri Lanka and Malaysia. *Third World Quarterly* 11 (4) (October): 18–35.

Husserl, E. 1970. *Logical Investigations*, trans. D. Carr. New York: Humanities Press.

International IDEA. 2002. Voter Turnout Since 1945: A Global Report. http://www.idea.int/publications/vt/upload/VT_screenopt_2002.pdf. Accessed 28 May 2013.

Ivan, Victor. 1999. *Nidahasa, Jaathika Ekagrathawa Ha Deshapalanaye Pwul Poraya* (Independence, National Integrity and the Struggle of the Families in Politics). Ratmalana: Nandana Marasinghe Anusmarana (Grantha Prakashana) Padanama.

Jayanntha, D. 1992. *Electoral Allegiance in Sri Lanka*. Cambridge: Cambridge University Press.

Jayasuriya, L. 2000. *Welfarism and Politics in Sri Lanka*. Perth: School of Social Work and Social Policy, University of Western Australia.

————. 2012. *The Changing Face of Electoral Politics in Sri Lanka (1994–2010)*. Colombo: Social Scientists' Association.

Jenkins, Richard. 2002. *Pierre Bourdieu*. Rev. London: Routledge.

Jiggins, J. 1974. Dedigama 1973: A Profile of a By-Election in Sri Lanka. *Asian Survey* 14 (11) (November): 1000–1013.

————. 1979. *Caste and the Family in the Politics of the Sinhalese 1947 to 1976.* London: Cambridge University Press.

Jupp, J. 1978. *Sri Lanka: Third World Democracy.* London: Cass.

Katz, R., and P. Mair. 2009. "The Cartel Party Thesis: A Restatement", of "Perspectives on Politics." *American Political Science Association* 7 (4): 753–766.

Kearny, R.N. 1973. *The Politics of Ceylon (Sri Lanka).* Ithaca and London: Cornell University Press.

Key, V.O. 1958. *Politics, Parties and Pressure Groups.* New York: Thomas Y. Crowell Company.

Kirchheimer, O. 1966. The Transformation of Western European Party Systems. In *Political Parties and Political Development,* ed. J. La Palombara and M. Weiner, 177–199. Princeton, NJ: Princeton University Press.

Kitschelt, Herbert, and I. Steven Wilkinson, eds. 1997. *Patrons Clients and Policies, Patterns of Democratic Accountability and Political Competition.* Cambridge: Cambridge University Press.

————. 2007. Citizen-Politician Linkage: An Introduction. In *Patrons Clients and Policies, Patterns of Democratic Accountability and Political Competition,* ed. Herbert Kitschelt and I. Steven Wilkinson. Cambridge: Cambridge University Press.

Kothari, Rajini. 1964. The Congress System in India. *Asian Survey* 4 (12) (December): 1161–1173.

Kvale, S., and S. Brinkmann. 2009. *Interviews: Learning the Craft of Qualitative Research Interviewing.* London: Sage.

La Palambara, J., and Myron Weiner, eds. 1966. *Political Parties and Political Development.* Princeton: Princeton University Press.

Leiserson, A. 1958. *Parties and Politics: An Institutional and Behavioral Approach.* New York: Alfred A. Knopf.

Lijphart, Arend. 1977. *Democracy in Plural Societies: A Comparative Exploration.* New Haven: Yale University Press.

————. 1979. Religious vs. Linguistic vs. Class Voting: The "Crucial Experiment" of Comparing Belgium, Canada, South Africa and Switzerland. *The American Political Science Review* 73 (2) (June): 442–458.

Lipset, S.M. 1963. *Political Man: The Social Bases of Politics.* New York: Anchor Books, Doubleday & Company Inc.

Lipset, S.M., and S. Rokkan. 1967. *Party Systems and Voter Alignments: A Cross-National Perspective.* New York: The Free Press.

Lowndes, Vivien. 2002. Institutionalism. In *Theory and Methods in Political Science,* ed. David Marsh and Gerry Stoker, 90–108. New York: Palgrave Macmillan.

Macy, M.W. 1997. Identity, Interest and Emergent Rationality: An Evolutionary Synthesis. *Rationality and Society* 9 (November): 427–448.

Mainwaring, B., and S. McGraw. 2018. How Catchall Parties Compete Ideologically: Beyond Party Typologies. *European Journal of Political Research.*
https://doi.org/10.1111/1475-6765.12307.

Marsh, David, and Paul Furlong. 2002. A Skin, Not Sweater: Ontology and
Epistemology in Political Science. In *Theory and Methods in Political Science,*
ed. David Marsh and Gerry Stoker, 17–41. New York: Palgrave Macmillan.

Maton, Karl. 2008. Habitus. In *Pierre Bourdieu: Key Concepts,* ed. Michael
Grenfell. Durham: Acumen.

May, T. 1997. *Social Research: Issues, Methods and Process,* 2nd ed. Buckingham:
Open University Press.

McNabb, D.E. 2009. *Research Methods for Political Science: Quantitative and
Qualitative Approaches.* New Delhi: M.E. Sharpe Inc.

Melis, M.M., Milanga Abeysuriya and Nilakshi De Silva. 2006. Putting Land
First? Exploring the Links between Land and Poverty. In *Centre for Poverty
Research, Symposium on Poverty Research in Sri Lanka.* Colombo: Centre for
Poverty Analysis.

Migdal, J.S. 2001. *State in Society: Studying How States and Societies Transform
and Constitute One Another.* Cambridge: Cambridge University Press.

Moore, M. 1985. *The State and Peasant Politics in Sri Lanka.* Cambridge:
Cambridge University Press.

———. 1994. Guided Democracy in Sri Lanka: The Electoral Dimension. *The
Journal of Commonwealth & Comparative Politics* 32 (1): 1–30.

"No Cabinet Till April 21," *The Sunday Times,* 11 April 2010.

Norris, Pippa. 2004. The New Cleavages Thesis and the Social Basis of the
Radical Left. Paper presented at the Annual Meeting of the American Political
Science Association, 3 September, Chicago.

———. 2006. *Electoral Engineering: Voting Rules and Political Behaviour.*
Cambridge: Cambridge University Press.

Oberschall, A., and H. Kim. 1996. Identity and Action. *Mobilization: An
International Quarterly* 1 (March): 63–86.

Palshikar, Suhash. 2006. Shiv Sena: A Tiger with Many Faces? In *India's Political
Parties,* ed. Peter de Souza and E. Sridharan. New Delhi: Sage.

Panebianco, A. 1988. *Political Parties: Organization and Power.* Cambridge:
Cambridge University Press.

Parfit, D. 1984. *Reasons and Persons.* Oxford: Oxford University Press.

Peiris, H.A. 1988. *Political Parties in Sri Lanka Since Independence.* New Delhi:
Navarang.

Peiris, Pradeep. 2007. Sri Lanka's Federalism Debate: Ruling Elites to Laymen.
In *Summer University: Best of the Students' Papers,* 165–182. Fribourg:
Institute of Federalism.

———. 2008. The Long and Winding Road. In *Essays on Federalism in Sri Lanka*, ed. R. Edirisinghe and Asanga Welikala, 316–327. Colombo: Centre for Policy Alternatives.

———. 2010. Some Observations on the 2010 General Election: Disturbing Realities of Sri Lanka's Electoral System. *Polity* 45 (3 & 4).

———. 2018. Politics of Citizens (Non-)Participation in Governance. *LST Review* 29 (345).

Quine, W. 1961. *From a Logical Point of View*. New York: Harper and Row.

Randall, Vicky, and Lars Svåsand. 2002. Party Institutionalization in New Democracies. *Party Politics* 8 (1) (January): 5–29.

Randall, Vicky. 2006. Political Parties and Social Structure in the Developing World. *Handbook of Party Politics*. Sage. http://www.sage-ereference.com/hdbk_partypol/Article_n33.html. Accessed 6 April 2010.

Ranugge, S., ed. 2000. *State, Bureaucracy and Development*. Delhi: Macmillan.

Read, Melvyn, and David Marsh. 2002. Combining Quantitative and Qualitative Methods. In *Theory and Methods in Political Science*, ed. David Marsh and Gerry Stoker, 231–248. New York: Palgrave Macmillan.

Richard, S. Katz, and Peter Mair. 2009. The Cartel Party Thesis: A Restatement. *Perspectives on Politics* 7 (4): 753–766.

Richardson, John M., Jr. 2004. Violent Conflict and the First Half Decade of Open Economy Polices in Sri Lanka: Revisionist View. In *Economy, Culture and Civil War in Sri Lanka*, ed. D. Winslow and Michael D. Woost. Bloomington: Indiana University Press.

———. 2005. *Paradise Poisoned: Learning about Conflict, Terrorism and Development from Sri Lanka's Civil Wars*. Kandy: International Centre for Ethnic Studies.

Ritzer, George. 1996. *Sociological Theory*. New York: McGraw-Hill.

Robbins, Derek. 2009. Theory of Practice. In *Pierre Bourdieu: Key Concepts*, ed. Michael Grenfell. Durham: Acumen.

Robert, Michels. 1962. *Political Parties: A Sociological Study of the Oligarchical Tendencies of Modern Democracy*. New York: The Free Press.

Roberts, M. 1997. Elite Formation and Elites: 1832–1931. In *Sri Lanka Collective Identities Revisited: Volume I*, ed. Micheal Roberts, 191–266. Colombo: Marga Institute.

Roberts, Michael. 2001. *Sinhala-ness and Sinhala Nationalism, A History of Ethnic Conflict in Sri Lanka: Recollection, Reinterpretation and Reconciliation*. Marga Monograph Series on Ethnic Reconciliation, No. 4. Sri Lanka: Marga Institute.

Robinson, M.S. 1975. *Political Structure in a Changing Sinhalese Village*. Cambridge: Cambridge University Press.

Roy, M. N. 2006. Politics without Party. In *India's Political Parties*, ed. Peter DeSouza and E., Sridaran, 51–57. New Delhi: Sage Publications India Pvt. Ltd.

Sanders, David. 2002. Behaviouralism. In *Theory and Methods in Political Science*, ed. David Marsh and Gerry Stoker, 45–63. New York: Palgrave Macmillan.

Sarvananthan, M. 2005. Introduction. In *Economic Reform in Sri Lanka: Post-1977 Period*, ed. Muttukrishna Sarvananthan, 1–24. Colombo: International Centre for Ethnic Studies.

Saravanamuttu, P. 2008. Electoral Violence and Dispute Resolution in Asia-Pacific Sri Lanka Case Study. In *The Electoral Reform Debate in Sri Lanka*, ed. Rohan Edrisingha and Asanga Welikala, 52–86. Colombo: Centre for Policy Alternatives.

Sartori, Giovanni. 1969. From the Sociology of Politics to Political Sociology. *Government and Opposition* 4 (2): 196–214.

———. 2000. The Party Effects of Electoral Systems. In *Political Parties and Democracy*, ed. Larry Diamond and Richard Gunther. Baltimore: The Johns Hopkins University Press.

Schattschneider, E. 1942. *Party Government*. New York: Farrar & Rinehart.

Schmitter, P.C. 2000. Parties Are Not What They Once Were. In *Political Parties and Democracy*, ed. Larry Diamond and Richard Gunther, 67–89. Baltimore and London: The Johns Hopkins University Press.

Scott, C. James. 1972. Patron-Client Politics and Political Change in Southeast Asia. *The American Political Science Review* 66 (1) (March): 91–113.

Selboe, Elin. 2008. Changing Continuities: Multi-Activity in the Network Politics of Colobane, Dakar. Unpublished PhD thesis, University of Oslo.

Sen, Amartya. 1999. *Development as Freedom*. Oxford: Oxford University Press.

Shastri, Amitha. 1983. The Political Economy of Intermediate Regimes: The Case of Sri Lanka. *South Asia Bulletin* 3 (2): 1–14.

Shastri, A. 2018. United National Party: From Dominance to Opposition and Back. In *Political Parties in Sri Lanka: Change and Continuity*, ed. A. Shastri and J. Uyangoda, 100–133. New Delhi: Oxford University Press.

Shastri, A., and J. Uyangoda, eds. 2018. *Political Parties in Sri Lanka: Change and Continuity*. Oxford: Oxford University Press.

Siavelis, Peter. 2006. Party and Social Structure. *Handbook of Party Politics*. Sage. http://www.sageereference.com/hdbk_partypol/Article_n30.html. Accessed 6 April 2010.

Silva, K.T. 1992. Capitalist Development, Rural Politics and Peasant Agriculture in Highland Sri Lanka: Structural Change in a Low Caste Village. In *Agrarian Change in Sri Lanka*, ed. James Brow and Joe Weeramunda, 63–94. New Delhi and Newbury Park/London: Sage.

————. 2004. The United National Party of Sri Lanka: Reproducing Hegemony. In *Political Parties in South Asia*, ed. Subrata K. Mitra, Mike Enksat and Clemen Spiess, 236–258. Westport: Praeger.

Sjoberg, G., and Roger Nett. 2006. *A Methodology for Social Research*. New Delhi: Rawat Publication.

Sobolewska, Maria. 2005. Ethnicity as Political Cleavage: Social Bases of Party Identity and Relevance of Political Attitudes. Working Paper 107, Centre for Research into Elections and Social Trends.

Social Indicator. 2004. *Parliamentary Election Poll 2004*. Colombo: Social Indicator-Centre for Policy Alternatives.

————. 2011. *Democracy in Post-War Sri Lanka*. Colombo: Social Indicator-Centre for Policy Alternatives.

Spencer, Jonathan. 1990. *A Sinhala Village in a Time of Trouble, Politics and Change in Rural Sri Lanka*. Delhi: Oxford University Press.

————. 2007. Performing Democracy. In *Anthropology, Politics and the State: Democracy and Violence in South Asia*, 72–95. Cambridge: Cambridge University Press.

Stoker, Gerry, and David Marsh. 2002. Introduction. In *Theory and Methods in Political Science*, ed. David Marsh and Gerry Stoker, 1–16. New York: Palgrave Macmillan.

Stokke, Kristian. 1995. Poverty as politics: The Janasaviya Poverty Alleviation Programme in Sri Lanka. *Norsk Geografisk Tidsskrift—Norwegian Journal of Geography* 49 (3): 123–135.

————. 1998. Globalization and the Politics of Poverty Alleviation in the South. *Norsk Geografisk Tidsskrift—Norwegian Journal of Geography* 52 (4): 221–228.

————. 2002. *Habitus, Capital and Fields: Conceptualizing the Capacity of Actors in Local Politics*. Oslo: University of Oslo, Department of Sociology and Human Geography.

————. 2011. Liberal Peace in Question: The Sri Lankan Case. In *Liberal Peace in Question: Politics of State and Market Reform in Sri Lanka*, ed. Kristian Stokke and Jayadeva Uyangoda, 1–34. New York and London: Anthem Press.

Stokke, Kristian, and Pradeep Peiris. 2010. Public Opinion on Peace as a Reflection of Social Differentiation of Identity in Sri Lanka. In *Democracy in Practice: Representation and Grassroots Politics*, CPD Journal, vol. II, no. 10, 37–68. Yogjakarta: University of Gadjah Madha.

Thaheer, Minna. 2010a. Why PR System Fails to Promote Minority Parties? A Discussion on Contemporary Politics and Sri Lanka Muslim Congress. In *Democracy in Practice: Representation and Grassroots Politics*, CPD Journal, vol. II, no. 10, 95–118. Yogjakarta: University of Gadjah Madha.

————. 2010b. Reconfiguring Patronage Democracy. *Polity* 5 (3 & 4) (July): 20–25.

Transparency International Sri Lanka. 2010. Special Report on Election Expenditure. 24 January. http://www.tisrilanka.org/. Accessed 10 May 2012.

Torcal, M., and Scott Mainwaring. 2000. The Political Recrafting of the Social Bases of Party Competition: Chile in the 1990s. Working Paper 278, September.

Uyangoda, Jayadeva. 1998. *Studies in Caste and Social Justice in Sri Lanka: Caste in Sinhalese Society, Culture and Politics*. Unpublished manuscript. Colombo: Social Scientists' Association.

———. 2010a. Politics of Political Reform—A Key Theme in the Contemporary Conflict. In *Power and Politics: In the Shadow of Sri Lanka's Armed Conflict*, ed. Camilla Orjuela, 29–78. Sida Studies No. 25. Sida.

———. 2010b. *Samaajeeya Manawa Vidya Paryeshana: Dārshanika saha Kramavedi Handinveemak*. Colombo: Social Scientists' Association.

———. 2010c. It Was Election Time. *Polity* 5 (3 & 4): 3–9.

———. 2011. Travails of State Reform in the Context of Protracted Civil War in Sri Lanka. In *Liberal Peace in Question: Politics of State and Market Reform in Sri Lanka*, ed. Kristian Stokke and Jayadeva Uyangoda, 35–62. New York and London: Anthem Press.

———. 2012a. The State in Post-Colonial Sri Lanka: Trajectories of Change. In *The Political Economy of Environment and Development in a Globalized World: Exploring Frontiers*, ed. D.J. Kjosavik and Paul Vedeld, 345–373. Colombo: Social Scientists' Association.

———. 2012b. The Dynamics of Coalition Politics and Democracy in Sri Lanka. In *Coalition Politics and Democratic Consolidation in Asia*, ed. E. Sridharan, 161–240. New Delhi: Oxford University Press.

———. 2015. Local Government as Local Democracy: Challenges in Sri Lanka's Rural Society. In *Local Government and Local Democracy in Sri Lanka: Institutional and Social Dimensions*, ed. J. Uyangoda, 196–243. Colombo: Social Scientists' Association.

Uyangoda, J., and K. Ariyadasa, 2018. Sri Lanka Freedom Party: Continuity Through Ideological and Policy Shifts. In *Political Parties in Sri Lanka: Change and Continuity*, ed. A. Shastri and J. Uyangoda, 134–158. New Delhi: Oxford University Press.

Venugopal, R. 2011. The Politics of Market Reform at a Time of Ethnic Conflict: Sri Lanka in the Jayewardene Years. In *Liberal Peace in Question: Politics of State and Market Reform in Sri Lanka*, ed. Kristian Stokke and Jayadeva Uyangoda, 63–76. New York and London: Anthem Press.

Walters, J.S. 1996. *The History of Kelaniya*. Colombo: Social Scientists' Association.

Warnapala, W.A.W., and D.E. Woodsworth. 1987. *Welfare as Politics in Sri Lanka*. Montreal, QC: Centre for Developing-Area Studies, McGill University.

Weber, Max. 1958. Class, Status and Party. In *From Max Weber: Essays in Sociology*, ed. H.H. Gerth and C.W. Mills. New York: Oxford University Press.

Weerakoon, T.S. 1997. Management Turnaround of a Public Enterprise: A Sri Lankan Case Study. *Asian Journal of Public Administration* 19 (1): 102–122.

Weiner, M. 2006. Party Politics and Electoral Behaviour: From Independence to 1980s. In *India's Political Parties*, ed. P. DeSouza and E. Sridaran, 116–154. New Delhi: Sage Publications India Pvt. Ltd.

Welikala, Asanga. 2008a. Representative Democracy, Proportional Representation and Plural Society in Sri Lanka. In *The Electoral Reform Debate in Sri Lanka*, ed. Edirisinha and Welikala, 11–15. Colombo: Centre for Policy Alternatives.

———. 2008b. Independent Elections Administration in Respect of Public Resources and State Media: The Constitutional Framework in Sri Lanka. In *Report of the Regional Workshop of Experts on Inclusive Electoral Process*, 104–112. Colombo: South Asians for Human Rights.

White, J.K. 2006. What Is a Political Party? In *Handbook of Party Politics*. Sage. http://www.sageereference.com/hdbk_partypol/Article_n33.html. Accessed 6 April 2010.

Wilson, A.J. 1974. *Politics in Sri Lanka, 1947–1973*. London: MacMillan.

———. 1975. *Electoral Politics in an Emergent State: The Ceylon General Election of May 1970*. London: Cambridge University Press.

———. 1984. *The Gaullist System in Asia, The Constitution of Sri Lanka, 1978*. Hong Kong: The Macmillan Press Ltd.

Winslow, D., and Michael D. Woost, eds. 2004. *Economy, Culture and Civil War in Sri Lanka*. Bloomington: Indiana University Press.

Wolinetz, Steven. 2002. Beyond the Catch-All Party: Approaches to the Study of Parties and Party Organizations in Contemporary Democracies. In *Political Parties: Old Concepts and New Challenges*, ed. Richard Günther, José Ramón Montero, and Juan Linz, 136–165. Oxford: Oxford University Press.

Woodward, Calvin A. 1969. *The Growth of a Political System in Ceylon*. Cambridge: Cambridge University Press.

———. 1975. Sri Lanka's Electoral Experience: From Personal to Party Politics. *Public Affairs* 47 (4) (Winter): 1974–1975.

Wriggins, W.H. 1960. *Ceylon: Dilemmas of a New Nation*. Princeton, NJ: Princeton University Press.

Author Index

© The Editor(s) (if applicable) and The Author(s), under exclusive
license to Springer Nature Singapore Pte Ltd. 2022
P. Peiris, *Catch-All Parties and Party-Voter Nexus in Sri Lanka*,
Politics of South Asia,
https://doi.org/10.1007/978-981-16-4153-4

Subject Index

A
Alignment, 222, 228, 230
Ancillary organizations, 6, 32, 50, 51,
    71–73, 196

C
Caste, 7, 8, 20, 24, 37, 40–46,
    48–50, 53, 54, 56, 61, 63–67,
    72, 78, 82, 85, 87–89, 91,
    95–98, 103, 104, 110, 113, 115,
    120, 133, 135, 139–143, 156,
    158, 171, 180, 194, 196, 209,
    210, 214, 217, 218, 248
Catch-all parties, 1, 3, 5, 11, 24, 25,
    143, 182, 212, 221–224, 227,
    229, 232, 238, 239, 244, 245,
    249
Cleavage(s), 7–9, 12, 61, 82, 88, 90,
    95–99, 101, 103, 109, 113, 133,
    139, 143, 145, 197, 204, 206,
    226, 246
Coalition centres, 239

Cultural capital, 15, 16, 36, 58–60,
    62, 68, 73, 75, 197

D
Deserting/desertion, 24, 25, 221,
    224–226, 228, 229, 237, 239
Doxa, 16, 17, 131, 132, 136, 170,
    181, 212, 245

E
Economic capital, 15, 16, 34, 36, 38,
    42, 44, 58, 59, 61, 69, 73, 75,
    85, 95, 169, 246
Electoral system, 3, 10, 20, 22, 32,
    81, 83, 101–103, 105, 106, 108,
    109, 112, 118, 119, 121, 196,
    222, 231, 246, 247
Electorate organizer, 32–36, 39, 40,
    43, 44, 46, 48–50, 52, 53, 58,
    64, 67, 68, 70, 72, 81, 83–88,
    91, 93, 94, 97–100, 102–105,
    108–112, 115, 116, 119–121,

Printed by Printforce, United Kingdom